Preaching Mark

Preaching Mark

Bonnie Bowman Thurston

Fortress Press
Minneapolis

The paper used in this publication meets the minimum requirements of American National Standard for Information Sciences — Permanence of Paper for Printed Library Materials, ANSI Z329.48-1984.

Manufactured in the U.S.A.   AF1-3428
06   05   04   03   02   1   2   3   4   5   6   7   8   9   10

In Memoriam
Miss Helen Louise McGuffie, Ph.D.
(1915–2000)

She taught me what to do with texts.

"Let her works praise her in the city gates."
Proverbs 31:31

Contents

Abbreviations

ABD	*Anchor Bible Dictionary.* Edited by D. N. Freeman et al. New York: Doubleday, 1992.
BR	*Biblical Research*
BRev	*Bible Review*
BTB	*Biblical Theology Bulletin*
CBQ	*Catholic Biblical Quarterly*
CBQMS	Catholic Biblical Quarterly Monograph Series
DJG	*Dictionary of Jesus and the Gospels.* Edited by J. B. Green and S. McKnight. Downers Grove: InterVarsity, 1992.
ExpTim	*Expository Times*
HTR	*Harvard Theological Review*
IBS	*Irish Biblical Studies*
ICC	International Critical Commentary
Int	*Interpretation*
JBL	*Journal of Biblical Literature*
JBR	*Journal of Biblical Religion*
JR	*Journal of Religion*
JSNT	*Journal for the Study of the New Testament*
JSNTSup	JSNT Supplement Series
JSOT	*Journal for the Study of the Old Testament*
JTS	*Journal of Theological Studies*
LXX	Septuagint
MT	Masoretic Text
NCBC	New Century Bible Commentary
NIB	*The New Interpreter's Bible*
NovT	*Novum Testamentum*
NTS	*New Testament Studies*
RevExp	*Review and Expositor*
RelSRev	*Religious Studies Review*
SBLDS	Society of Biblical Literature Dissertation Series
SJT	*Scottish Journal of Theology*
ZNW	*Zeitscrhift für die neuentestamentliche Wissenschaft und die Kunde der älteren Kirche*

Preface

In the last fifty years there has been widespread interest in Mark's Gospel, resulting in a great many fine scholarly commentaries and serious studies of the Gospel. But in my experience, few of them specifically assist one who comes to Mark as preacher and teacher.[1] This book was written specifically to aid preachers and teachers in the church. My particular focus is homiletical, although the homiletical suggestions may also serve as points for personal prayer and meditation. As such, the work differs in several ways from more traditional scholarly commentaries, not the least of which is that I abandon the ruse of scholarly omniscience and write in the first person as preacher to preacher, teacher to teacher.

First, I treat canonical Mark in English. That is, I deal with the Gospel as we have it in modern English translations. In discussing passages, I do not speculate about Mark's sources or the existence of earlier "drafts" of the Gospel. Nor do I deal extensively with textual matters, although from time to time I point to alternative readings. While there is no more important interpretive tool for preachers of the New Testament than reading the text in the original Greek, I know that many preachers either do not have Greek or have allowed their seminary Greek to become rusty. Thus, although it is impossible to deal carefully with the text without alluding to Greek, I avoid as much as possible technical matters of translation, and I transliterate Greek when I introduce it.

Second, this work focuses on units of material rather than proceeding verse by verse. The lectionaries of the church present Mark's Gospel to the worshipping church in small units technically called *pericopae*. (See Appendix 1, which includes the Markan texts in Year B in the Roman Catholic, Episcopal, and Common lectionaries.) Furthermore, in examining particulars in great detail, verse-by-verse exposition has a tendency to obscure the general significance of a passage. Pheme Perkins notes in her introduction to Mark in the *New Interpreter's Bible* that "most parishioners encounter the text . . . in isolated fragments," therefore "people find it difficult to attend to the larger structural features in each individual Gospel."[2] In order to address this practical fact, and because I think Mark carefully arranged the material in his Gospel, I first introduce larger units of material in discussing the texts and then treat the smaller pericopae within them.

Third, I have tried to avoid scholarly apparatus. I transliterate Greek, avoid technical textual matters, and keep documentation at a minimum. In order for the book to be useful for students and seminarians, I provide suggestions for further reading, and Appendix 2 is an annotated bibliography of works I have found to be of special interest to those preaching and teaching Mark. My "suggestions for further reading" are not always the most recent publications. My criteria for selection was usefulness to the preacher and teacher, not what has been published most recently.

Fourth, my remarks on the text move toward application. My methodological assumption is that, of all the Jesus material available to him, Mark preserved this material for a reason. Mark recorded these selections of the tradition he received because they spoke to his community, the church for which he wrote the Gospel. Thus behind my commentary on any given pericope are these questions: Why did Mark preserve this story? Why was it important for his community? My sense is that the answers to these questions should direct the course for contemporary preaching. Although it is not a particularly avant-garde position, I understand the Gospel of Mark to be a historical document (not, one should note, *history*). The intent of its author and his circumstances set limits on how the text should be interpreted in our own day. Mark's intent in preserving a story circumscribes to some extent its appropriate interpretation.

Finally, in this book I am not proposing an overarching theory about Mark's Gospel. Nor do I write to take issue with the scholars and commentators who do develop synthetic readings of Mark. My aim is far more modest: it is to provide preachers and teachers of Mark's Gospel with information to help them appropriately interpret and proclaim it.

Contemporary biblical scholarship has insisted that there is no objective interpretation. Who we are and what we bring to the text often determines what we find in it. True enough. So a word about my location vis-à-vis the text is in order. I am a middle-aged, middle-class, white, female scholar and ordained pastor. My first academic training was in literature (thus my interest in Mark's ordering of material, methods of characterization, and patterns of metaphor). My formal New Testament training was all post-graduate and sporadic, fit in amid other responsibilities. This may account for oversights in my work, and for them I ask your pardon in advance. I consciously write from within the "one holy, catholic, and apostolic church." Theologically, I am a Nicean

Christian. What this means practically is that I approach Mark's Gospel with a hermeneutic of belief.

If you are looking for new theories about the origins of Mark's Gospel, an entirely fresh reading of it, an attack on patriarchy, or a political or polemical reading of the text, this is not the book for you. If you seek notes on canonical Mark with a special focus on Mark's patterns of organization and on the relevance of his Gospel to Christian life today, this volume may be of interest. I certainly hope it will be helpful to preachers. If it is not, then I have failed at what I set out to do.

Acknowledgments

I am grateful to Pittsburgh Theological Seminary for granting me sabbatical leave to complete this manuscript during the winter and spring quarters of 1999–2000. During that time, Fr. Joseph Hayden, S.J., loaned me a laptop computer when my own died of exhaustion. Thanks, Joe! One thousand salaams to Sr. Anne Rutledge, O.P., Pittsburgh Theological Seminary faculty secretary, who in many and wonderful ways aids our work. Twice I have taught Mark's Gospel at Pittsburgh Seminary, and I thank the students from whom I learned so much. And thanks also go to the Master of Arts in Applied Theology students at Wheeling Jesuit University with whom I first seriously explored Mark's gospel from 1985 to 1995.

I am also indebted to the Task Force on the Gospel of Mark of the Catholic Biblical Association to which I belong. My thinking has been challenged by these colleagues, and I have learned much from them, always in the context of faith and service to the church. Four Markan scholars have shaped my thinking about this gospel and the methods with which to approach it: Paul Achtemeier; John Donahue, S.J.; Sharyn Dowd; and Elizabeth Struthers Malbon. My work has been immensely influenced and enriched by theirs, but they are not responsible for my mistakes, for which I take full credit.

Thanks are also in order to Harold Rast, my editor at Fortress Press, who not only improved the manuscript but persevered to provide the contract. And without George Miller's loving and exacting proofreading, my manuscripts would be peppered with errors.

Finally, my deep gratitude goes to the preachers who have nourished my own faith journey, especially to my sisters in ministry. It is my hope that this book will help others proclaim the message in a world that so desperately needs to hear it.

All Saints Day 2000

Introduction

Questions that concern academic students of Mark's Gospel—the provenance of the Gospel, whether the evangelist had sources and what they were, whether canonical Mark is a rewrite of an *ur-Markus*, what the relationship of Mark is to the sayings source Q—do not often loom large for those of us charged to preach and teach Mark. Acquaintance with these discussions is helpful, however, for as recent biblical scholarship has insisted, all writing derives from its author's particular perspective (for example, his or her social, political, economic or theological location). Thus to preach and teach the Gospel as effectively as possible, some knowledge of the author's probable context is essential. Or perhaps it would be more accurate to say "some knowledge of the *theories* about the evangelist and the Gospel's origin is essential," since there is precious little scholarly consensus about the evangelist Mark, when and where he wrote, and to whom.

Since most lectionary preachers will spend a year with Mark's Gospel, reading a good, general article on Mark is time well spent. You can find these in the readily available *The Interpreter's Bible, The Anchor Bible Dictionary,* or *Dictionary of Jesus and the Gospels;* or you can read the chapter on Mark in a good New Testament introduction.[1] The following material is not exhaustive but seeks to introduce the backgrounds of the Gospel and some of the issues in Markan studies.[2]

Markan Priority and Sources

Lexical studies show that Matthew reproduces 606 of Mark's 661 verses, and Luke reproduces 320 of them. Matthew uses close to 51 percent of Mark's actual words and Luke 53 percent. There are two basic explanations for this phenomenon. Either all three Gospels used a common source, or two of the three used the third as a source. It is the consensus of scholarship that Matthew and Luke used Mark as source material. Thus we speak of "Markan priority"; Mark was the first Gospel to be written.[3]

But the evangelist Mark did not make up his Gospel. Behind his written Gospel stands the oral tradition of the church. Additionally, Mark may have had written sources from which to work. Many scholars think that a written account of the passion narrative existed when Mark composed his Gospel. The text of Mark suggests that certain "narrative complexes" preceded Mark. For example, groups of the same genre of story (for example, miracles or parables) were collected before Mark, and he inserted these collections into his Gospel (see Mark 4:1-34; 4:35—5:43; 11:27—12:27 for examples). Or Mark may have inherited groups of stories that were circulated together before he wrote.[4] It has also been suggested that canonical Mark is not the "original Mark," that there existed a "first draft," an *ur-Markus*. The *ur-Markus* hypothesis suggests that Matthew and Luke used that earlier version of Mark, which accounts for the agreements of Matthew and Luke against Mark.[5] (Parenthetically, there also exists an apocryphal Gospel, sometimes called the "Secret Gospel of Mark," which was found by Morton Smith at the Mar Saba Monastery near Jerusalem in 1958. It seems to be an expanded version of canonical Mark. For example, it contains a story, inserted after Mark 10:37, of a young man raised from the dead by Jesus who subsequently encounters this man's sisters. This story obviously resembles the raising of Lazarus in John 11.

I have saved discussion of the possibility that Peter was a source for Mark's Gospel until last because of its significance. Early church tradition connects Mark's Gospel with the apostle Peter. The most ancient attestation of this tradition is a quotation from Papias (who was born about 60 A.D. and served as a bishop in the second century) found in Eusebius's *Ecclesiastical History* (3.39). The passage states that Mark became Peter's interpreter and wrote accurately, but not in order, all that he remembered of the things said and done by the Lord. Mark, it suggests, had not heard of or been one of the disciples of Jesus, but he had followed Peter. Papias notes Mark was careful to omit none of the things he had heard and to state no untruth. If Eusebius's record of Papias's recollection is correct (and there is reason to trust it), then there is a direct connection between the text of Mark's Gospel and the apostle Peter. This connection between Mark's Gospel and Peter appears over and over in the early church. It is found in Justin Martyr, Irenaeus, Clement of Alexandria, Origen (who thought the evangelist was referred to in 1 Pet. 5:13), Tertullian, Eusebius, Jerome, and Augustine. In short, the tradition of Mark's dependence upon Peter is very ancient and very widely attested.

For Further Reading

Ernest Best, "Mark's Preservation of the Tradition," in William Telford, ed., *The Interpretation of Mark* (Edinburgh: T. & T. Clark, 1995), 153–68.

Robert H. Gundry, "The Origin of Mark's Gospel," in *Mark: A Commentary on His Apology for the Cross* (Grand Rapids: Eerdmans, 1993), 1026–45.

Dieter Lührmann, "The Gospel of Mark and the Sayings Collection Q," *JBL* 108 (1989): 51–71.

Thomas C. Oden and Christopher A. Hall, eds., *Ancient Christian Commentary on Scripture: Mark* (Downers Grove: InterVarsity, 1998), xxi–xxix.

H. E. W. Turner, "The Tradition of Mark's Dependence upon Peter," *ExpTim* 71 (1960): 260–63.

Authorship, Date, and Location

The only thing that can be said with absolute certainty is that the Gospel of Mark was written by a Christian around the middle of the first century in an unspecified part of the Roman Empire. This assertion is academically "safe," but it gives us little help in interpreting Mark.

There is consensus that Mark wrote at about the time of the First Jewish War, A.D. 66–70. This date fits much of the data in the text. First, Mark is a Gospel that is particularly concerned with suffering, emphasizing the suffering of John the Baptist and of Jesus and his first disciples, probably because Mark's community is itself a suffering community. Toward the end of the reign of the Emperor Nero (A.D. 54–68) Christians in Rome suffered terrible persecutions. The date fits the circumstances of the intended audience. Second, apocalyptic expectations soared during the Jewish War. Mark 13, the "Markan apocalypse," is full of allusions to war and the destruction of the Temple in Jerusalem. Although scholars divide on whether Mark 13 predates or postdates the Temple's destruction, almost all connect the chapter to that historical event. Again, the date fits the text. Finally, if Mark were used by Matthew and Luke, then it not only had to have been written before either of them, but long enough before them to be circulated and, thus, from a well-known Christian center. Since most scholars put the writing of Matthew and Luke in the 80s, a date of from 65 to 70 seems reasonable for Mark.

From what well-known Christian community did Mark come? Ancient testimony supports a Roman location, and many modern scholars agree. The text of Mark seems to support this as well. The evangelist pauses in the narrative to explain Jewish customs (for example, Mark 7:3-4) and to translate Aramaic expressions (for example, 5:41), things a Roman audience far removed from Palestine might well need help to understand.

Furthermore, Mark contains numerous Latinisms and Latin loan words, which, again, would be consistent with a Roman location (although, of course, Latin loan words and Latinisms could appear anywhere in the Empire, especially in the western sections). While I tend to think a Roman location for Mark answers more questions than it raises (a good principle for testing any biblical hypothesis), it is not the only possibility. Both Galilee and a community just north of there in Roman Syria have been suggested. Certainly the Gospel has strong links with Palestinian Christianity (but it would if Peter were one of its sources).

Whatever the geographic location of Mark's community, the text suggests it was a predominantly but not exclusively Gentile community, that it was experiencing or was about to experience suffering, and that it needed to understand more deeply the suffering and cross of Jesus.

In an interesting and helpful article on the social location of Mark's community or audience, Richard Rohrbaugh (who thinks Mark was written in a village in Galilee or Syria about A.D. 70) argues that the first recipients of the Gospel were not from the elite class or their retainers, but were probably from the "degraded, unclean, expendable" (beggars, prostitutes, laborers, tanners), or from rural peasants. He notes that these groups are prominent in Mark's narrative. Rohrbaugh thinks that the term *crowd* (Greek, *ochlos*), which occurs thirty-eight times in Mark, is a metaphor for the poor who make up Mark's audience. Mark's Jesus breaks the purity rules of the elite and aligns himself with the crowd. So in defending Jesus, Mark is also defending his community. If Rohrbaugh's understanding of Mark's audience is correct, it means that they received Mark's Gospel much as our ordinary parishioners do: they heard it read aloud. "No Gospel was earlier or more clearly consensually received as designed for use in public worship than Mark."[6]

Who was this Mark? We don't know. Originally, the Gospel circulated anonymously. The name "Mark" comes from Papias, but it was one of the most common names in the Empire. Tradition associates Mark the evangelist with the John Mark of Acts (Acts 12:12, 25; 15:37, 39), but Papias said Mark had not seen Jesus. And if Mark were an eyewitness, he would not have needed Peter's testimony. One ingenious theory is that Mark has written himself into the Gospel much as Renaissance painters drew themselves into their canvases. The argument is that Mark is the "streaker" in 14:51-52.[7] But, again, this would contradict Papias.

My own sense is that Mark was not an eyewitness of the events in Jesus' life, but that he had access to someone (Peter?) who was or to a source that was. Mark was one of the second generation of disciples and was a careful and skilled writer and an incisive theologian.

For Further Reading

S. G. F. Brandon, "The Date of the Markan Gospel," *NTS* 7 (1960/61): 126–41.

John Donahue, "Windows and Mirrors: The Setting of Mark's Gospel," *CBQ* 57 (1995): 1–26.

Joel Marcus, "The Jewish War and the Sitz im Leben of Mark," *JBL* 111 (1992): 441–62.

Richard Rohrbaugh, "The Social Location of the Markan Audience," *Int* 47 (1993): 380–95.

Mark the Writer

The first literary question is that of genre. Since Mark's Gospel is probably the first Gospel, Mark the evangelist "invented" Gospels. What sort of writings are they? It is important that we not read the Gospel of Mark as if it were either modern history or biography. The evangelist is not interested in dates, places, exact quotations, collecting all the relevant data, or the other tasks of modern history. We must interpret Mark in the context of the writing of the first century.[8] But what kind of writing?

Biography as a form seems to have arisen in the fourth century B.C. The first known biography is Evagoras's life of Isocrates, about 365 B.C. Popular biography in the first century was interested in the character of the person described. In form, popular biographies were usually collections of disconnected sayings and incidents in the life of a person without chronological ordering. "Character" meant "types" of persons representative of virtues, not individuated people.[9] The usual subjects of popular biography were public figures and philosophers, exemplified in the *Memorabilia* by Xenophon or the *Apology of Socrates* by Plato. The oldest collection of such popular biographies is a Latin work by Cornelius Nepos called *De Viris Illustribus*.

Another form of first-century literature in the Greco-Roman world related to biography was aretalogy, a term derived from *arete,* virtue. These were accounts of the remarkable careers of impressive teachers and were intended to be used as a basis for moral instruction. But Gospels also have Jewish antecedents. Several scholars suggest that the life of Moses and the Elijah-Elisha cycles in Kings have exerted formative influence on the Gospel genre. There also existed in first-century Palestine a collection of thumbnail sketches called *Lives of the Prophets,* which may have influenced Gospel writing.

While Mark's Gospel is related to these forms, it is nevertheless something quite different. The word *Gospel* reveals something about this form. In Greek, *euaggelizesthai* means "reward for bringing good news" as well as the good news itself. In Greek literature, the word was apparently first used by Aristophanes for news of victories or joyful events. The Greek verb form is based on the Hebrew *bissar*, "to announce news of salvation." The term had already achieved religious significance in the first century in the imperial cult; it was used in connection with the appearance of a divine world ruler and the inauguration of his reign.

Let me suggest a description of the genre "Gospel" as Mark developed the form. A Gospel is a brief, popular writing in the common language (*koine* Greek) that was used as "propaganda" for the early Christian mission. That is, the use of the Gospel is evangelistic and/or didactic; its interest is to speak to the religious concerns of its recipients, not to present "objective history" (if, indeed, such a thing exists). To quote Werner Kümmel's well-known New Testament handbook, "The aim of the Gospels is not recollection about Jesus, nor glorification of his miracles . . . but the main concern is rather to evoke faith and to strengthen it . . . to show the early Christian church the ground of its faith."[10]

In preaching Mark, we must remember that the center of the Gospel is the person Jesus of Nazareth. But the primary concern of the evangelist is not facts about the person but evoking and strengthening faith in him. In my view, what John the evangelist tells us about his work is true of Mark as well: "these are written so that you may come to believe that Jesus is the Messiah, the Son of God and that through believing you may have life in his name" (John 20:31). Mark shared with Jews of his day the view that history is the meeting place of God and humans. He understood that God was sovereign and that Jesus of Nazareth was the instrument of God's purpose. Mark understood and wanted to communicate that God's activity on behalf of humans culminated in the life of Jesus of Nazareth and especially in his suffering, death, and resurrection.

The question of the genre of Mark's Gospel is very important to interpreting the text today. The Gospel of Mark is a faith document, not a secular history or biography. I am not suggesting that Mark's Gospel is not historical; I believe that it is. But its aim is not to record history. Its aim is faith. That being the case, our homiletical task, to apply the Markan texts to our own churches and congregations, is entirely appropriate. It is what Mark was doing: applying the life of Jesus to his community.

Following Rohrbaugh's description of the social location of Mark's audience, we might think of the Gospel as similar to a folktale. That is, Mark is a realistic narrative with particularizing detail. It is meant to be read aloud to hearers, much as a story is told. Mark is "told" among the unofficial people. One thing worth noting in Mark's Gospel is that nothing very good is said about "official people," whether Jewish, Roman, or apostolic ("the Twelve" in Mark's parlance). This in itself may provide a preaching point in a given text.

With this as an introduction to genre, let me suggest some of Mark's characteristics as a writer.[11] I noted that Mark is fond of clustering stories of similar types. For example, 4:1-34 is a parables grouping, and 4:35—5:43 is a group of miracle stories. In building the Gospel, Mark also uses intercalation or story-within-a-story construction. For example, Mark begins the story of Jairus's daughter (5:21-24a), inserts the account of the woman with a hemorrhage (5:24b-34), and then returns to the original story (5:35-43). It is from Mark that we come to expect vivid eyewitness touches like Jesus being asleep on a cushion in the boat or people being invited to sit on green grass (see 4:37; 5:5; 6:40; 10:21). Mark also preserves the words of Jesus in Aramaic (3:17; 5:41; 7:11, 34; 14:36; 15:22, 34); perhaps this reflects the aural memory of Peter. Mark is interested in the feelings and emotions of Jesus (1:41; 3:5; 4:38) and in people's responses to him, responses often described as fear, astonishment, or amazement.

Markan habits of speech include a tendency to tell his stories in the present tense (he uses the historic present 151 times) or simple past tenses and to join ideas by using "and" (*kai*) instead of more complex subordinate conjunctions and constructions. Mark's favorite word is "immediately" (41 uses) followed by "again" (25 uses). The effect of these characteristics is to give the Markan Gospel a sense of forward movement, rapid progression. Mark also frequently employs diminutives (5:23; 7:25; 10:13). As already noted, he uses Latinisms and Latin loan words, and is prone to repetition and redundancy. Consult a synopsis and you will see that Matthew and Luke tend to omit or "clean up" these Markan habits.

Observing how Mark structures his Gospel is crucial to understanding it. Any speculation about structure must take into account the theological aims of Mark. Perhaps, then, you should read the next section, "Mark the Theologian," and then return to this discussion. Mark's Gospel has been called a passion narrative with an extended introduction. It is true that all the material in the Gospel moves us toward Jesus' last week in Jerusalem, Mark 11–16. Most discussions of Mark note that 8:27—9:1 is not only the spatial center, but the turning point of the narrative. "Who Jesus is" comes explicitly to the fore, and that moves inexorably toward the passion. In my view Mark's structure can be viewed either geographically or theophanically.

One geographic outline of the Gospel is as follows:

1:1-11	Prologue
1:16—8:26	Galilee
8:27-10	Peter's confession and travel to Jerusalem
11–16	Jerusalem and environs

Within this general structure, there are a number of geographical references in the "travel section" of 8:27-10 (8:30, 33; 10:1, 32, 46) as Mark envisions a "traveling seminar" with Jesus teaching on discipleship. The number of references to Jerusalem and its environs are again multiple (11:11, 15, 27; 14:3, 12, 15, 19, 26, 32; 15:22), and within Jerusalem there is a specific focus on the Temple (11:11, 15, 17; 12:35, 41; 13:1-3; 14:1, 53; 15:38).

Interestingly, if one tries to trace the Gospel of Mark on a map of Roman Palestine, it does not "work"; the movements of Jesus and the disciples are not logical. This suggests that geography is more than place in Mark's Gospel. For example, the first part of the Gospel probably reflects Mark's interest in a Gentile Christian mission since it is set in mixed-population Galilee. Jerusalem is clearly the locus of opposition to Jesus. I shall have occasion to elaborate on Mark's symbolic geography in the notes that follow.

The other structural pattern in Mark is theophanic. The Gospel can be seen as built around the three theophanies: the baptism of Jesus (1:9-11; v. 11 the voice of God), his transfiguration (9:2-8; v. 7, the voice of God) and the death/resurrection of Jesus (15:34, the voice of God in a Markan irony?). If symbolic geography characterizes the first ordering of Mark, this theophanic ordering is characterized by Christology, a "high" Christology not usually associated with Mark's Gospel.

Within either of these two views of Mark's structure one still finds blocks of similar forms of material and summary passages. Most of the forms of literature that later appear in Mark are prefigured in the "typical day" of 1:16-38. They are as follows:

2:1—3:6	controversy narratives
4:1-34	parables
4:35—5:43	miracle stories
6:30-56	miracle stories
7:24—8:26	miracle stories
8:31—10:34	three similarly crafted passion predictions
11:27—12:27	controversy dialogues
13	apocalyptic

This schema suggests that the public ministry may be presented by an inclusion formed by two groups of controversy stories: 2:1—3:6 and 11:27—12:27. It is possible that Mark took these blocks of material from already existing collections. Markan summaries appear at 1:14-15, 21-22, 39; 2:13; 3:7-12; 5:21; 6:6b, 12-13, 53-56; 10:1. They remind the hearer (and the reader) that more happened in the Jesus story than is recorded.

In interpreting Mark's Gospel it is important to keep structural features in mind. Where a pericope occurs in Mark may be the most helpful clue to what Mark intended his audience to understand from the story. In the form Mark invented, order and arrangement provide the context for understanding and interpreting the text. "To understand Mark, we must be aware that he is a creative author who has chosen to make his points by the way he uses and arranges traditions."[12] Always look to see what precedes and follows the lectionary selection, as lectionary texts can be continuations of longer units of material, or the pericope may be "cut off" by the lectionary selection. One of the most important preaching tasks may be to "situate" the text for the congregation, to provide the context for understanding its relevance.

Mark the Theologian

Paul Achtemeier notes that "the author of the shortest Gospel, unknown despite some early guesses in the tradition, was a person of considerable creativity and theological insight" and that "the interpreter of Mark underestimates the theological sophistication and literary skill of Mark only at his or her own peril."[13] I introduced Mark's "literary skill" in the previous section, and I shall draw attention to it in the notes that follow. It remains to suggest something of Mark's "theological insight," his "theological sophistication."

As noted in the preface, I do not advance a particular view of why Mark wrote. I will highlight here particular theological concerns of Mark, which to me are clearly evident in the text. That said, I must confess that my thinking about Mark as a theologian has been colored by two sentences I read many years ago in the "Lifebuilder Bible Study" on Mark by James Hoover. Hoover notes that "Mark, theologically and pastorally, sets out to retell the story of Jesus, showing that the kingdom in its glory comes at the end of a path of suffering and service. . . . Mark portrays Jesus principally as the servant-king whom we should follow (Mark 1:17)."[14] In my view, this succinctly summarizes Mark's concerns.

One of the most discussed features of Mark's Gospel is the secrecy motif. In Mark, demons recognize Jesus and are commanded to be silent; the healed are told not to reveal who healed them; the disciples are at least temporarily forbidden to make Jesus' messiahship known, and Jesus withdraws to teach his disciples in private. The first and powerfully influential treatment of this motif was Wrede's *Das Messiasgeheimnis in den Evangelien* (1901). The book argues that the messiahship of Jesus could not be kept secret and that the motif of secrecy was invented by Mark or one of his sources for their own purposes.

It is certainly the case that a "charge to secrecy" is given frequently by Mark's Jesus. But it seems to me there are legitimate reasons why Jesus himself might have done so. Jesus came to proclaim the kingdom of God (1:14-15); he did not want to be known only as a wonderworker (of whom there were many in his time). So he charged those he healed to remain silent about their cures. Or, because Jesus understood "Messiah" differently from the common understanding in first-century Judaism, his command to the disciples to keep his messiahship secret was expedient and temporary until he could teach them what that messiahship meant. Or perhaps the command to silence about messiahship was an attempt to avoid political violence in already disturbed and violent Roman Palestine.

Jack Kingsbury argues that the meaning of the secrecy motif has to do with what the evangelist wants his readers to understand. "The purpose of the secret," he writes, "is to bring the reader to recognize that to confess Jesus as the Son of God is to confess him . . . to be the one appointed by God to die upon the cross."[15] Helmut Koester writes in *Ancient Christian Gospels* that all the acts of the Markan Jesus are overshadowed by the account of his suffering and death. The "'messianic secret' of Jesus [is] that God's revelation in history is not fulfilled in the demonstration of divine greatness, but in the humiliation of the divine human being in his death on the cross."[16]

Mark's interest in and use of a secrecy motif is tied to his particular focus on the passion of Jesus. As noted, Mark is frequently thought of as a passion narrative with an extended introduction. And this is an accurate way to focus on another of his primary theological concerns: that Jesus be understood in light of the cross with all its terrible associations in his day.[17] In my view this is one reason why John the Baptist plays a crucial role in Mark's Gospel. John is the prototype of what will happen to Jesus. And what happens to Jesus is the prototype of what will happen to his disciples. The connection of John and Jesus is made not only narratively (John is pivotal in chapters 1, 6, and 11 and appears at the end of chapter 8 and the beginning of 9), but linguistically by Mark's use of forms of the Greek verb *paradidomi*, handed over. John preached, was handed over, and was killed. Jesus preached, was handed over, was killed, and then vindicated by God through resurrection (although Mark downplays that event). Thus the disciples when they preach may expect to be handed over, killed, and finally, raised up.

This is to say that Mark's theological interest in the suffering and death of John and Jesus reflects not only his concern for his suffering community, but his interest in discipleship. In Mark, as Jesus is, so are the disciples to be. Mark signals this both narratively (by devoting a large section of the Gospel to discipleship, 8:22—10:52) and linguistically. In Mark's Gospel, "to follow" (*akoloutheo*) means more than to follow spatially behind Jesus. *Follow* is a technical term for discipleship. The healed or exorcised "follow" Jesus as a mark of their full restoration. To be a disciple is to follow Jesus, to be identified not only with his lordship, but with his passion. This is what Jesus says in 8:24: "If any want to become my followers, let them deny themselves and take up their cross and follow me."

This stark connection between suffering and discipleship may be one reason for the incomprehension of the disciples, another of Mark's theological concerns. The inability of the disciples to understand the identity of Jesus is one of the most perplexing features of the Gospel for modern readers. He was "with them"; why couldn't they "get it"? Why indeed! Because Jesus was not what and who they expected. (And be aware of the number of times in Mark's Gospel when the "wrong" people *do* "get it": "foreigners" and "outcasts," not religious leaders or close associates of Jesus.)

Mark wants his audience not only to get it but to get it *right*. So he uses the obtuseness of the disciples to instruct his hearers (and readers—us). Their incomprehension aids our comprehension. We, and Mark's audience, are being led to understand exactly what Peter repudiates in 8:32. The Messiah is a suffering Messiah. It is the crucified Jesus who is the Son of God. Mark's theological concerns—the secrecy motif, the suffering theme, discipleship, and the incomprehension of the disciples—come together in Mark's narrative at the cross. The title of Robert Gundry's commentary, *Mark: A Commentary on His Apology for the Cross,*[18] underlines this fact. Lightfoot's dictum summarizes the discussion: the crucified Messiah, as fulfillment of God's promise, is the chief theme of Mark's Gospel.[19]

Theologically, Mark is interested in what modern scholars call Christology. Both the identity and nature of Jesus are at issue. Mark views Jesus not only as the crucified Messiah, but also as an authoritative teacher. Jesus is called "teacher" more frequently in Mark than in any other Gospel, and yet there are fewer words of Jesus in Mark than in any other Gospel. Mark establishes at the beginning that Jesus teaches "with authority" (1:27). And this raises the question of the source of his authority, which in turn leads to conflict with various Jewish leaders who think they are the religious authorities and know *they* did not grant it to Jesus. In Mark, Jesus' miracles show the extent of his authority (4:35—5:43), and stories of conflict demonstrate its power (11:27—12:17).

More could and will be said later about Mark the theologian. Let it suffice for now to remind the preacher, as he or she approaches the text, to be alert for hints of the secrecy motif, of the suffering theme, of the incomprehension of the disciples, of discipleship, and of the authority of Jesus. To do so will be to remain close to Mark's own interests.

For Further Reading

Adela Yarbro Collins, *The Beginning of the Gospel* (Minneapolis: Fortress Press, 1992), chap. 2, "Suffering and Healing in the Gospel of Mark."

Robert H. Gundry, *Mark: A Commentary on His Apology for the Cross* (Grand Rapids: Eerdmans, 1993), "Introduction."

David Hawkin, "The Incomprehension of the Disciples in the Markan Redaction," *JBL* 91 (1972): 491–500.

Jack Kingsbury, "The Significance of the Cross within Mark's Story," *Int* 47 (1993): 370–79.

Heinz-Dieter Knigge, "The Meaning of Mark," *Int* 22 (1968): 53–70.

R. H. Lightfoot, *The Gospel Message of St. Mark* (Oxford: Oxford Univ. Press, 1962).

Eduard Schweizer, "Mark's Theological Achievement," in *The Interpretation of Mark,* ed. William Telford (Edinburgh: T. & T. Clark, 1995), 63–87.

Robert Tannehill, "The Disciples in Mark: The Function of a Narrative Role," *JR* 57 (1977): 386–405 (reprinted in Telford).

1

The Prologue and Typical Features of Jesus' Ministry
Mark 1:1-39

The Prologue: Introduction
1:1-15

Most commentators note that, although it is not poetic like the Gospel of John, Mark's Gospel is similar to John's in that it also has a prologue. The length of Mark's prologue is debated. Three possibilities are suggested. First, some scholars suggest 1:1-8 is the prologue, making it essentially the title and the ministry of John the Baptist. Others think that 1:1-13, the ministry of the Baptist and the temptation of Jesus are the prologue. The third possibility is that the prologue includes vv. 1-15.

In this regard, I am a maximalist and read vv. 1-15 as Mark's prologue. My decision is based on what appears to me to be the structure of the passage. Verse 1 begins and v. 15 ends with reference to the "good news," thus creating an inclusion. Within these brackets, material about Jesus and John alternates (Jesus, v. 1; John vv. 2-8; Jesus vv. 9-11; John v. 14a; Jesus vv. 14b-15). Verses 14-15 are included as the summary of Jesus' teaching and preaching, to which Mark frequently alludes in the early scenes of the Gospel. When teaching is mentioned but not reported, we are to remember vv. 14 and 15 as its content. What Mark does at the outset is to provide all the hearer or reader needs to understand Jesus and the Gospel. We begin with information that no character in the story has. We are told that Jesus is the Christ and the Son of God, facts that characters in the narrative must discover as it unfolds.

Morna Hooker notes that the information at the outset of Mark 1 "is primarily christological."[1] The John the Baptist material makes the connection between Israel's past and Jesus. The baptism introduces the Trinity and provides divine confirmation of the identity of Jesus given in v. 1. The temptation of Jesus depicts him as one who overcomes Satan. And finally, vv. 14-15 summarize the preaching of the all-powerful Christ. The identity of Jesus and the extent of his ministry are summarized in these fifteen verses.

For Further Reading

R. H. Lightfoot, "The First Chapter of Mark's Gospel," in *The Gospel Message of St. Mark* (Oxford: Oxford Univ. Press, 1962).

Frank Matera, "The Prologue as the Interpretive Key to Mark's Gospel," *JSNT* 34 (1988): 3–20.

1:1

The first verse of Mark functions as both title and introduction, giving information no one in the narrative possesses. "The beginning" echoes Genesis 1:1 and indicates that God is making a fresh start. The nature of that fresh start is in the Gospel, a word used more frequently by Mark than any other evangelist. It is the Gospel both of and about Jesus, who is Christ and Son of God. As Lewis Hay notes, "To be God's son means to be both the object and agent of divine purpose."[2] These two titles for Jesus summarize the early Christian confession about him and also suggest the famous "fish" (*icthus*) symbol of Christianity (*'Iesou Christou 'Hiou Theou*, Jesus Christ, Son of God).

"Son of God" presents a textual problem; it is missing in several early manuscripts. While strongly attested in slightly older textual families, the phrase is bracketed or footnoted in some English translations. The designation of Jesus is interesting because "Son of Man" appears more frequently in Mark. "Son of God" is found in the Markan theophanies (1:11; 9:7), and when demons bespeak Jesus' identity (3:11; 5:7), it is claimed by Jesus (14:61-62) and confessed by the centurion at the cross (15:39). It reflects a seldom-noted Markan "high" Christology.

The Ministry of John the Baptist
1:2-8

The ministry of John the Baptist[3] is introduced by a quotation combining Mal. 3:1 and Isa. 40:5-6. The combination of otherwise unrelated texts is characteristic of the way Mark uses the Hebrew scriptures. He blends or synthesizes two quotations in such a way that a new assertion is made. (cf., for example, 1:11 and Isa. 42:1 plus Ps. 2:7.)[4] The Baptist provides the link between Israel's past (symbolized by the prophets) and its future (announced in the Coming One). John both ties Jesus to Israel's past and foretells his final fate. John preaches, is delivered up, and martyred. Jesus preaches, is delivered up, and martyred. John is Jesus' forerunner in life and death.[5]

John appears in the wilderness, the symbol of the time when God was preparing the people for entry into the promised land (that is, salvation). Probably for this reason, 1:1-8 is appointed as the text for the second

Sunday in Advent. In scripture, the wilderness is the place where people go to meet God or where God chooses to appear. The Baptist is the prime example of "wilderness spirituality" in the New Testament, a spirituality Jesus appropriates in the next pericope. John is described in terms reminiscent of Elijah (2 Kings 1:8; Zech. 13:4). Later in Mark, people think Jesus is John (8:28), but Jesus suggests John was Elijah returned (9:13), whose return, of course, was understood to precede the Messiah's coming.[6] Since the discovery of the Dead Sea Scrolls, scholars have also connected John to the community at Qumran.[7]

John's message is twofold. First, he proclaims "a baptism of repentance for the forgiveness of sins." John preaches repentance (*metanoias*, a complete change of mind, a new direction of the will; the word is probably the Greek equivalent of the Hebrew *shub*, turn around). Second, John announces the Coming One to whom he is subservient (untying sandal straps was the job of slaves) and whose baptism is not with water, but with fire (a symbol of purification) and the Holy Spirit (a symbol of judgment and the means by which God communicates with humanity). Note that John's preaching, harsh though it may have been, met a spiritual hunger; crowds—even those from Jerusalem, the religious center of Israel, where spiritual needs ought to have been met—flocked to John (v. 5).

John's significance is preparatory. He is like the musicians who "warm up" an audience before the main performers appear. The story of Jesus is rooted in Israel's history and begins with a call to repentance. John's message is that Israel must repent, turn around, and claim the *original* inheritance of God's children. The assumption that God's chosen people and visible Israel are one is incorrect; the Messiah had not come to fulfill political expectations. Mark's Gospel, a Gospel especially concerned with discipleship, opens with one person in service to another. John declares his subservience to "the one who is more powerful" and points to Jesus. This leaves us with the question "To whom do we point?"; and it is around this question that a sermon can be built.

For Further Reading

S. Moyise, "Is Mark's Opening Quotation the Key to His Use of Scripture?" *IBS* 20 (1998): 146–58.

Ben Witherington III, "John the Baptist," *DJG*, 383–91.

The Baptism of Jesus
1:9-11

Mark's introduction to Jesus, John's "Coming One," has three parts: his baptism (vv. 9-11), temptation (vv. 12-13), and teaching (vv. 14-15). The theological problem in this pericope (which must be considered since the text is appointed for the Baptism of the Lord just after Epiphany) is summarized by the question, "Why was Jesus baptized since he was without sin?"(see Heb. 4:15). The baptism of Jesus marks the beginning of his ministry, his commission from God. It signals both the start of his public ministry and his solidarity with sinners. It is like the prophetic sign-acts in Hebrew scripture; it unifies Jesus with the movement toward repentance (v. 4), sets an example for his followers, and serves as a metaphor for the sanctification of water for sacramental use.

Verses 10 and 11 are particularly interesting. Note, first, that only Jesus sees the heavens open and hears the voice. Again, we have access to information that those in the narrative do not have. In Mark's day it was popularly believed that there was a plurality of heavens; God dwelt in the most remote of these. The "tearing apart" (or rending or splitting) of the heavens (which, ironically, is paralleled in 15:38 as the temple curtain is torn) is a symbol of God's coming down (see Isa. 64:1 and Ps. 144:5). In rabbinic literature the dove appears not only as a symbol of peace, but of purity, divine creativity, and the Spirit of God. The voice from heaven (probably a Greek equivalent of the Hebrew *bat qol*, literally "daughter of a voice") confirms to Jesus his divine nature, "you are my Son, the Beloved" (a combination of Isa. 42:1 and Ps. 2:7). "Beloved Son" is used again at 9:7; in 12:1-11 and 15:39, "son" is used in connection with Jesus' martyrdom. We are to understand "beloved" (*agapetos*) here as similar to "chosen" in Isa. 42:1. An expanded translation might read "that of which there is only one," as Aristotle uses the term and as it is used of Isaac in the LXX translation of Gen 22:2 to denote uniqueness.

A number of motifs from Hebrew scripture are important for preaching this passage. As noted, the connection is made between Jesus the Beloved Son whom God loves and Isaac the beloved son whom Abraham loved. Is Mark foreshadowing another sacrifice? Second, we find here the fulfillment of God's promise to crown a messianic Son in Ps. 2:6-7 (a hymn of royal accession). And finally in Isa. 42:1, God has promised to commission a servant by the Spirit. Note, as well, that all three persons of the Trinity are present: the Son, the Holy Spirit (as a dove), and God (as the voice).

For Further Reading

Stephen Gero, "The Spirit as a Dove at the Baptism of Jesus," *NovT* 18 (1976).

R. Harrisville, "Mark 1:4-11," *Int* 47 (1993): 399–402.

William Stenger, "The Baptism of Jesus," *BRev* 1 (1985).

Lamar Williamson Jr., "Mark 1:1-8," *Int* 32 (1978): 400–404.

The Temptation of Jesus
1:12-13

Note that the events related in vv. 2-13 all occur in the wilderness and are linked by references to the Holy Spirit. Like those passages, vv. 12-13 are replete with scriptural associations. Mark expects his hearers to remember the forty years' wilderness testing of the Hebrew people, Moses' forty days on the mountain, and Elijah's trip to Mt. Horeb. These images will reappear at the transfiguration in chapter 9 (cf. Wis. of Sol. 2:12-20; 5:1-7).

It is the Spirit who "drives" or "forces" or "casts out" (*ekballei*) Jesus into the wilderness (for "wilderness" associations see 1:2-8 above). "Satan" (v. 12) is an example of Mark retaining an Aramaic term. That Jesus is with "wild beasts" that do not harm him is a depiction of the curses of Genesis 3 lifted and the harmony of created beings restored. If Mark is written for a Roman audience, certainly "wild beasts" would remind them of the horrors of the arena. Jesus' victory over his temptations is marked by the ministration of angels. The malign spirits that appear later in Mark's Gospel recognize Jesus because they have met him and been overcome in these encounters.

Mark's account of the temptation of Jesus is much shorter than either Matthew's or Luke's. This may be because he does not have access to a source (Q?) that they share. Or, and I tend to prefer this view, it may be because Mark understands *all* of Jesus' public ministry to be filled with temptation, but especially the temptation to be Messiah in a way that fulfills human expectation rather than divine plan. The lectionaries for the first Sunday of Lent usually include prior or following verses with this text. To introduce Lent by means of it allows the preacher to stress Jesus' identity as the one who shares our struggles and temptations with us.

For Further Reading

Susan R. Garrett, *The Temptations of Jesus in Mark's Gospel* (Grand Rapids: Eerdmans, 1998).

Jerome Murphy-O'Connor, "Triumph Over Temptation," *BRev* 15 (1999): 34–43, 48–49.

The Gospel in Miniature
1:14-15

Having introduced Jesus in two narrative sequences (vv. 9-11 and 12-13), Mark now gives a verbal portrait of him by summarizing his preaching. Note first that Jesus does not proclaim (or preach, *kerusson*) Jesus, but the "good news of God" (*euaggelion tou theou*). In these days of "christological warfare," preachers do well to remember this. Mark will narrate the story of John's arrest in 6:14-29. Alluding to it here provides another foreshadowing of the final end of both John and Jesus. John's ministry was in Judea (v. 5). So as not to compete, and because it is his own home territory, Jesus begins to preach in Galilee. For Mark, Galilee, with its mixed population of Jews and Gentiles, provides a link to Christianity's Gentile mission (in which he has particular interest). Recall that the disciples are to return to Galilee after the resurrection of Jesus (16:1-8). Galilee, the "ordinary" place of day-to-day life, is the locus of ministry.

Verse 15 gives in summary form the content of Jesus' preaching. It is constructed of two indicatives ("the time is fulfilled, and the kingdom of God has come near") and two imperatives ("repent, and believe in the good news")—the "facts" (what we are to believe) and the "acts" (what we are to do) of Christianity. Ancients believed that the course of history was determined beforehand; "the time is fulfilled" reflects that belief. (See also Dan. 7:22; Josephus's *Antiquities* VI. 4.1; Gal. 4:4; and the premise of Ephesians that history unfolds according to God's plan.) That the "kingdom is at hand" (or "has begun to arrive," *'eggiken*)[8] speaks to expectations in Jesus' world. As a result of the "drawing closer" of the kingdom, Jesus preaches (as John did) that people must repent and, additionally, believe the Gospel. The substance of that Gospel is the nearness of God, good news in any age. Hereafter in Mark when the teaching or preaching of Jesus is mentioned without specified content, we are to "fill in the blank" with 1:14-15.

Summary
1:1-15

Mark 1:1-15 provides all the information necessary to understand Jesus. It sets forth his titles (v. 1) and links him to Israel's history (vv. 2-8). The titles are confirmed in vv. 9-11 and demonstrated in reality in vv. 12-13, and the substance of Jesus' message is given in vv. 14-15. As noted in the introduction of this work, entitled "Mark the Theologian," Mark is particularly interested in both the authority of Jesus and in discipleship. Jesus has authority, and disciples are to be like Jesus. Jesus came not to be served, but to serve (10:45). Thus the disciples are to be servants (9:35; 10:43-44). These themes are prefigured in Mark's prologue. By means of allusion to Hebrew scripture, John the Baptist is to be understood as an "authority figure." But he stoops to untie sandals, which is slave work, and announces that one mightier than he is coming (v. 7). By means of the voice from heaven at his baptism, Jesus is introduced as this "more powerful" one, but the first thing that happens to him is that he is driven into the wilderness and tempted. Already Mark has begun to present the paradoxes that are at the heart of Jesus' identity and, thus, the mission of his disciples. The forerunner has done his work; the ministry of the Son can begin. The Spirit has been manifested (vv. 10, 12); the Father has spoken

(v. 11); and the Son has preached (v. 15). It remains to present the work of the Son.

The Typical Features of Jesus' Ministry
1:16-39

Having revealed the identity of Jesus to his hearers (readers) at the outset, Mark now characterizes the public ministry of Jesus by relating an example of each of its components. In his active ministry, Jesus called disciples (1:16-20), taught and preached (1:21-22, 38-39), exorcised demons (1:23-26; 32-34), healed (1:29-31, 32, 34), and withdrew for prayer (1:35). From the outset, Mark tells us what it is Jesus actually does and what it is he understands himself as called to do, "that I may proclaim the message . . . for that is what I came out to do" (1:38).

This section of the first chapter also introduces several of the primary literary forms from which Mark constructed his Gospel. It includes a call story, miracles, controversy dialogues, and summary passages. It also prefigures Jesus' unique view of the law (he not only teaches but heals on the Sabbath), the incomprehension of his disciples (who do not understand his need for prayer or his role as preacher, 1:35-38), and the fact that Jesus' view of his role (he felt called to "proclaim the message") differed from that of his disciples (and the crowds who, at this point, respond to the wonderworker but not the preacher). Finally, note that 1:21-39 is cast as a "typical day." It begins in the evening with the coming of Sabbath (1:21), continues during the evening of that Sabbath (v. 32), and ends after the Sabbath "in the morning while it was still very dark" (v. 35). These texts appear in the lectionary early in Epiphany because they "manifest" or "show forth" the character of Jesus' ministry.

1:16-20

If the previous pericope presents the Gospel in miniature, this one presents the proper response to it: people follow (that is, become disciples). It is cast as two call stories. The pattern of a call story is as follows: first, Jesus is described as passing by (1:16, 19), then he says something or issues a call (1:17, 20), and finally, those who are called follow (1:18, 20).

Both call stories occur, according to Jewish usage, by what Mark calls the "Sea of Galilee" (Roman usage was the Sea of Tiberias; Luke simply says "the lake"). In the first story (vv. 16-18), Jesus sees two biological brothers, Simon and Andrew, fishing with nets. Simon, later called Peter, is the first disciple called, thus his prototypical character and his literal primacy in Mark. *Follow* is a technical term for discipleship. The call in

v. 17 echoes the words of Elijah in 1 Kings 18:21, "If YHWH is God, follow him!" (Remember that Jesus is mistaken for Elijah, Mark 8:28.) Peter and Andrew immediately choose to be disciples by their own volition, but they are "made" fishers of humans, *anthropon* (an idea found in Jer. 16:16 and in Greek philosophy), by Jesus.

In the second call story (vv. 19-20), James and John are also biological brothers (this is important to remember when Jesus redefines family in 3:31-35) and always appear in this order in Mark. That they owned a boat and could afford hired help suggests that they were not poor peasants. They were small business owners. The brothers did not leave their father to do the work alone; they left him with the hired workers. What they do is exchange biological family for the family of God (see 3:31-35).

The call of the first disciples makes three important points. First, it introduces the radical nature of discipleship. Peter and Andrew leave their nets (the symbol of their professional lives), and James and John leave their father (the symbol of biological family) to go with Jesus (cf. 10:28-31). Second, Mark makes very clear that Jesus was not a "solo performer," a "lone ranger." He calls disciples to help him carry out his mission. (This provides a Gospel paradigm for mutual ministry.) Third, the immediate response of the fishermen indicates the success of the ministry of John the Baptist. I suspect we are to understand the response of the brothers as "prepared" by the preaching of the Baptist whose fame certainly reached north of Judea.

For Further Reading

Jerome Murphy O'Connor, "Fishers of Fish, Fishers of Men," *BRev* 15 (1911): 22–27, 48–49.

J. Reuman, "Mark 1:14-20," *Int* 32 (1978): 405–10.

1:21-28

This text for "Ordinary Time (Epiphany) 4" is a pivotal point in Mark's narrative. Here Jesus both speaks and does, teaches and exorcises. But Mark's interest is in the response of the onlookers (vv. 22, 27) and the spreading fame of Jesus (v. 28). Additionally, Jesus' own view of Sabbath is introduced (v. 21) and the cosmic nature of the conflict in Mark's Gospel is revealed (vv. 24-26). This is not just "Jesus versus the unclean spirit"; it is the power of God versus the powers of evil.

Capernaum was at the north end of the Sea of Galilee on the highway between Ptolemais and Damascus. It was an important Galilean town, a center of customs and the location of a tax office, so it was an outpost of Roman administration. In describing Jesus' movements in Capernaum, Mark narrates in the plural (Peter's memory?). Jesus' first act in Capernaum is to enter the synagogue and teach "as one having authority" (*os exousian exhon*, v. 22). The scribes' teaching would have been on the basis of precedent (rather like our own legal system, which involves quoting precedents set by earlier cases). "Authority" is an interesting word. *Exousia* is sometimes described as being a compound of *ex*, "out of" and *ousia*, "being." Jesus taught "out of his being" rather than by quoting sources. However, *exousian* here is the feminine participle of *exestin*, meaning "it is free" or "it is permitted"; therefore, it refers not to the manner of Jesus' teaching, but to its legitimacy. Jesus has the right (Latin, *auctoritas*) to teach as he does.

"Unclean spirit" (*pneumati akatharto*) is a rare expression outside the New Testament. Whether the spirit itself was unclean or demon possession led to ritual uncleanness is a moot point. The effect of having an unclean spirit was to separate a person from the worshipping community of Israel and thus from God. The spirits know Jesus because he had overcome them in his wilderness temptation. Verse 24b is in the vocative case and might be translated "I know who you are, you holy one of God" (cf. 1 Kings 17:18). Jesus silences the spirits with a common formula of exorcism (*phimotheti*, literally "be muzzled") found in Hellenistic magic papyri to express the binding of a person by means of a powerful spell. Interestingly, after the spirit leaves the man, the crowd is amazed but responds in terms of Jesus' "new teaching" (v. 27), not his exorcism. The point is that the teaching of Jesus with which the pericope opens has its authority confirmed by his ability to cast out unclean spirits. The result is "instant fame" (v. 28), and it is this fame (which begins in a well-known center) that will bring Jesus to the notice of the authorities (with the resulting conflicts).

In preaching the passage, there are two obvious "points of entry." The first is the authority of Jesus, which can be approached by means of a bit of etymological work. The second has to do with demon possession or evil spirits. In *The Screwtape Letters*, the eminently sensible C. S. Lewis notes that we make two mistakes vis-à-vis devils. We either assume they do not exist or we manifest an excessive (even obsessive) interest in them. Certainly Mark's Gospel proclaims Jesus' victory over the dark forces of the spirit world. But I suspect in our day the "contact point" of the story is the exclusionary effect of possession. What are the "demons" that exclude persons from full participation in the worshipping community today? And how would Jesus respond to them?

For Further Reading

R. Dillon, "As One Having Authority (Mark 1:22): The Controversial Distinction of Jesus' Teaching," *CBQ* 57 (1995): 92–113.

1:29-34

This unit has two parts: the healing of Simon's mother-in-law (vv. 29-31) and a Markan summary (vv. 32-34). It extends the authority of Jesus from exorcism in the realm of the spirit to healing in the realm of the body. The first account relates retrospectively that the two sets of brothers had accompanied Jesus to synagogue (v. 29), so they were eyewitnesses of Jesus' teaching, authority, and power. That Simon has a mother-in-law indicates that at some point he also had a wife and lived in the typical extended-family dwellings of first-century Palestine. Note that the house belongs to Peter and Andrew (v. 29), so it probably did house more than one family. And, in fact, the house in Capernaum known since the fourth century as Peter's is larger than others excavated nearby. "They" (the brothers? those in Simon's house?) report to Jesus the illness of Simon's mother-in-law "at once," suggesting a serious illness about which there is some urgency. Jesus' response is to take her by the hand (v. 31). This is significant for several reasons. First, it is the first instance of the typical way that Jesus effects healing in Mark's Gospel; he touches. Second, that he touches is another subtle way Mark tells us that Jesus is not "as the scribes" (v. 22). To touch a sick person was to risk ritual uncleanliness, and the risk was increased because the invalid was a woman. Jesus ignores these barriers and heals both by word (1:25) and by touch (1:31). In preaching the text, it would certainly be appropriate to note the appearance of Word (both Jesus' words and Jesus the Word) and sacrament, symbolized by the healing touch of Jesus.

Modern readers sometimes stumble over v. 31b. The problem is usually expressed something like this: "That poor woman—she has been sick and now she has to jump up and *serve?*" and worse, presumably serve the men, the two sets of brothers and Jesus. The Greek helps us understand Mark's point. First, "to heal" and "to save" are the same Greek verb, *sozo.* That she "serves" after she is "healed" proves that she is also "saved" and restored to community. "Served" in Greek is *diekonei,* the same root from which we get the English word *deacon.* In the New Testament, the word is usually found with the implication of some official work on behalf of the Christian community. That Simon's mother-in-law "served" is Mark's way of telling us that she took her full place among the disciples who, after all, are charged to be servants (10:42-45). The standard pattern in Mark is that those Jesus heals either "follow" or "serve," and this is how their understanding and discipleship are demonstrated. Simon's mother-in-law may be the first person in the Gospel to understand what being a disciple of Jesus means.

Verses 32-34 are a Markan summary. Since it is "evening at sundown" (an example of Markan redundancy), the Sabbath is over and the sick and possessed can be "legally" carried to Jesus. Verse 33 suggests both a particular occasion and introduces an important Markan detail. *Where* Jesus acts or teaches is important in Mark. When he is "in the house," the miracle or teaching is intended for the inner circle of disciples; "around the door" is public, an activity for all to see.[9] Verse 34 says very subtly that "he cured many," but we wonder, "not all?" Is this the report of a truthful eyewitness? The verse also contains the first hint in the Gospel of the "messianic secret," Jesus' charge: "Don't tell." Here the demon's question in 1:24 is answered.

Jesus expels demons and charges them not to tell who he is because he wants the people to decide about him for themselves (see 8:29), and because he does not want to be known as a thaumaturge. As the next pericope makes clear, he has come to proclaim the message (1:15). Mark leaves the reader with a sense that Jesus has had a very full day: teaching in the synagogue, a single exorcism, a single healing, a "family occasion" (dinner?), and then multiple healings and exorcisms.

1:35-39

Following the previous summary passage with its description of active ministry, Mark inserts a picture of Jesus that "rights the balance." Jesus is not hyperactive; he sets aside time for solitary prayer. Even though he has had a full day previously, Jesus gets up well before dawn and goes out "to a deserted place" (more desert spirituality as in 1:2-8, 12-13) to pray. That he had to be "hunted" (v. 36) and "found" (v. 37) implies the remoteness of the place of prayer Jesus sought. He really wanted to be alone. Jesus actively seeks prayer, relationship with God. The source of Jesus' authority and power springs from this dependence upon God.

But, as they will so frequently, the disciples do not "get it." They seek Jesus out; "hunted for him" (v. 36) employs a verb (*katediochen, zetousin*) that is used in Mark with negative implications. Those who "hunt for him" or "seek him out" do so to kill him (11:18; 12:12; 14:1, 11, 55) or to distract him from his true mission (3:32; 8:11). As is frequently the case, Peter is the spokesman for the disciples and, here as in 8:32, the voice of temptation. Jesus seems unmoved by the popularity that Simon so eagerly announces in v. 37. Jesus' task is not to be a wonderworker, but to "proclaim the message" in the towns around Capernaum, which serves as the headquarters of the Galilean mission in Mark's Gospel. The preacher might well reflect on how we can be led from our calling by well-meaning but misguided persons. Or, seen another way, how many have I distracted from God's call? How many have I judged for "wasting time" alone rather than being engaged in active ministry?

Verse 39 is another Markan summary. It indicates, first, that Jesus is working in a relatively small geographical area, and second, that he is working with his own Jewish people "in their synagogues." I wonder if the fact that Mark designates the synagogues as "theirs" suggests that his own community had broken with the synagogue. Finally, the summary verse reminds us that Jesus' mission is to preach and that he also casts out demons, both activities that have been established as authoritative.

1:16-39
Summary

In the first fifteen verses of chapter 1, Mark has identified who Jesus is; in these verses he demonstrates what Jesus does. In philosophical terms, vv. 1-15 are his essential definition of Jesus, and vv. 16-39 his functional definition. Jesus' typical activities include calling disciples (vv. 16-20), teaching and preaching (vv. 21-22, 27, 38-39), exorcising demons (vv. 23-26, 32-34, 39), healing bodily diseases (vv. 30-31, 32-34), and withdrawing for prayer (v. 35). What the Master does, the disciples are to do. These activities continue today, but the church now calls them evangelism, education, preaching, social service ministries, and spirituality. Mark wants to indicate something of the stress and pace of Jesus' ministry, so he telescopes a great deal into a twenty-four-hour period. But he also shows us that Jesus' life was balanced; he visited with friends in their homes and took time out to pray. The need for that sort of balanced life is, itself, an important preaching point in our day.

The authority of Jesus' teaching has been remarked upon by those who hear him and confirmed by his ability to cast out demons and to heal. News of this man of authority and power travels quickly; those in Capernaum and those in neighboring towns experience it. Mark stresses the authority of Jesus, and in so doing he prefigures the conflicts that will follow, first with the Jewish authorities, and then with Rome. Mark 1:16-39 depicts the typical ministry of Jesus. Mark 1:40—3:35 depicts the inevitable response to it.

2

The Opposition in Galilee

Mark 1:40—3:35

Mark 1:40—3:35 continues Mark's presentation of the Galilean ministry of Jesus and introduces the conflicts that ensued from it. The material falls into two sections: 1:40—3:6 is a collection of miracles with embedded conflicts situated largely in Capernaum, and 3:7-35 describes the formation of the community around Jesus.

Introduction
1:40—3:6

The healing of the leper in 1:40-45 can either finish the "typical ministry" material of 1:16-39 or introduce the opposition in Galilee. I opt for the latter, because in the pericope Jesus heals a man of a disease that was thought to be a judgment from God and then clarifies his view of the law (Jesus commands the man to keep it, 1:44). These two aspects, healing and interpretation of the law, characterize the following five stories.

All of the pericopae from 2:1—3:6, then, deal with healings and conversations about the law. Lightfoot notes that each of the five conflict stories has a saying of Jesus with a vital bearing on the Gospel message.[1] The stories depict the first stirrings of opposition to Jesus by the scribes and Pharisees, and they exhibit a pattern of escalating conflict that continues throughout the Gospel. Confrontation with Jesus proceeds from the scribes' internal questions (2:6), to questioning Jesus' disciples (2:16), to direct confrontation with him (2:24) in hopes that "they might accuse him" (3:2) and plot "to destroy him" (3:6). The matter at issue in all these conflicts is the authority of Jesus.[2] Mark highlights the contrast between the positive response to Jesus shown by the general populace and the hostility from officialdom. If we see 1:40—3:6 primarily as controversy stories, then the whole active ministry of Jesus is framed by like material, since most of his last public teaching (11:27—12:27) is also cast in this form.

In a very helpful essay, Joanna Dewey focuses on the miracle story aspect of 2:1—3:6.[3] She thinks that the unit is a collection of stories compiled (or received) by Mark in chiastic (cross) form as follows:

A	2:1-12	healing (sin)
B	2:13-17	eating (sin)
C	2:18-22	fasting
B1	2:23-28	eating (Sabbath)
A1	3:1-6	healing (Sabbath)

Dewey notes that pericopae A and A1 have nearly identical introductions and contain controversy stories within healing miracles. A and B deal with forgiveness of sins and association with sinners. B1 and A1 address Sabbath observance. As the stories progress, opposition to Jesus grows. At first Jesus' opposition is silent (2:6), but then his disciples are questioned (2:16). Jesus himself is queried (2:18, 24), then watched (3:1), and finally plotted against by those who would normally be enemies, the Pharisees and Herodians (3:6). The pattern of opposition and hostility to Jesus depicted here escalates through the rest of Mark's Gospel until his betrayal and arrest in chapter 14.

Since much of the material in the first half of Mark deals with Jesus' miracles, a word about them is in order here.[4] Most of the miracles of Jesus that Mark relates occur in the first nine chapters of the Gospel (there are seventeen miracles in chapters 1 to 8), chapters that reveal who Jesus is. It is important to remember that the question raised by Mark's original audience would not have been: "Can Jesus do miracles?"; their world accepted and was filled with miracle workers (some of whom we know by name: Eleazar, Honi, Hanina ben Dosa, Apollonius of Tyana, for example). Instead, they would ask: "By whose power does Jesus do miracles?" The issue, once again, is the authority of Jesus. Mark relates miracle stories, in part, to demonstrate that Jesus manifests the power of God. The miracles of Jesus are "proof ocular" that the reign of God has begun. Or, as Adela Yarbro Collins puts it, the "extraordinary deeds" of Jesus were the sign of the dawning of a new age (recall 1:15) and authorized Jesus as the eschatological agent of God.[5]

Miracle stories of healing in ancient literature followed a literary form observable in the Gospels. Accounts of healing miracles generally have six features: (1) the sickness is described, (2) the failure of physicians is recounted, (3) the ill person encounters the healer, (4) the cure is related, (5) there is some proof given that the sufferer is healed, and (6) the reaction of the spectators (who serve as witnesses that a miracle happened) is noted. This literary pattern can provide the framework for a narrative sermon on almost any of Jesus' miracles. Markan miracle stories usually follow this pattern but may also lead to a pronouncement by Jesus. In the secondary literature, these miracle stories are sometimes also called "pronouncement stories" or "apophthegms." Preachers should be alert to the fact that when these sayings occur, they are the "point" of the miracle story, the reason why Mark relates it. These pericopae appear late in the Epiphany lectionary (so are not preached when Epiphany is a "short season") or begin the post-Easter "Ordinary Time," thus setting the stage for the long season of discipleship teaching that Year B's Markan texts afford.

For Further Reading

B. L. Blackburn, "Miracles and Miracle Stories" in *DJG*, 549–60.

Joanna Dewey, "The Literary Structure of the Controversy Stories in Mark 2:1—3:6," *JBL* 92 (1973): 394–401 (reprinted in Telford).

Harold E. Remus, "Miracles (N.T.)," *ABD* 4:856–69.

1:40-45

Leprosy was for Mark a catchall term for any one of a number of skin diseases. The salient thing about these diseases was that they led to the exclusion of the leper from his or her community. Leviticus 13 and 14 provide a graphic depiction of such skin diseases and their consequences and are a good place to begin preparation of the sermon.

Note that for the first time in Mark a person approaches Jesus of his own volition for healing. He asks not to be healed, but to be made clean (*katharisai*, which the LXX uses for both physical and ceremonial cleaning), indicating the religious significance of his disease. Mark is more likely than the other evangelists to reveal the emotional state of Jesus. The textual variant in v. 41 has to do with Jesus' response. The minority of ancient manuscripts read that Jesus was *angry* (*orgistheis*), not "moved with pity" (*splagchnistheis*), as in the NRSV. Following the principle that the more difficult reading is likely to be the authentic one, I think the "minority opinion" is correct.[6] Anger is an appropriate response to the devastating effects of disease, especially disease that leads to social ostracism. Considering all the pastoral issues that arise around anger, the appropriateness of Jesus' anger may be the preaching point in the text. Anger is certainly important to consider when working with those suffering from serious illness and their families. As in 1:31, then, Jesus reaches out to touch the "unclean" one to effect healing, which is instantaneous (1:42). Contact with Jesus makes the leper clean; indeed, contact with Jesus restores him to community.

There are at least two important points in verses 43-45. First, Jesus does not defy the law or religious custom. He sends the man to fulfill the law (v. 44), to present proof of his healing to the priests, presumably so that they could officially certify that he was "clean." Mark is informing the careful hearer and reader: charges that Jesus ignores the law are false.

Second, the "secrecy motif" (see "Mark the Theologian" in the introduction to this book) appears prominently here as Jesus charges the former leper, "See that you say nothing to anyone" (v. 44). But the man disobeys Jesus, with the result that Jesus "could no longer go into a town openly" (v. 45). Human disobedience hinders God's designs. Jesus cannot go into the towns to preach as he feels called to do (1:38-39). Instead, people come out to him in the country as they did to hear the Baptist. The preaching point may be the issue of how human disobedience to direct commands of Jesus (God) are not only "sinful" (the usual approach to the problem), but restrict and hinder the Lord's ability to act on our behalf. Jesus takes human decisions and behavior seriously enough to accept the consequences of them.

2:1-12

To this point Mark has painted a picture of Jesus' expanding field of operations; he moves from synagogue (1:21) and house (1:29), to "outside" (1:33, 45), to "throughout Galilee" (1:39). Now he returns to Capernaum (to his own home or to Peter's), the headquarters of his Galilean ministry.[7] His popularity was such (1:28) that the house was filled, and people were gathered before the door (1:33, 2:2) where Jesus preached to them. In Mark, the location of Jesus' teaching is important. "Outside" or "in front of the door" teachings are general and for everyone; "inside" or "in the house" teaching is usually special instruction to the disciples (see, for example, 4:10, 34). But hearing the word (which we later learn is a technical term for the Gospel, 4:14, 33) is not enough for the crowd. As is usual at this stage of the Galilean ministry, teaching gives way to healing. The two-part account that follows exhibits a characteristically Markan intercalation: the healing story begins (vv. 3-5), the controversy interrupts (vv. 6-9), and the healing is concluded (vv. 10-12).

Verses 3 and 4 describe the practical caring and persistence of a paralyzed man's friends. The house in question is a typical Galilean house of the period. It probably had a flat roof made of sticks and mud that was reached by outside stairs. To Jesus, removal of the roof is not an act of vandalism (an affront to private property!), but an act of faith (v. 5). It is to faith that he responds, using familial language with the paralytic: "son (*teknon*, literally 'child') your sins are forgiven" (v. 5). How does this speak to the paralytic's problem? The assumption behind the healing and the resulting controversy is that of Job's friends, that is, that illness and sin are connected. The Talmud notes that "no man gets up from his sickbed until all his sins are forgiven" (*Nedarim* 41a). This is why Jesus speaks a word of forgiveness first and why the scribes are concerned about blasphemy (vv. 6-7). Because only God can forgive sin (see Ps. 103:3; Isa. 43:25), when Jesus forgives sin it appears to be blasphemy (see Lev. 24:13-16). When the man walks (v. 12), it is proof that his sin is forgiven.

The healing account sandwiches Jesus' first controversy with official-dom, here scribes (vv. 6-10), the students of scripture and law. Apparently Jesus has a special sensitivity to others (see 5:30); he "perceived in his spirit" the questions of the scribes. Jesus' response is typical of his peda-gogical method; he asks a question. In an article that sheds immense light on the controversy stories in Mark, Jerome Neyrey notes that questions are characteristic devices in ancient rhetoric.[8] They are used as weapons. In a culture driven by shame and honor, one that understood honor to be in "finite quantity," to win a dispute with a clever question was to shame those perceived as losing the debate. Jesus answers his opponents' ques-tions (even their unspoken ones); thus they lose respect (they are shamed) in the eyes of the onlookers, whose positive response to Jesus confirms his "victory" (v. 12). This dynamic helps to explain the increasing hostility of officials to Jesus.

In the midst of this encounter, Jesus makes reference to himself as "Son of Man" (Aramaic, *bar-nash[a]*, "man") a title that has led to much spec-ulation.[9] Generally scholarship holds one of three positions: (1) the title is a circumlocution for "I," (2) means simply a typical human being, or (3) is linked to its appearance in Dan. 7:13-14 with its Messianic implications. (See, for example, Acts 7:56.) In his book *Jesus: Lord and Savior,* F. F. Bruce summarizes the discussion this way:

> . . . "The Son of Man" was Jesus' way of referring to himself and his mis-sion—a form of words that had no antecedent significance for his hear-ers, so that he could fill it with whatever meaning he chose—represen-tative man, righteous sufferer, obedient servant of God, or the one fore-ordained to be invested with universal authority.[10]

While we cannot solve the scholarly debate here, the context in 2:10 suggests that Jesus understands the title to imply some authority or right to act. That the man stands is a subtle way to communicate that Jesus is, indeed, God's special representative. The pericope ends as a typical mira-cle story with the crowd's amazement and with their glorifying God (v. 12), suggesting that they made some connection between Jesus' words and deed and God's operative presence.

This is a rich passage for preaching, but let me suggest six points, each of which begins with Jesus the healer. First, the healing Jesus heals whole peo-ple, spirits and bodies (vv. 8-9). Jesus "puts people back together." Second, "speaking the word" is part of the healing of Jesus (v. 2). The Healer is first and foremost the Proclaimer. Third, sometimes it takes effort to get to the Jesus who heals. Some get there of their own volition and some have to be carried (vv. 3-4). Fourth, the Jesus who heals is not sidetracked by theologi-cal debate. What he says and what he does are consistent (vv. 6-11). Fifth, the

Jesus who proclaims and heals is not welcomed by everybody. It is noteworthy in this pericope that it is the religious establishment that is threatened and unwelcoming (vv. 6-7). Finally, the Jesus who heals sends people home, back to the locus of their everyday activities (v. 12). We take up our mats to go home to our responsibilities. But we return as changed, healed persons.

For Further Reading

Lewis Hay, "The Son of Man in Mark 2:10 and 2:28," *JBL* 89 (1970): 69–75.

2:13-17

The story begins outside and moves inside. Again, in Mark, when crowds gather, Jesus teaches (1:39; 2:2). The call of Levi in v. 14 is similar to those in 1:16-20 with the important difference that this man is a tax collector. The NRSV translates *telonai* "tax collector," one who collects taxes directly for Rome and is thus a "quisling," a traitor. John Donahue has argued persuasively that the better translation is "toll collector," tolls being more minor taxes (sales, customs, transport) and paid via Antipas, not the Romans. *Telonai* appears in the New Testament only at the commercial centers of Capernaum and Jericho.[11] In any case, tolls and taxes were a particular burden in first-century Palestine. In addition to the tax the Jews paid to maintain the Temple in Jerusalem, there were taxes on water, meat, and salt. There were road, city, house, and poll taxes. Tax and toll collectors were particularly suspect because they "leased" their positions. The lessee paid the tax in advance and was then free to keep whatever he could extort above that requirement. Tax and toll collectors were generally understood to engage in a dishonest occupation and were in such ill repute that their evidence was not accepted in court and their alms were not accepted in synagogue and temple. It was dirty money.

Levi probably collected customs or transport or import/export taxes at the port of Capernaum as the tax officer for Herod Antipas. This is not necessarily his first encounter with Jesus, since the latter had some reputation in the area (1:28, 39; 2:13). Except for the four chief disciples, Levi is the only other mentioned by name, and he is called as they were with the technical formula "follow me" (*akolouthei moi*). The startling thing, of course, is that Jesus calls a tax collector an outcast. Having just dealt with a leper, Jesus calls another outcast to demonstrate that no one is beyond God's call and grace.

And Jesus not only calls Levi; he shares table fellowship with him. Verse 15 literally says that they "reclined" (*katakeisthai*), suggesting this may be a celebratory or ceremonial meal. The NRSV indicates that the house is Levi's, but the Greek reads simply "his." It appears that Jesus had a home in Capernaum (cf. 2:1). We do well to remember that Mark's community met in house churches, so these home settings would especially resonate with Roman Christians. The anger of the scribes and Pharisees in v. 16 would be greater if Jesus, a Jew, were entertaining toll collectors and sinners in his home. The point is not where, but who: "many tax collectors and sinners were also [reclining] with Jesus and his disciples—for there were many who followed him" (v. 15). Jesus flouts social convention and religious regulation by the irregular house guests he entertains (or by whom he is entertained). These "tax collectors" or "publicans" were civil servants who bought their positions for the highest bid. The identity of the "sinners" (*hamartoloi*) has been variously interpreted as (1) moral reprobates, (2) Jews who by reason of occupation could not keep the purity laws, (3) Gentiles. In Mark, "sinners" probably ought not to be thought of as having broken the moral code (thieves, killers, adulterers, and so forth), but as those who did not meet the Pharisees' high purity standards or whose occupations (like the toll collectors') were suspect. The point is that they all followed (the technical term *hekolouthoun* is used) Jesus. Mark's first use of the term "disciples" (*mathetais*) indicates that already there were many of them and that they were an odd company: small business owners, those who worked for Rome or Rome's retainers (who hardly helped small businesses), the religiously unclean, those of questionable or dishonest occupations.

It is little wonder that the scribes and Pharisees are shocked by the company the teacher Jesus keeps. *Berakoth* 43b records, "a disciple of the wise must not sit at table with *Amhaarez* (people of the land)." Note that the religious officials do not at this point confront Jesus; they approach some of his many disciples. But "perceiving in his spirit" (2:8), overhearing, or upon having the question repeated to him, Jesus responds that these are exactly the people to whom he has come. Only sick people need a doctor. He has not come to call the righteous who, since they are keeping the law, are already in proper relationship to God, but sinners. Indeed, by the Pharisees' own standards this is exactly who Jesus has called (the word in 2:17 is exactly that in 1:20) and healed: fishermen, an older woman, a leper, a toll collector. In following Jesus, there is room at the table for all comers.

This might well provide the entrée to the sermon: all the wrong people are Jesus' associates. The religious people, the Pharisees (who, note, seem themselves to be present and thus ironically keeping the same company they criticize), are in an antagonistic relationship to Jesus and to his understanding of his call. The Pharisees would not have come to this odd dinner party if they had not heard of Jesus. Now they see him breaking, or at least bending, the rules (preparing us for the Sabbath controversies in 2:23—3:6). This important story establishes Jesus' vocation as that of saving sinners (*not* the first-century equivalent of "nice church people") and is a subtle criticism of those who thought themselves righteous. The self-righteous are in worse shape than the "sinner" Levi, who knew he needed help. Preach that if you dare!

For Further Reading

John Donahue, "Tax Collectors and Sinners," *CBQ* 33 (1971): 39–61.

Elizabeth Struthers Malbon, "*Th Oikia Aytoy:* Mark 2:15 in Context," *NTS* 31 (1985): 282–92.

2:18-22

This story may well reflect issues in Mark's community and the early church; it may reflect a later stage of dispute between Christians and Jews over different fasting practices or the question of why Christians fasted when Jesus did not. The Jewish community kept both general fasts like the Day of Atonement (and, later, the day of the Temple burning) and voluntary fasts (understood as a sign of piety). The Pharisee in Luke 18:12, for example, holds up his twice-weekly fasts as proof of his piety. The disciples of John the Baptist fasted for repentance and were esteemed for doing so. If John's disciples and the Pharisees, both understood to be serious about religion, fasted, why not the disciples of Jesus?

The question is now addressed directly to Jesus. His answer has two parts: vv. 19-20 and vv. 21-22. Verses 19-20 are a sort of "implied parable." Weddings were important social events in Palestinian villages. They lasted for a week. The men partied together and the women partied together. Weddings were so important that scholars could leave their study of Torah to attend. It would be not only bad manners but absurd to fast while the bridegroom was still in attendance (cf. Isa. 62:5 and John 3:25-30). But beyond social custom, reference to a wedding feast had religious associations. It was widely believed that when the Messiah came, he would host a great banquet, the messianic banquet, and only he could throw that particular party. (See notes on 6:30-44.) If Jesus is suggesting that he is the bridegroom, then the implications are obvious and religiously potent. If v. 19 is all celebration, v. 20 casts a pall over the party. It makes clear that the bridegroom does not stay forever. He leaves, and the fasting begins. Tertullian thought this text was about the paschal feast, so v. 20 was a prediction of Jesus' passion. It is important not to miss the implications for Jesus' own life of the bridegroom being "taken away from them"; his leaving is not voluntary but violent. (See the use of the same verb in Isa. 53:8.)

It is a little hard to find the connection between vv. 19-20 and vv. 21-22. The latter focuses on the "new way" of Jesus' disciples. Using comparisons from what was then ordinary domestic life—sewing, a woman's activity in v. 21, and winemaking, a man's activity in v. 22—Jesus stresses that sometimes new cannot be reconciled with old. To apply the idea to the metaphor at hand, the new way of Jesus (wedding feast) cannot be harmonized with the old religious customs (fasting). To attempt to do so is to spoil *both* the old and the new.

Two points are noteworthy in these two rather disparate units of tradition. First, because Jesus is among us (in the terms of the previous pericope, which is also about eating *among us* tax collectors and sinners!), we have every right to celebrate. The long emaciated face is not for the followers of Jesus! His absence, which will be experienced, is starkness itself. His presence is cause to celebrate. Second, liberation of discipleship is at the heart of vv. 21-22; the focus is upon not forcing what is new into old forms. In a passage from the Revelation to John that opens with a bridal metaphor (21:2), the one seated on the throne of heaven says, "See, I am making all things new" (21:5). That, I think, is what Mark's Jesus communicates here. But "new" is often "threatening," as it seems to have been to the Pharisees in Capernaum. How do we and our congregations respond to Jesus' invitation to newness?

For Further Reading
R. Banks, "Fasting," in *DJG*, 233–34.
John Muddiman, "Fast, Fasting," in *ADB* 2:773–76.

2:23-28

This is another in a series of stories that begins without reference to specific time or place (2:13-14, 15-17, 18-22), leading scholars to suggest that the stories were arranged in this order and were edited or redacted by Mark or by the tradition from which he received them. Taken together, they clearly depict increasing hostility to Jesus; 2:13-17 and 2:18-23 involve eating or fasting, while 2:23-28 and 3:1-6 involve Sabbath observance. The Sabbath controversies continue the old/new theme raised in 2:21-22.

Again the account falls into two parts, the narrative itself (vv. 23-26) and two sayings of Jesus (vv. 27-28). Jesus and his disciples are passing through the fields on the Sabbath. Keeping Sabbath was one of the most sacred duties of Israel (see Exod. 34:21; Deut. 5:12-15). Plucking the heads of grain was technically reaping, one of the thirty-nine activities forbidden on the Sabbath, and in any case Sabbath overrode even the pressures of harvesting (see Exod. 34:21). The Pharisees attack Jesus indirectly by questioning what his disciples are doing. But what were the Pharisees doing out in the fields on Sabbath? Were they "stationed" to spy on Jesus and his disciples? Is that how Sabbath should be kept? Note how frequently Mark's presentation of religious leaders is ironic (and tremble!).

Jesus responds by questioning the Pharisees' knowledge of scripture. It is certainly a confrontational verbal strategy, one not calculated to "win friends and influence people." He alludes to a story about David (1 Sam. 21:1-6) in which, in fact, the bread of the Presence (cf. Num. 4:7) is given to David, not taken by him. (For some this raises an interesting christological issue because it seems that Jesus has misquoted scripture.) Mark explains what the bread of Presence is (v. 26b), because his audience may be unfamiliar with Jewish practice. Using scripture very much as the Pharisees themselves did, Jesus' point is that David had the right to provide for those with him. The implied comparison is between David and Jesus (and perhaps alludes again to the messianic banquet; see notes on 2:18-22; 6:30-44).

Verses 27-28 make Jesus' principle of action explicit and reveal more of his self-understanding. Jesus does not criticize or set aside the law (1:44); it is for human good (in the case of the Sabbath, allowing rest). But if a greater good is furthered by breaking a law (here, feeding the disciples), then the lesser is broken to keep the greater. At least in Jesus' hands, the highest good has authority over the means by which it is to be attained. In Jesus' teaching the Fourth Commandment is never mentioned. It was, in fact, set aside, since by the time the Gospels were written, Christians kept not the Sabbath (the last day of the week), but the first day of the week. Note in v. 28 that, as in 2:10, when Jesus makes reference to his own authority, he uses the "Son of Man" phrase (which is not used again in Mark until 8:31, Jesus' first passion prediction). In 2:23-28 we see what the teaching authority of Jesus, remarked upon at 1:27, means in action (and we will see it again in 3:1-6).

> Jesus did not follow the procedure of contemporary rabbis. Indeed, he dismissed their rulings, handed down to one generation from another by word of mouth, as too often prone to obscure or frustrate the original intention for which the commandments were given. He appealed back to that original intention against the "tradition of the elders"; he held that a commandment was most worthily kept when its original purpose was fulfilled.[12]

In my view, 2:23-28 follows logically from 2:21-22. Both speak of new circumstances that are at hand in Jesus. A new situation has arisen; the old rules no longer fit. The questions raised about Jesus' disciples are what we would call "lifestyle issues," matters of work and of eating. It strikes me that the first objection to Jesus' disciples is not so much what they did, but what they failed to do; their sin of omission is greater than of commission. This might well provide a fresh approach to a sermon on the text. Another approach is to compare the attitude of the Pharisees (the religious authorities) to that of church people today. Have we become "Pharisaical" about lifestyle issues? Have we made of Christianity a set of "laws" (which it most assuredly is not)? Since I am not the "Son of Man," how can I or any of us know when to set aside a law and when to keep it?

For Further Reading

D. M. Cohn-Sherbok, "An Analysis of Jesus' Arguments concerning the Plucking of Grain on the Sabbath," *JSNT* 2 (1979): 31–41.

Lewis Hay, "The Son of Man in Mark 2:10 and 2:28," *JBL* 89 (1970): 69–75.

Arland Hultgren, "The Formation of the Sabbath Pericope in Mark 2:23-28," *JBL* 91 (1972): 38–43.

J. W. Leitch, "Lord Also of the Sabbath," *SJT* 19 (1966): 426–33.

3:1-6

The unit of healing/controversy stories which began at 2:1 comes to a hostile climax in this pericope. The "again" (v. 1) may be a simple Markan conjunction or may signal a repeated activity of Jesus. The setting is the synagogue, a place where Jesus regularly teaches (1:21, 39) and so a likely place in which to observe him (v. 2). Mark apparently regards the synagogue as a place of conflict and the lakeside or "outside" as a place where Jesus is well received. (Perhaps this reflects the circumstances of his own community.) "Watched" in v. 2 (*pareteroun,* literally "lie in wait for") suggests evil intent, even a setup. "They" is presumably the Pharisees from the previous pericope. (Is this the same Sabbath or another?) In this second Sabbath controversy, Jesus himself is accused.

Since Jesus regularly teaches in the synagogue we may, I think, assume that is why he enters this one. A man with a withered hand is in the congregation. Was he planted by the Pharisees? The text does not say. The apocryphal *Gospel to the Hebrews* says he was a stone mason and needed his hand to make a living; otherwise he would have to beg. Jesus calls the man forward (v. 3 "come forward," literally "arise into the midst"), and he serves as a visual aid for the point the Teacher wants to make. The question raised in v. 4 has already been raised obliquely in 2:23-28. Jesus acts in conformity with the principle he stated in 2:27. The question he poses in v. 4 is that of omission/commission, and it puts the whole principle of law at stake by implying that the refusal to do good is to do evil. Those who lie in wait for Jesus are silenced, which according to the terms of ancient rhetoric is a mark of defeat.[13]

As he frequently does, Mark notes that Jesus looked around (3:34; 5:32; 10:23) and describes Jesus' emotional state; he is angry with their hardness of heart (6:52; 8:17). In Jesus' day, the heart was not only the seat of emotion, but also of understanding and will. A hardened heart is one that does not understand. In v. 5 the man obeys Jesus' second command. He stretches out his hand, and with no further activity on Jesus' part, it is restored (literally "made like it was before" or "made good again"). The religious leaders have understood Jesus' implied criticism of them. Verse 6 brings to fearsome close this unit of material. The Pharisees, those interested in the law and its application, go out and "conspire" (*sumboulion edidoun,* literally "began to plot," the same phrase used at 15:1) with their enemies the Herodians, who supported the royal family and thus the Roman occupiers of Palestine. Under normal circumstances these two groups would have nothing to do with one another. But Jesus presents an unusual circumstance, a threat so great that, ironically, it makes co-conspirators of enemies.

In preaching the text, do not allow the conflict element of the story to overshadow its central event—Jesus' compassion for a man with a withered hand. As in the previous pericope, Jesus gives human need precedence over rules and regulations. This is an important point, especially in church communities with rigid hierarchies and inflexibly enforced canons.

Summary
1:40—3:6

This marks the end of the first cycle of Galilean conflicts between Jesus and the authorities. Mark has shaped 2:1—3:6 to depict a pattern of increasing hostility to Jesus: from silent questioning (2:6), to questioning his disciples (2:16), to directly questioning him (2:18), to plotting to destroy Jesus (3:6). From the outset of Mark's Gospel, Jesus has been judged and found guilty by the authorities. Four major reasons for their opposition to him are evident. First, Jesus claims to forgive sins (2:5), which God alone can do. Second, Jesus kept "bad company" (2:13-17). Third, Jesus *seemed* to show blatant disregard for important Jewish observances like fasting and the Sabbath. Finally (and perhaps most damning) Jesus shows concern for individuals before regulations. By Mark 3:6, Jesus has challenged social convention, ethical mores, and religious and societal strictures. This is not the gentle Sunday school Jesus, the "gentle child of gentle mother" of the children's hymn. This is a man who goes on the verbal attack and wins. On one level the conflict is shaping up to be between organized religion and freedom of the Spirit. A similar stress point was evident in the early churches, especially in Pauline communities. (See 1 Corinthians and Romans, for example.) The decision on round one of the Galilean conflict goes clearly to Jesus. Now we move to round two.

Introduction
3:7-35

This section of the Gospel represents another stage in the contest between Jesus and the authorities, although conflict may be less evident because of the framing material. The central passage, 3:19b-30, involves scribes who have come from Jerusalem, apparently to observe firsthand the work of Jesus. That encounter is framed by the formation of a new community around Jesus, the Twelve (3:13-19), and the "new family" of those who do God's will (3:31-35). The section begins with a Markan summary (3:7-12) that reiterates Jesus' need for solitude (1:35) and the increasing difficulty of having it as he became well known. Again Jesus' approval rating from the people is high but from the religious authorities is very low indeed.

There is a narrative logic in the material as an enthusiastic reception from the general populace (3:7-13) is contrasted with the skepticism of the Jerusalem scribes (3:19b-30). In response to that ongoing conflict, Jesus calls to himself a smaller group (3:13-19a) and begins to define his brethren (3:34-35). Prefigured in this last account is the constriction of the group around Jesus as the Gospel narrative as a whole progresses. From being surrounded by crowds, Jesus is accompanied by disciples. That group shrinks to the Twelve and the Twelve to the "inner circle" of Peter, James, and John, until, at his passion, Jesus is alone.

3:7-12

Following a unit of five conflict stories (2:1-3:6), this Markan summary (for others see 5:21, 6:30-33, 53-56) reminds the reader both of Jesus' great popularity with the crowds and of the wide geographic region over which news of him has spread. Verses 7 and 8 clearly exemplify Markan redundancy. (The preacher is well advised not to follow Mark's example in this!) In v. 7 the word "departed" (*anechoresen*, literally "withdrew" or "went away" but also "come back") appears only here in Mark, but its uses in Matthew occur in contexts of Jesus at prayer. The word is a compound of *ana*, "each" or "each one," and *choreo*, "to make room for, to hold, to contain." The implication is that Jesus withdraws precisely in order to make room for each person and situation that he encounters. The etymology allows for a sermon on the importance of cultivating a life of prayer.

The wide distances enumerated in v. 8 are intended to suggest the universal appeal of Jesus' actions and message. "Mark wants to stress the universal appeal of Jesus' ministry and message."[14] The NRSV's translation of v. 9 obscures another interesting point about prayer. The word translated "ready" (*proskartere*, literally "wait on") in all other uses in the New Testament speaks about diligence in prayer (see Acts 1:14; 2:42, 46; 6:4;

8:13; 10:7; Rom. 12:13; 13:16; Col. 4:2). Jesus withdraws in a boat to avoid being crushed by the crowd (cf. Luke 5:1-3). An analogical approach to the passage sees the boat as an image of what time alone in prayer is to the inner life: it keeps one from being crushed by the press of responsibilities. Verse 10 is a summary of Jesus' healings, and vv. 11-12 reprise 1:21-26 and the encounter with unclean spirits. The spirits literally prostrate themselves before him (*prosepipton auto*), thus acknowledging themselves in the presence of a superior power, the "Son of God" (a "holy one of God," 1:24). As in 1:25, Jesus commands the unclean spirits to be silent about his identity (3:12).

This short text is a "bridge." It recapitulates the picture of Jesus drawn heretofore (many "follow" him; he is the object of popular attention over a wide area; he is a healer and exorcist; the spirit world recognizes him, but the human world has not articulated its understanding of him) and prepares the hearer or reader for the next section of the Gospel. (Some scholars argue that 3:18—8:30 represents the second stage of Jesus' public ministry.) It also serves narratively to remove Jesus from organized opposition (3:6, 7). Perhaps surprisingly, it also provides rich material for a sermon on prayer.

For Further Reading
Leander E. Keck, "Mark 3:7-12 and Mark's Christology," *JBL* 84 (1965): 341–58.

3:13-19a
From the outset Mark makes clear that Jesus does not think of himself and his mission in individualistic terms. He is a team player, not a solo performer. His first public act was to call four disciples (1:16-20). Subsequently, he adds another (2:13-17). Now, from the large group of disciples who follow him (1:45, 2:15, and compare 2:23 and 3:7, in which the number and gender of the disciples is not specified; cf. 15:40-41) Jesus calls and appoints twelve to a special ministry. In our culture, which has made a cult of rugged individualism, the communal nature of Jesus' work and of his first followers is noteworthy.

Verse 13 begins "he went up the mountain," a phrase undoubtedly calculated to stress the authority of Jesus. Mountains are places where God reveals the divine self and gives commands; mountains are the locus of divine revelation. (Moses, for example, went up a mountain to receive the Law.) Mark's next "mountain text" is the transfiguration, 9:2-8. On the mountain, Jesus calls to himself those he wants. The initiative is Jesus'. We are not told whether the called found it convenient, were pleased to be called, or were even in any way "prepared" for such a call and mission. What they are is obedient; "they came to him." Here is rich material for a sermon on religious vocation.

Jesus calls to himself a small number of people, a convenient number to work with, to receive intensive instruction and training, to share his work, and to serve as a spiritual community. The number twelve (v. 14) is much discussed and is as important as a symbol of the reconstitution of the twelve tribes of Israel as it is the literal number of Jesus' inner circle of disciples. "The essential character of the Twelve is eschatological-symbolical not historical-masculine. . . ."[15] I do not think Mark is describing here the later apostolic office of the church. In fact, Mark is more interested in discipleship in general than he is in an apostolic office; "disciple" is used in the Gospel much more frequently than either "Twelve" or "apostle." Some ancient manuscripts of Mark do not have the phrase "whom he also named apostles" (v. 14), which many textual scholars view as an interpolation from Luke 6:13. The important thing is that the Twelve are sent out (*apostelle,* from *apo,* "out" or "out from," and *stello,* "to send") to do as Jesus has done (here, to proclaim the message and to have authority to cast out demons). In this Gospel, the Twelve are to listen to, learn from, and understand Jesus. They preach, heal, exorcise, and call disciples (6:6b-13, 30); they do exactly what has been presented as the typical ministry of Jesus (1:16-39). Mark's Gospel makes clear that as the Teacher does, so are the disciples to do. This has stark implications at the end of the Gospel and certainly for Mark's original audience.

Although all lists of the Twelve begin with Peter and end with Judas, the list of names given in vv. 16-19 does not square exactly with its parallel in Matt. 10:1-4 or Luke 6:13-16. This is not homiletically significant. What is of note is Mark's particular interest in this Twelve. He places Simon first (and reminds the hearer or reader that he is the same as Peter). Simon was the first disciple to be called (1:16-17), and now he is given primacy among the Twelve, for whom he often serves as spokesman (see, for example, 10:28). The list includes Jewish fishermen, the "first four" (1:16-20), as well as men with Greek names (Andrew, Philip, Bartholomew), two Jameses (one son of Zebedee, one son of Alphaeus—the usual way of identifying persons in Semitic culture, *bar* or *ben* in Hebrew), and a Cananaean, Simon, so designated to distinguish him from Simon Peter, but also an indication that persons from non-Jewish territory (could he be a Gentile?) were among the first followers. In last place, so to speak, is Judas Iscariot, which St. Jerome thinks means "man of Kerioth," designating the only "southerner" among the Twelve. How poignant that last phrase, "who betrayed him." The word is *paradidomi,* "handed over," which again links the Baptist's story to Jesus' and serves as another dark foreshadowing. The Twelve mirror what we know of Jesus' followers from chapters 1 and 2: they manifest what is now popularly called "diversity." Some are Jews, some apparently Greeks; some come from the north of Israel, at least one from the south. This "mixed bag" is to be the nucleus of the new Israel.

Mark 3:14-21 is the appointed text for Lent 4 in the Roman lectionary. In this context the preacher might wish to stress the tension between the high calling of the Twelve and the betrayal of Jesus by one of the insiders. Or one can approach this text as a call story (like 1:16-20 or 2:13-27). As such it would be appropriate to stress the initiative of Jesus and, save for their obedience, Mark's silence about the response of those called. What they are sent to do (3:14-16), we shall later learn they accomplished (6:7-13, 30). Contrary to popular summaries of the disciples in Mark, they are not always failures, but their "power" or "ability" resides in the Caller, not the called. Alternatively, one might wish to address the diversity of persons in that early group (remembering that women were numbered among the disciples, 15:40-41). Jesus did not expect his first followers to be "homogenized," so the churches today need not exhibit sameness in membership, nor is the church to be monolithic. Because of the circumstances of women in the contemporary church, and since Mark is not interested in the Twelve as authoritative male representatives of early church offices but as those sent to do as Jesus has done, it is important not to make overmuch of the fact that the Twelve are men—especially since, by the end of the Gospel, the Twelve men are nowhere to be found, and the women disciples are standing at the foot of the cross. (And remember that Paul knew and approved of at least one female apostle, Junia, Rom. 16:7.)

For Further Reading

Rudolf Bultmann, *History of the Synoptic Tradition* (Oxford: Blackwell, 1963), 343ff.

C. G. Kruse, "Apostle," in *DJG*, 27–33.

Elisabeth Schüssler Fiorenza, "The Twelve," in Leonard and Arlene Swidler, eds., *Women Priests* (New York: Paulist, 1977), 114–22.

3:19b-35

Although the lectionaries variously divide this segment of material, I prefer to treat it as one unit. It exemplifies unfortunate extremes of judgment about Jesus by the very people who should have recognized him (the scribes) and known him best (his family). Furthermore, structurally, the material exhibits a "double framing" as follows:

3:21	family of Jesus
3:22	scribal attack
3:23-29	response of Jesus
3:30	scribal attack
3:31-32	family of Jesus
(3:33-35)	(response of Jesus)

It may be that 3:30 is a Markan redundancy. That would not cancel the inclusion provided by references to the family of Jesus (3:21 and 3:31ff). In the notes that follow, discussion of Jesus' family (3:19b-21 and 3:31-35) precede the conflict with the Jerusalem scribes (3:22-30).

3:19b-21, 31-35

After appointing the Twelve, Jesus returns home, presumably to Capernaum. Again, Mark leaves it ambiguous whether this is Jesus' own home (2:1) or perhaps Peter's. Although we are not told who "they" are in v. 20, presumably Mark means Jesus' many followers. "They" are so busy (with the work of healing and teaching?) that there is scarcely time to eat (cf. this highly stressful scene with Jesus' own need to withdraw in 1:35 and 2:9-10). It is this frenetic activity that is behind the action in v. 21. Jesus' family "heard it" (of his popularity? of his overwork? of the intense emotions swirling around Jesus?) and "went out to restrain him." "Restrain" (*kratesai*) means "to seize," "to take control of," "to seize by force." The NRSV translates *hoi par autou,* an impersonal plural, "people were saying." Perhaps Jesus' move from "what do people say" to "who do you say" in 8:27-30 is the result of the sad misunderstanding here. The family has heard general reports of Jesus, reports that he is "out of his mind" (*exeste,* literally "beside himself"; the aorist suggests a present state resulting from a past action). Is the implication that the family fear for his health because he is near collapse from overwork? Or do they think he is insane? If so, they infer he was under the control of demons, precisely what the scribes accuse in the next story. In any case, Jesus' family set out to make the thirty-mile journey from Nazareth to Capernaum. (This is inferred from the Matthean account since Mark does not tell us where Jesus' family lives.) The ensuing narrative (3:22-30) allows this travel time before the story is resumed at 3:31-35, an example of Markan intercalation.

Mark's intent in 3:31-35 is not to denigrate the biological family of Jesus (some of whom we know, from the Acts of the Apostles, became leaders in the Jerusalem church). This pericope, falling as it does after the early call-of-disciple accounts and the calling of the Twelve, continues to develop the picture of the new community that Jesus is calling into being. In v. 31 Jesus' mother and brothers are "standing outside"; they are not privy to the special "inside" group of disciples (remember that "inside" and "outside" are symbolic for Mark). That no "father" is mentioned has been taken to mean that Joseph has died. Other scholars suggest it is an oblique reference to Mark's understanding that Jesus' father is God and not a human man. This reference to the "brothers" (*adelphoi*) of Jesus, whom Mark names in 6:3, presents something of an ecumenical challenge.[16] It has been held that they are (1) sons of Joseph and Mary born after Jesus and thus his half brothers; (2) sons of Joseph by a previous marriage and thus Jesus' stepbrothers (so Epiphanius); or (3) cousins of Jesus (so Jerome). Mark was not concerned with proving or disproving later church pronouncements about Jesus' mother. His interest is to compare biological family (or what we might call "family of origin") with the new community which Jesus called into being by obedience to the will of God (to which, of course, Mary already belonged by her fiat in Luke 1:38).

The crowd around Jesus (presumably inside) report that his mother, brothers and sisters are "outside" asking for him (v. 32). Jesus' response in vv. 33-35 would have been as shocking to his hearers in Palestinian Capernaum as it is to many in our churches. He asserts that biological kinship confers no special rights or privileges with regard to himself. He redefines the nature of family; "family" is no longer those with biological connections ("blood kin" as we say in West Virginia), but those who do the will of God. Jesus replaces the basic sociological unit of the biological family with a community constituted by common faith in and obedience to God. "Doing the will of God" (a phrase used only here in the New Testament) is the condition of relatedness that "trumps" all earthly relationships. Jesus indicates that those around him (note brother *and* sister *and* mother, women included, v. 35) who do God's will are his family. His biological family is left standing outside.

Mark's point in telling this story is to describe the new family that comes into being through obedience to Jesus. Jesus' words must have been a comfort to those who first heard them, those who had left brothers and sisters and mother and father and children for his sake and the sake of the Gospel (10:28-31). Likewise they would have been encouraging words to Mark's community, which undoubtedly numbered among itself those who had been disinherited for allegiance to the Gospel (cf. 13:12-13). Jesus' words fall less softly on modern ears, especially in churches which tout "American family values" (in spite of the fact that "family" meant something very different and included a very different group of people in the first century than it does today).[17] This is not a text for a Mother's Day sermon! What it does is introduce the difficulty of discipleship. For the first time in Mark's Gospel, we get an inkling that being a disciple of Jesus is not just a matter of going "from strength to strength," of healing and being healed. It costs, and the price is high. The text (which appears in the "Ordinary Time" after Pentecost) can be used to remind modern Christians of the seriousness of discipleship. It can serve as comfort to Christians who have been rejected by their nearest and dearest because of their decisions for Christ and his Gospel's sake. And it raises the very important question of how we Christians understand ourselves as God's family. Do we understand (and treat) all fellow believers as mother and brother and sister? It is a fascinating exercise to retell the story from the point of view of Jesus' mother.

For Further Reading

Richard J. Bauckham, "All in the Family: Identifying Jesus' Relatives," *BRev* 16 (2000): 20–31.

3:22-30

Following a rumor that Jesus is "out of his mind" (v. 21), Mark notes that scribes come from Jerusalem and attribute to Jesus demonic powers (v. 22; cf. Luke 7:33 and John 10:20, in which Pharisees attribute demonic power to Jesus). Jerusalem is the very heart of Judaism and the center of its teaching life. But for Mark, Jerusalem also represents the focus of opposition to Jesus. (See the excursus on the temple in the introduction to chapter 7 of this study.) "Beelzebub" was a pagan god (2 Kings 1:2, 6) associated with Satan. The issue is the authority of Jesus, whom the scribes accuse of wielding the authority of demons, "by the ruler of the demons he casts out demons" (v. 22).

Mark describes Jesus' answer in vv. 23-29 as a "parable," by which he means a comparison or "figurative language." (The next chapter presents parables as a literary form.) Verses 23-26 are a clear and logical refutation of the charge. "How can Satan cast out Satan?" (v. 23b). That would be to say that Satan did good! Verses 24-25, with the reference to a divided kingdom and house (which in Aramaic can refer to a political domain), must have been very provocative. It was precisely because of such divisions that the Hasmonean dynasty fell to Rome in 63 B.C. (John Hyrcannus II and Aristobulus, brothers, contended for the same throne) and Palestine came directly under Roman control in A.D. 6 (the sons of Herod the Great divided his kingdom). If a divided kingdom or a divided house cannot stand, then certainly if Satan were divided against himself, he could not stand (v. 26). The proverb in v. 27 implies a comparison between Satan (the strong man) and Jesus (the one who ties him up). Jesus is the one who rescues those brought under subjection to Satan by evil spirits (see 1:24-26, 34, 39; 3:11-12); he subjects the evil spirits. Jesus has argued that it is foolish for Satan to fight against himself (vv. 23-26); Satan is the one he himself has bound (v. 27). God's agent has overcome Satan's power.

In vv. 28-29 Jesus addresses his accusers. Detailed exegesis of these verses is notoriously difficult, but the general sense is clear.[18] Verse 28 begins with the Aramaic *amen*, used thirteen times in Mark in connection with solemn declarations (and apparently uniquely used by Jesus, since in Jewish usage it follows rather than precedes statements). The blasphemy "against the Holy Spirit," sometimes called the "unforgivable sin," is to attribute evil motives to the work of God, to attribute the work of God's spirit to Satan's spirit. To put the matter another way, if Jesus did miracles by the power of Satan, then there is no possibility of salvation. The immense irony here is that, by means of their accusation, the scribes from Jerusalem have committed just this sin. This is reiterated by Mark's editorial comment in v. 30, not, I think, as a redundancy this time, but to be sure the hearer/reader has made the connection.

I find this a difficult text to preach. An obvious criticism of the religious establishment is implied by the fact that the scribes come from Jerusalem. But I do not think this gets us very far homiletically. Sermons on Satan and demons do not preach well in mainline churches and perhaps for that reason should be preached. (I remember an old man asking my pastor husband, "Do you believe in Satan?" He replied, "If there's no Satan I'd like to know who's been doing his work all these years!") The good news of the passage is that the strong man *has* been bound and the only unforgivable sin is willfully to deny God's power to deliver—in effect, to deny that god is God. (For an interesting working out of this sin, see the character of Weston in C. S. Lewis's novel *Perelandra*.)

Summary
3:19b-35

D. E. Nineham's overview of this section of the Gospel provides a helpful summary. The first verse

> reemphasizes what has been shown in the previous passage (vv. 7-19a)—that ordinary, unprejudiced folk, recognizing . . . the goodness and God-given character of Jesus' power, flocked to avail themselves of it. . . . We are shown by contrast how those who might have been expected to share this attitude to the full, Jesus' own family and the religious leaders of the people, not only failed to recognize the true source and character of his actions, but insisted on attributing them to evil sources. His family thought he was beside himself (v. 21, i.e., under the power of demons), while "the scribes from Jerusalem" . . . alleged that he was possessed by Satan and that it was by Satanic power that his . . . works were performed. . . . We are thus shown early in the Gospel, how when the Son of God "came unto his own, his own"—both family and nation—"received him not."[19]

Summary
3:7-35

Mark's picture of the early Galilean ministry of Jesus is now complete. Four characteristics of that ministry are noteworthy. First, the crowds have enthusiasm for the miracles, healings, and exorcisms of Jesus, but the reader has no indication of how they responded to the preaching of the kingdom. Second, disciples are with Jesus, they "follow," but again, Mark does not reveal how they viewed him or understood his mission. They need more teaching (which comes immediately in Mark, chapter 4). Third, Mark presents a pattern of increasing opposition to Jesus, and by the end of chapter 3, the religious leaders are antagonistic to Jesus to the point not only of accusation, but of plotting "how to destroy him" (3:6). Fourth, there seems to be little support and no understanding of Jesus by his biological family.

These four groups of people around Jesus are suggestive. The crowds represent human life in need, and need responds to Jesus (recall 2:17). They also exemplify faith where it is least expected (and will continue to do so in the Gospel). The disciples are, at least in potentiality, the new family of God, constituted of those who would not normally be found together (Jews and Greeks, men and women, business people and tax collectors) but are joined in obedience to Jesus' call and God's will. They are certainly not "religious" types. The religious officials, who should have recognized and supported Jesus' work, oppose him and are worried enough to join forces with their enemies against Jesus (Pharisees and Herodians) and to send men down from Jerusalem to check on his teaching. The biological family of Jesus completely misunderstands him at this point. Not to put too fine a point on it, they think he is crazy.

At this juncture, one could hardly describe the ministry of Jesus in Galilee as a success. Jesus has a following attracted by wonders, but not apparently by the preaching of the kingdom (1:14-15), the very thing he has come to do (1:38). Already, Jesus is opposed by the religious establishment. It is clear to all that Jesus has power, but the source of that power is obscure. To quote an old saw, "the plot thickens."

3

The Parables:
The Substance of Jesus' Message
Mark 4:1-34

Introduction

Having described Jesus' ministry of healing in miracle stories, and having depicted the hostility of the religious officials in controversy dialogues, Mark now focuses on Jesus the teacher in a series of parables. Jesus is, in fact, called "teacher" more frequently in Mark than in any other Gospel (e.g., 1:21; 2:13; 6:2, 6), and in Mark the word for teacher is restricted to Jesus. Mark wants to make clear that one cannot understand Jesus without taking into account his teaching.[1] Following a block of controversy material (2:1—3:6 and 3:19b-29), Mark inserts a block of teaching material (4:1-34). This same pattern occurs at the end of Jesus' public ministry, where controversy (11:27—12:27) is followed by teaching (13:1-37).

Drawing on form-critical conclusions about the shaping of this chapter, Greg Fay has seen in Mark 4:1-34 a concentric pattern, which he outlines as follows (and which I largely follow in my notes on the texts):

A	4:1-2a	Introduction
B	4:2b-9	Parable Material
C	4:10-13	Parabolic Method
D	4:14-20	Parable (In)Comprehension
C1	4:21-25	Parabolic Method
B1	4:26-32	Parable Material
A1	4:33-34	Conclusion

Within this larger framework there are other parallelisms, the most important of which may be the one between vv. 10-13 and 21-25, which follows a pattern: (1) disciples question, (2) Jesus explains parabolic method, (3) Jesus questions disciples.[2] Fay's schema is helpful in understanding not only the structure of the chapter, but in focusing on the wider issue of the theme of the incomprehension of Jesus' disciples. As he notes, the entire block of material is "concerned with productive hearing."[3]

Excursus on Parables

Mark says that Jesus taught "many things in parables" (4:2). There is a very extensive secondary literature on the form. (I list some of this literature in the suggestions for further reading.) The Greek word for "parable" (*parabole*) is a common one and means simply putting one thing beside another for comparison. (This is how the word was used in 3:23.) Aristotle defines parable as a "comparison" or "allegory" (Rhet. II, xx, 2-4). Behind the Greek word stands the Hebrew *mashal,* meaning either a brief statement of popular wisdom (a proverb) or a discourse. In the Old Testament, *mashal* is sometimes used with *hidah,* which literally means "a riddle" and denotes indirect (or metaphorical) speech rather than literal and open speech. The two Hebrew words alert the interpreter to the fact that parables often depend upon analogy and are, to some degree, meant to puzzle people, to provoke them to reflection and subsequently deeper understanding. Parables were widely used by rabbis at the time of Jesus. Their general purpose is to bring their hearers to a recognition of the truth.[4] Cyril of Alexandria provides a clear explanation of how parables function: "Parables are word pictures not of visible things, but rather of things of the mind and the spirit. That which cannot be seen with the eyes of the body, a parable will reveal to the eyes of the mind, informing the subtlety of the intellect by means of things perceivable by the senses."[5]

Until the nineteenth century, parables were often treated as allegories, stories in which each element of the narrative stands for something else. But the two Hebrew terms that describe parables seldom, if ever, function this way. In my view, parables are best treated as brief narratives intended to bring home to the hearer some truth about God, or in the Synoptic Gospels, the kingdom of God. And this brings us to the Markan text at hand. Form critics generally assume that Mark received three parables from the tradition, 4:3-9, 26-29, and 30-32. Attached to the sower parable (4:3-9) was a later explanation of it (4:10-20). Finally, 4:21-25 was added to the collection, perhaps when Mark provided the "connector" to the previous material, 4:1-2.

Pheme Perkins notes that "Mark's use of alternations between what occurs 'outside' in the presence of the crowd and what occurs 'inside' with [Jesus'] circle of disciples confuses the geographical sequence somewhat."[6] While that may be so narratively, we do well to remember that "outside" and "inside" may be more than spatial locations in Mark; they may signal instructions for "everyone" and for the "inner circle" respectively. In any case, the purpose of these Markan parables in the narrative is clear. In light of the controversies already experienced, the parables assure the triumph of the proclaimed kingdom (1:14-15), explain the reception of Jesus' ministry and message, and alert the hearer/reader to its ultimate success in spite of temporary setbacks (4:26-28). The teaching material in chapter 4 has the same general purpose as that in chapter 13, to give the disciples confidence that "silent but irresistible forces [are] at work upon their side . . . not to be perceived by all."[7] "Only the insiders get the point of the parables."[8]

For Further Reading

Madeleine I. Boucher, *The Mysterious Parable: A Literary Study*, CBQMS 6 (Washington, D.C.: Catholic Biblical Association, 1977).

John D. Crossan, *In Parables: The Challenge of the Historical Jesus* (New York: Harper and Row, 1973).

C. H. Dodd, *The Parables of the Kingdom* (London: Nisbet, 1952).

John R. Donahue, *The Gospel in Parable* (Philadelphia: Fortress Press, 1988).

Arland Hultgren, *The Parables of Jesus* (Grand Rapids: Eerdmans, 2000).

Joachim Jeremias, *The Parables of Jesus* (London: SCM, 1955).

Sallie TeSelle, *Speaking in Parables* (Philadelphia: Fortress Press, 1975).

Dan O. Via Jr., *The Parables* (Philadelphia: Fortress Press, 1974).

4:1-2a

These two verses provide a perfect example of Mark's redundant style. Their intent is to link the parables to the previous narrative. "Again" (v. 1) reminds the reader that Jesus has already been teaching. As Capernaum is "beside the lake," we can assume Jesus is in the same geographical area as he was in chapter 3. Again, he is surrounded by large crowds which necessitate his teaching from a boat (cf. 3:7-10, especially v. 9). There are, in fact, many inlets on the north shore of the Sea of Galilee which provide natural amphitheaters when a teacher sits in a boat and listeners arrange themselves on the shore (and, of course, sound travels well over water). What is important, however, is that Jesus sits to teach, the rabbinic position of authority (cf. Matt. 5:1-2). Note that Jesus "began to teach them many things in parables" (v. 2), but not everything. This is Mark's subtle equivalent to John 20:30; both texts make clear that the evangelists selected some material from a larger body available (see also 4:33, which makes the same point).

4:2b-9

Several commentators note that the Greek of this seed parable suggests that it derives from an Aramaic original. The imperative "listen" (*akouete*) provides a solemn beginning and probably represents a Hebrew word meaning "to hear" and "to obey." Its parallel with the Shema (Deut. 6:4) has led Gerhardsson to suggest that the whole parable is based on the

Shema. A sower is a common metaphor in ancient literature for a teacher (Plato, Laws IV; 2 Esdras 9:31, 33) and thus sets up the implied comparison between Jesus and the sower. The parable itself has five elements: the opening (v. 3), the path (v. 4), the rocks (vv. 5-6), the thorns (v. 7), and the good ground (v. 8).

There is much discussion in the secondary literature of *how* seed was sown at the time of Jesus, but the general consensus seems to be that the seed was broadcast (not sown in neat rows as in modern gardens) and that the ground was plowed *after* sowing, thus allowing for the exposure of the seed that the parable presumes. Fields were bounded by hard-packed paths which were not plowed, so birds could, indeed, eat seed that fell there (v. 4). Anyone who has visited Palestine can attest to its stony ground, which explains thin soil that does not allow a root system to develop (vv. 5-6). And anyone who gardens understands the weed metaphor (v. 7). However, the seed that falls on good soil (the majority that fell in the field that was later plowed? or only one-fourth of the whole of the seed that was sown?) produces a wonderful harvest. In all cases, the seed is good. What is questionable is the soil. I once heard a lecture in the theology department of a German university that explained by means of agricultural slides and stalks of corn how it is, indeed, possible for one seed to produce "thirty and sixty and a hundredfold!" We who live with such wealth do well to remember that in a world of subsistence living, an abundant harvest is good news indeed. Part of the Good News of the kingdom is its abundance and lavish provision (cf. 6:30-44, especially vv. 42-43, and 8:1-10, especially v. 8). The parable opens with the command to "listen" and closes with the charge "Let anyone with ears to hear listen!" (v. 9). This framing suggests that the parable is as much about hearing as it is about speaking the word (v. 14, cf. 7:31-37, especially v. 35).

This parable is addressed to the crowd. Its explanation to the disciples and the Twelve comes later. However, assuming the comparison of teacher/sower was well known, the parable is about the reception of a teacher's message. The hearer is charged to "listen" (hear and obey) and to "hear." The first responsibility of those who come to learn from Jesus is to listen, to practice what we might call "stewardship of the ear." Disciples of Jesus first hear what he says and then are obedient to what they hear. But this presumes listening, and listening presumes that the listener is silent. The parable of the sower reminds us that we must make time for listening to Jesus, for being silent in his presence. (This is an important reminder in all conversation. When we listen to others, we must really *listen* to them, not be quietly formulating what we will say next.) The parable is first a charge to responsive hearing, and second, as the following verses will explain, Mark's view of the ministry of Jesus and the response to it. "In the early church, this parable encouraged believers who had already accepted the word to nourish its growth in their lives, and it explained why some people failed to respond."[9]

For Further Reading

John D. Crossan, "The Seed Parables of Jesus," *JBL* 92 (1973): 244–66.

B. Gerhardsson, "The Parable of the Sower and Its Interpretation," *NTS* 14 (1968): 165–93.

4:10-12

These brief verses on the interpretation of parables are some of the most difficult and most widely discussed in scholarly treatments of Mark's Gospel. They seem to reflect a time after Jesus' life when the meaning of parables had become puzzling, perhaps because their original context had become obscure. Note, first, that the setting has shifted. We are no longer by the lake with the crowd but "alone" with "those who were around him along with the twelve" (v. 10). This shift is significant. It reveals that Jesus gave special, private teaching to his disciples and the Twelve; they are two separate groups (the "disciples" probably included women; cf. 15:40-41). Verse 10 introduces what develops as a gradual constriction of the numbers of people around Jesus in Mark's Gospel and highlights the "insiders/outsiders" theme.

Verse 11 suggests that this "inner circle" has a special opportunity. Mark employs a passive verb in what is called "the Divine passive," a Greek circumlocution used to indicate that God is speaking or acting without using the Divine Name. Is this an oblique hint about Jesus' view of himself, or is it Mark reflecting a later understanding of him? This inner circle is given a "secret" (literally, *musterion,* mystery), a term used in the New Testament for knowledge given, not to people in general, but to the initiated. To the disciples, God gives that which was previously hidden, knowledge of the kingdom of God. The "secret of the kingdom" changes. It was different for Mark than when Jesus first spoke the parable. From the hidden presence of God's reign in Jesus' ministry, the secret becomes instructions of Jesus to his disciples for the benefit of the Christian community. More on this shortly.

Verse 12 begins with the strong phrase "in order that" (a *hina* or purpose clause in Greek). Although some commentators try to "tone it down," my sense is that Mark means exactly what he says here: judgment comes on the basis of who will and who will not "hear." (This is confirmed in the interpretation of the parable in 4:14-20.) The quotation in v. 12 is taken from Isa. 6:9-10, the call story of the prophet. In that context, immediately after accepting God's call, Isaiah is told that his ministry will not be well received. Some Markan interpreters suggest, therefore, that 4:12 is an allusion to Israel's refusal to "hear" the message of Jesus. (Cf. Paul in Romans 10-11 on the same issue.) Other commentators relate 4:12 to the "messianic secret" in

Mark, to Jesus' frequent charge that his healings, for example, not be "told," his messiahship not be proclaimed. Certainly in the Gospel "from this point onward, the Twelve behave with singular lack of understanding, while some outsiders show remarkable faith."[10]

Most commentators on this difficult passage stress that v. 11 is to be understood in light of v. 12. C. S. Mann, for example, notes that reading this text as if there were a deliberate attempt on the part of Jesus to obscure his teaching ignores (1) the context in Isaiah, which is Israel's faithlessness and the prophet's vocation to preach to a faithless people, and (2) that the use of a command to express a result is a typically Semitic construction.[11] The verse from Isaiah and its original context determines the meaning of these Markan verses. An interesting article by H. C. Kee on the function of scripture in Mark 11–16 provides further insight into the Semitic context of this text. Key explains a form of scriptural interpretation in Judaism called *pesher* (plural, *pesharim*). Such interpretations are based on secret or mystical interpretations of texts. Key suggests that 4:11 leads Jesus to quote Isa. 6:9-10 to justify the esoteric nature of truth; he is providing a *pesher* for the end times on his parables.[12]

Such sharply judgmental texts are hard to preach in the current cultural climate. If the preacher must avoid the either/or approach with regard to the message of Jesus, he or she might focus instead on v. 11 and the "mystery of the kingdom of God." In fact, vv. 11-12 remind us that understanding is a gift that comes only from God. The "charism" (to use Paul's language) of understanding mysteries is a gift from God. Those who are theologically Calvinists or who minister in the historically Calvinist churches can make much of this approach to the text. (See also 1 Cor. 2:12-14.)

For Further Reading
Schuyler Brown, "The Secret of the Kingdom of God (Mark 4:11)," *JBL* 92 (1973): 60–74.

4:13-20

Verse 13 can either be understood to complete vv. 10-12 or to introduce the explanation of parables in vv. 14-20. In either case, it is a sharp word of reproach to the disciples and the Twelve, the first clear indication in Mark of their failure to understand Jesus and the first of several reprimands by Jesus (cf. 7:18; 8:17). Verses 14-20 are an allegorical interpretation of the parable of the sower which, as several commentators point out, may be an early preacher's explanation of the parable. (When we preach this text, we are probably preaching a sermon on a sermon.) The text certainly reflects conditions in the early church where it likely originated.

In the allegorical interpretation, the seed represents the word. "Word" (*logos*) is repeated eight times in vv. 13-20 (for emphasis? a redundancy?), and four times in connection with "hear" (see the commentary on vv. 3-9 above). "Word" has already been used by Mark as shorthand for the message of Jesus (2:2; see also 4:33). The various types of soil represent the reception of that word/message of Jesus. The "soil" of the path has no depth, and so the word is easily snatched from it even before it germinates (v. 15). It is taken by "Satan," a reminder of the cosmic nature of these events (recall 1:23-24). The "soil" of the rocky ground allows the seed to sprout but not develop roots, and so the word is easily "uprooted" by difficulties (vv. 16-17). Verse 17 would have had special meaning for Mark's persecuted community. Undoubtedly there were persons known among the Gospel's original recipients who had initially responded to the preaching of the kingdom, but apostasized under persecution. The "seed" germinates among thorns but is quickly choked out by them (vv. 18-19) and "yields nothing." But the "seed" sown on "good soil" yields a large harvest (v. 20). The interpretation of the parable focuses on the failure of the seed in various venues. The character of the seed (the proclamation) never changes. What is at issue is the soil, the reception of the seed, how it is "heard" (4:3, 9, 12, 15, 16, 18, 20). The key element is hearing.

In the context of Mark's community, the explanation of the parable is really a description of the reception of the proclamation of Jesus, the "word" of the kingdom, a story about the proclamation of the Gospel and how it is received. That proclamation divides people into two camps: those who receive the word and bear fruit and those who do not. Mark's community is the "good soil" that may be worried about *its* fruitfulness. The interpretation of the parable suggests that, from very early in the church, it was understood that the word would not be universally well received, but that when it *was* received, it would be wonderfully fruitful. (I am reminded of the salt and the light in Matthew's Sermon on the Mount, which are also images of small amounts that have enormous impact.) The point of the parable, then, is about how one listens and responds to Jesus. In the final analysis, the contrast is between ordinary activity and extraordinary result.[13]

In a fascinating article, "How the Gospel of Mark Builds Character," Mary Ann Tolbert suggests that these "soil types" also represent characters in the Gospel narrative.[14] The seed on the path is the religious opponents to Jesus, the scribes and Pharisees who refuse even to hear the word. The seed on the rocky ground is the disciples (especially Peter, the "rock"). They hear the word, and the seed flourishes *until* persecutions arise. This serves as a reminder to Mark's community that those who appear faithful may not be so until the end. The seed among the thorns represents those like the rich man in 10:17-22, and Herod, Herodias, and Pilate, who have heard the word but "choke it out" because their other concerns take priority. Finally, the seed on good soil is those, like Peter's mother-in-law in 1:30-31, the Geresene demoniac in chapter 5, and blind Bartimaeus in 10:46-52, who are healed, who hear and "follow," and become disciples. Tolbert's schema provides a fresh approach for a sermon on this well-known text, or even a series of sermons, one for each type of "soil" (exemplified by someone in Mark's narrative).

For Further Reading
Mary Ann Tolbert, "How the Gospel of Mark Builds Character," *Int* 47 (1993): 347–57.

4:21-25

These five verses depart from the seed metaphor and are a short collection of independent sayings used by Mark to describe the right use of parables (or they are on "parabolic method"). We know they must have circulated separately, because they occur both in this and in other contexts in Matthew (5:15) and Luke (6:38; 11:33; 12:2; 19:26). The text begins almost identically to the previous pericope, "and he said to them" (4:13, 21), but this time in the past rather than present tense. There is no indication of where or to whom these sayings occur, although I tend to take "them" in 4:13, 21 to be "those who were around him along with the twelve" of 4:10. (On the other hand, "them" in 4:33 seems to be the "large crowd" of 4:1.) Two comparisons are made here, 4:21-22 and 4:24-25, punctuated by the solemn charge in 4:23 to "listen" (see 4:9), thus continuing the theme of "right hearing." "Hear" in v. 23 provides the link to teaching about hearing in vv. 24-25.

It is important to interpret these two comparisons in the context of what has come before, especially the theme of vv. 11-12. These are not "general truths" for Mark, but further elaboration of the material at hand.

Verses 21-22 begin with the image of a "lamp," not the kerosene lamps of our day, but small bowls or saucers of oil (probably poor quality olive oil) with rag wicks. In more prosperous homes several of these little lights were placed in lampstands made of iron or wood. In humbler dwellings, only one lamp sufficed. Obviously, to be effective, it would not be put under a "bushel" (Greek *modion* from the Latin *modius,* a pan or measure of about a bushel). In the Markan context, v. 22 suggests that the "word" is not meant for only a chosen few, but is a "mystery" into which all are invited, a light to illuminate everyone. The "purpose," which was hidden in the past (see Ephesians by way of comparison), is now made known in Jesus.

Perhaps it is the *modion* of v. 21, which leads to the saying about measures in vv. 24-25. Certainly v. 24a, which might be literally translated "see what you hear," follows logically from v. 23. Remember that "see" can, in Mark, be a metaphor for "understand." Again, these sayings are not to be interpreted generally, but in the context of the hearing of the word. Thus verses 24 and 25 are about the cultivation of a right attitude toward the word. A paraphrase of v. 24 might be something like "the more you work to understand the word, the more you will understand it" or "the more you invest in the word the more of it you will 'get.'" Verse 25 is not to be understood in some economic sense (like "the rich get richer and the poor get poorer"), but in terms of understanding the word. A good comparison is "use it or lose it"; as a muscle atrophies when not used, so spiritual understanding diminishes when not cultivated.

If 4:14-20 makes clear that the word will be heard and will bear fruit, these verses suggest that the light will shine forth and greater understanding will be given. But the responsibility of the individual to hear and respond is still emphasized. An appropriate sermon on this text probably focuses on the importance of diligent "working at" the Word and then "showing it forth" and would emphasize that the more one pursues the "mystery of the kingdom of God" the more he or she understands it.

4:26-29

In verses 26-32 Mark returns to the metaphor of the seed and records two contrasting parables that add further texture to his tapestry of preaching and hearing the word. The parable of the growing seed (vv. 26-29) is one of the few pericopae that are peculiar to Mark. It clearly reflects its original setting in rural Palestine. It depicts seed sown by broadcasting (v. 26, and thus provides clarification for the parable in 4:3-9); reckons time as the Jews did, from night to day (v. 27); reflects how plants actually grow (v. 28); and describes realistic harvest practices (v. 29).

The parable begins "the kingdom of God is *as if*," indicating that what follows is a metaphor and that the kingdom is so radical and mysterious that it cannot be spoken of directly. The key to the parable is the phrase in v. 27, "he does not know how." Growth occurs "of itself" (*automate*). Not only does v. 28 suggest that the laws of nature are the laws of God, but the metaphor insists that the kingdom depends on God's power to bring it to pass, not human effort or agency (cf. Ezek. 17:24, and see notes on vv. 11-12 above). In the context of the either/or quality of much of this chapter, it is probably important to remember that in Jewish literature, "harvest" is a metaphor for judgment. (See, for example, Joel 3:13-14.) Once the seed (the word) has had time to grow (come to maturity), the sower has the right to return and harvest the crop.

The parable makes clear that the growth of the kingdom of God is a mystery outside human control. Human beings can play a role in its growth (can "sow seed"), but the growth itself is in God's hands. (Note how exactly this point is also made in Isa. 55:10-11.) This must have been a comfort to Mark's community. It explains that sowing (preaching) is the human task, but that God ultimately brings growth (or does not!) from human effort. It reminded them that, even in their tribulation because of the word (cf. 4:17-19), God was ultimately in control. The parable places on the lips of Jesus optimism about the mission, even in the face of delay (v. 27) and judgment (v. 29); Jesus fully expected the message of the kingdom to spread. The pericope provides an opportunity not only to preach about the ultimate success of the church and its mission, but to remind Christians of truths of personal spiritual growth. There is a divine element in spiritual as well as natural growth. In the spiritual as in the natural realm, people must wait on God's timing and remember that God, not our own efforts, not only provides orderly growth, but has the right to harvest. (In Job 1:21 and 2:10b, poor Job has it just right.)

4:30-32

Interpreting the well-known parable of the mustard seed depends upon knowing something of the Judaism of Jesus' time. Nineham says "this whole section rests on an Aramaic original."[15] Perhaps that accounts for the poor Greek in vv. 31-32. The parable opens, as did much of the teaching of the rabbis, with a question carefully articulated as a Semitic parallelism. In that opening we see how very like the scribes and Pharisees Jesus is. Verse 31 probably reflects a common simile, "as small as a mustard seed." The NRSV translation reflects the reality that mustard seeds grow into large shrubs (lachanon, literally "vegetable" or "garden herb"), not trees. But the full-grown mustard "bush" is certainly large enough to shelter birds. This image of shelter calls to mind a prophetic image of the tree as a symbol of protective care, care of subject peoples by great empires (see, for example, Ezek. 21:1-9; 31:6, and Dan. 4:10-12). Hebrew scripture also uses the image of a tree to describe God's care (Ezek. 17:23).

As in the previous pericope, the point of the parable is the comparison between the growth of plants and the kingdom of God. Here, the hearer or reader is asked to understand that great things can come from insignificant beginnings. This is because divine forces are at work beyond human effort (the "sowing" in v. 31). Mark's original audience was to take comfort in the fact that from a tiny beginning (a mustard seed, their own small house churches) would come a tremendous result (a large shrub, the consummation of God's kingdom). And the image of God's sheltering protection would have been most welcome to a suffering community. The echoes of Hebrew scripture in the text lead directly to a challenge: that of seeing in the present, small moment the promise of God's kingdom coming to fruition and extending to all people. The preaching of "the word" is intended to bring all nations into the protective branches of God's tree.

The two seed parables in 4:26-32 stress the growth process that occurs with the passage of time. Thus both patience and perseverance are required to see fruition. In each, there is a subtle warning against complacency in the time of waiting.

4:33-34

In Mark's editorial conclusion to the collection of parables, "the word" in v. 33 is to be understood as the message of the kingdom (cf. 1:14-15; 4:11, 26, 30). That teaching is progressive; it is given as the hearer is able to receive it (cf. 4:24-25). Thus parables can be interpreted on many levels, certainly, at least, on the "surface" level of the crowds and the "deeper" understanding given to the disciples. (This serves, in part, to explain to Mark's audience why some people "got" their proclamation and some did not.) "Them" in v. 33 is the "whole crowd" of 4:1. Jesus teaches them in parables that he later explains to his disciples. This is exactly what has been demonstrated in the chapter: vv. 1-9 is general teaching; vv. 10-20 is explanation to a select group. The disciples receive special explanation because of the work they will later be called upon to do. But the text also suggests that fuller understanding of the parables (the kingdom of God) is contingent upon nearness to Jesus and an effort to understand (4:24-25).

Mark 4:26-34 appears in the lectionary early in the post-Pentecost "Ordinary Time." As such, the text can be used to introduce the whole process of spiritual growth that Ordinary Time is intended to foster. This growth is to be both communal and personal. The two parables in the lectionary text can be interpreted and preached on either level.

Summary
4:1-34

The importance of the "parable chapter" in Mark cannot be overemphasized. Nor can the importance of understanding it from at least two points of view, that of Jesus' time and that of Mark's original audience. It is here that Mark introduces the reader to both what (the kingdom of God) and how (in parables) Jesus teaches. Mark makes clear that Jesus cannot be understood without knowing him as a teacher.[16] Furthermore, the point of the parables is how one listens and responds to Jesus. There are at least eleven references to listening and/or hearing in this material. In a world of terrible noise pollution, a world in which too many people talk and too few people listen, sermons on these parables that focus on listening and hearing are needed. Responding positively to what is heard allows one to become a disciple and thus to receive more intensive teaching. Ignoring the word of Jesus has dire consequences. Hearing and responding to the Word are directly related to the incomprehension of the disciples that will soon appear in the narrative.

Throughout the chapter, ordinary activities produce extraordinary results. Certainly this is Mark's way of reminding his community to look beyond the "ordinary" for the "other thing," indeed, the divine thing that is mysteriously happening. As Schuyler Brown makes clear, the "secret of the kingdom" for Mark is not what it was when Jesus spoke the parables. The "secret" is not the hidden presence of God in Jesus' ministry, but the instructions of Jesus to his disciples for the benefit of the whole community. At the level of Mark's community, the secret is not kerygmatic but didactic.[17] That is, these parables as interpreted for Mark's community are not so much the proclamation of Jesus as they are teaching for Jesus' community, Mark's church. Another, and perhaps simpler way to say this, is to say that the parables in chapter 4 may be interpreted in two "time zones": the "time zone" of Jesus himself and the "time zone" of Mark's community. What this means for us as preachers is that 4:1-34 can be used christologically and kerygmatically as an "expression of [Jesus'] own experience of God,"[18] or ecclesiologically and didactically as a means of teaching the church about her own nature and growth, both corporate and personal.

For Mark's community and for us, the parables are ultimately a source of comfort. They remind us that divine forces, though perhaps unseen and mysterious, are at work on our behalf and are as certain and orderly as the works of nature (when it has not been interfered with by humans!). The fact that this is "heard" and "seen" by some and not by others is part of the "mystery of the kingdom of God" that Jesus promises to make known to those who seek it. "Let anyone with ears to hear listen!"

4

The Miracles:
The Extent of Jesus' Power
Mark 4:35—5:43

Introduction

Earlier I noted Mark's tendency to shape his Gospel by using blocks of the same literary type (2:1—3:6 are controversies; 4:1-34 are parables). That practice continues with this block of four miracle stories in two pairs: stilling a storm and stilling demons; two healings, both done for females. But there is a narrative and theological logic at work as well. In 4:1-34 Mark depicts Jesus as an authoritative teacher. This is followed immediately by a series of miracles that confirm Jesus' authority to teach as he does. The four stories not only confirm Jesus' authority but demonstrate its extent. Jesus has authority over the natural world (4:35-41), the spirit world (5:1-20), the human body (5:24b-34), and over death itself (5:21-24a, 35-43).

Paul Achtemeier thinks that 4:35—5:43 is actually part of a larger block of miracle stories that begins at 4:35 and continues through 8:26. The first cycle of miracle stories is found in 4:35—6:44 and the second in 6:45—8:10. Each of these cycles follows the pattern: sea miracle, three healings, feeding.[1] Achtemeier goes on to suggest that this pre-Markan miracle catenae was formed as part of a eucharistic liturgy.[2] I find Achtemeier's argument intriguing, although I have chosen to divide the material differently. I suggest that Mark relates a block of miracle stories (which he may well have received from the tradition) at this point in the Gospel to prove the authority of Jesus the teacher and to demonstrate that his authority extends through the whole creation: material, spiritual, and human (both body and spirit). Certainly these stories are part of the big picture of the ministry of Jesus in and around the northern shores of the Sea of Galilee. (I will pick up the focus on Jesus' public ministry again in the next chapter.)

I provided a brief discussion of the miracle story form and especially of healing miracles in the introduction to 1:40—3:6 (and see chapter 2, note 4). Form-criticism has isolated two basic types of miracle story in the

Gospels: nature miracles (like stilling the storm) and healing miracles (like cleansing the leper). In the world of the Gospel writers, what we now call miracles were not considered extraordinary. Theirs was a cosmology in which the divisions between the material and spiritual worlds were porous and in which the gods regularly intruded into human affairs. The Gospel miracle stories are not unlike similar stories in the Greco-Roman world, but Mark's tend to be richer in detail. The question of Mark's audience would not have been the "how" of a miracle but the "why." That is, the first recipients of Mark's Gospel would not have doubted *that* miracles occurred, but they would have wanted to know *why* they were performed and what they signified.[3]

In his commentary on Mark's Gospel, Hugh Anderson suggests that the point of miracle stories is testimony. The evangelist wants to testify to God's action in Jesus. He records miracles not because they are extraordinary, but because "they point away from themselves to God and become channels for [God's] Word."[4] This is a particularly helpful approach in our skeptical age. As the parables are special language vehicles for explaining the kingdom of God, miracles explain the power of God at work in Jesus. "The miracle-story is but another mode of language . . . communicating like the parabolic teaching the mystery of God's action in the world, a mystery that discloses itself only to faith."[5] In preaching the Gospel miracles, it is good to remember that miracle stories are written in faith and for faith.

4:35-41

As is the case with so many pericopae in Mark, proper interpretation of this one is immeasurably improved by knowledge of its background. In ancient Near Eastern mythology, the roaring sea is an image of the power of chaos over which the gods triumph (Baal over Yam or Marduk over Tiamat, for example).[6] The Hebrews understood that YHWH controlled the sea and subdued the chaos monster, Tehom ("The Deep"). In the Hebrew scripture, a storm is a metaphor for evil forces, especially as they attack the righteous (Ps. 69:1-2, 14-15). The ability to control the sea is a divine power (Ps. 89:8-9), and the faithful know that God saves in a storm (Ps. 46:1-3; Isa. 43:2). When the Hebrews thought that God had forsaken them, they said that God "slept" (Pss. 35:23; 44:23-24; Isa. 51:9a).When Jesus sleeps in the storm, it is an image of his complete trust in God's sustaining care (cf. Prov. 3:23-24) in contrast to the "no faith" of the disciples. Seen against this background, Mark's christological use of the miracle is clearly evident.

Verse 35 suggests that the teaching in 4:1-34 occurred during one long day (even though there are hints within the text that this is not so). In terms of the narrative, evening has come and Jesus takes the initiative to go to "the other side," the east side of the Sea of Galilee; it was less populated and thus potentially would afford more possibility for rest (cf. 3:9-10; 6:31-32). Verses 36-40 are told from the disciples' point of view (Peter's memory?). Note that the disciples take Jesus with them in the boat (v. 36); some of them, after all, are fishermen, and he is a carpenter. (But are we to understand that in this they are "leading" rather than "following" and thus courting disaster?) Verse 38 is full of what many commentators call "eyewitness" touches: that Jesus was in the stern, that he slept on a cushion, that he was rudely awakened by the disciples when the storm arose (note, in v. 38 they call him "teacher"). This rude awakening is softened by Matthew and Luke when they relate this incident, perhaps to preserve the dignity of the first disciples (Matt. 8:23-27; Luke 8:22-25).

The formula by which Jesus rebukes the wind in v. 39 (*pephimoso*) is a formula of adjuration for a storm demon and is the same word used in 1:25 to subdue the unclean spirit. The result is dramatic; the storm not only ceases, but there is a "dead calm," *galee,* used only here in Mark. (Parenthetically, remember v. 36 says there were "other boats" with them, other boats that also would have benefited from Jesus' action.) Only after having effected their rescue does Jesus turn to speak to the disciples, and then it is to rebuke *them* with faithlessness, a rebuke which the preacher should not soften. The disciples' response to Jesus' action is as obtuse as their response to his teaching in parables (cf. 4:13). When Jesus stilled the storm, they should have made the connection to the authority of God. God made the sea, and God alone can control it. Their emotional response is described by the NRSV as "awe," but the Greek says literally "they feared a great fear" (*ephobethesan phobon megan*), a Semitism meaning "they feared greatly." What (if anything) they have learned about Jesus is unclear, because their reaction to him is cast in the form of a question. Now, finally, the disciples have posed the big question: "Who then is this?" Who, indeed!

For Mark, the point of the story in the development of his narrative is probably the disciples' failure to understand who Jesus is. That follows directly from the parables section. But I imagine Mark's audience heard it rather differently. It seemed to the Hebrews in various scriptural texts that God slept while the chosen people suffered. The parallel to Mark's church suffering under persecution in Nero's Rome could not be clearer. Is Jesus sleeping while the "ark" of the church flounders in a storm? On the contrary, the Jesus who could still the storm on the sea can save the "ark" of the church.

This is a particularly rich passage for preaching. (Psalm 107:23-32 provides a good Old Testament companion lesson for those not tied to a lectionary.) A review of the notes on the passage in Gundry's commentary will provide a wealth of suggestions. I once heard a sermon on it begin:

"There are only two kinds of people within the sound of my voice: those who have been in a storm and those who will be in a storm." It is almost too easy to transfer the *communal* effect of this miracle (several disciples as well as "other boats" were saved) to a *personal* or *individual* application. The miracle was done for a group. What does the account tell us about Jesus' relationship to the church (which is frequently symbolized by a little boat)? The freshest applications of the miracle will focus on its Christology. It says something very important about the Incarnation: it shows how Jesus entered into the severest experiences of human beings (here the very power of chaos itself) and was able to master them (and use them for good if we see the account as revealing that Jesus had God's authority). Personally, I am taken by the picture of Jesus asleep on a cushion while the storm rages, not because he is "ignoring" his own, but because he incarnates the faith that trusts God to achieve divine purposes even in the teeth of apparent chaos and destruction (see 9:23).

For Further Reading

B. Batto, "The Sleeping God: An Ancient Near Eastern Motif of Divine Sovereignty," *Biblica* 68 (1987): 153–77.

Robert H. Gundry, *Mark: A Commentary on His Apology for the Cross* (Grand Rapids: Eerdmans, 1993), 241–47.

5:1-20

A great many issues surround the composition history of this account. It is variously suggested that the original story ended at v. 10 with parts of vv. 11-16 added from an unrelated folktale or that it ended at v. 15 (thus stressing Jesus' power). Our task is to preach the canonical form of the story. In this form, the narrative continues the picture of Jesus' power over evil and his desire (and ability) to make people whole. In view of the power and number of evil spirits, the immense power of Jesus is dramatized. It was also a potent story for Mark's community, since it shows Jesus doing great things outside of Palestine, thus supporting a "Gentile mission" in the early church. The narrative has three "scenes." Verses 1-5 describe the condition of the man with the unclean spirit, vv. 6-14a his exorcism (the miracle story itself), vv. 14b-17 the response of those in the neighborhood. The pericope closes with Jesus' charge to the delivered man, who responds in obedience to Jesus (vv. 18-20).

The question about where the exorcism took place was raised as early as the time of Origen.[7] The majority opinion with regard to the textual issue is "Gerasene" (not "Gadarene," which is probably a scribal assimilation to the text of Matt. 8:28), but the actual town is unknown, although Kursa on the east side of the Sea of Galilee is shown by local guides as the "traditional location." Upon embarking from the boat (cf. 4:25-41), Jesus is met by "a man out of the tombs with an unclean spirit" (v. 2). In Jesus' day, tomb areas, unclean places because of corpses, were primary hangouts of demons; unclean spirits resided in unclean places. In the Talmud there are four tests of madness: (1) a mad person spends time (the night) in a grave, (2) a mad person tears his clothing, (3) a mad person walks around at night, and finally, (4) a mad person destroys anything given to her. Verses 3-5 (with v. 15) exhibit all four signs and emphasize the power of the spirits who oppress the man.

When the demoniac saw Jesus, "he ran and bowed down before him" (*prosekunesen*, literally "worshipped," the same word used of the Roman soldiers in 15:19). Other people could not bind the man with chains or subdue him in any way (v. 4), but the mere appearance of Jesus seems to soothe him. Nevertheless the unclean spirits that possess him cry out with remarkable rudeness to Jesus (*ti emoi kai soi*, literally, "what of you and me," which could be translated "whadda ya want?" to capture the tone) and with recognition of who he is (cf. 1:24, which uses the exact same words). "Most High God" is an odd way to refer to God; it is the non-Israelite way to refer to Israel's God and thus suitable for Gentile territory and unclean spirits. (Note that in terms of chronological progression of the narrative, events in v. 8 actually precede those in v. 7, an example of Mark's rough style.

The spirits fear Jesus because he knows them. To know its name is to have power over a person or spirit. "Legion" was a Roman army unit of between four thousand and six thousand men. It was widely used in Hellenistic writing as a metaphor for a great number, and the Aramaic word behind the Greek means "soldier." These martial spirits rightfully cower before their exorcist. Ironically, they beg not to be tormented. It is okay for them to torment humanity but not to be tormented. Knowing that they are about to lose power over the man, the unclean spirits ask to be allowed to stay in the same region (v. 10). It was widely held that when spirits were exorcised, they vented their anger by causing havoc and mischief.[8] Jesus circumvents this by allowing the unclean spirits to enter swine (unclean animals) who immediately commit mass suicide. The impulse to self-destruction they stir in the man (v. 5) comes to fulfillment when the swine drown in the lake, thus joining the demons of the storm who were subdued in the previous pericope (see Ps. 65:7-8a for a useful gloss). The matter of the swine is problematic if Jesus is in Jewish territory. Wherever Gesara was, it must have been a predominantly Gentile area. If that is the case, when Jesus removes both the unclean spirits and the unclean animals, he is symbolically making unclean territory ritually clean. And since the boar was the symbol of the Roman Tenth Legion, Jesus has metaphorically triumphed over imperial power as well (see Mark 3:27). In any event, the swineherds have the unenviable task of reporting to their employer and to others what has happened to their pigs.

The repetitiousness of vv. 14-16 exemplify again Mark's rough style and suggest that two separate accounts were woven together at this point. At v. 15 a new section of the narrative is signaled by a shift to the "historic present" tense. The story is told from the point of view of a beholder. Not content with a report, the locals come to see for themselves what has transpired. The popular response to the miracle is telling. Seeing the man whom they knew to have been mad "seated, clothed, and sane" (*kathemenon himatismenon kai sophronounta,* that is, not wandering around naked howling and harming himself), they are not pleased for him but are afraid (see Ps. 68:6 for a gloss on such deliverance). Their apparent interest is not in the deliverance of the man, but in the loss of the livestock. The locals fear for their property. They beg Jesus to leave their neighborhood (*ton horion auton,* literally leave their boundaries or limits!). What if Jesus delivers everyone from their evil spirits? There may not be enough livestock to hold the demons! The locals are apparently more concerned for their way of life (herding pigs) than for life itself (the man) or the Lord of Life (Jesus).

The comparison between the people and the former demoniac could not be more sharply drawn than it is by vv. 18-20. As Jesus is responding to the request made of him and is leaving (be careful what you ask Jesus for, you are likely to get it!), the man whom he delivered begs to accompany him. Having been delivered from a living death, he wants to accompany the Lord of his new life. In Mark's Gospel the proper response to healing or to hearing the word is to "follow," to become a disciple. The command that Jesus gives in v. 19 is, to my mind, one of the most difficult in the Gospels. The former demoniac is sent to proclaim the power and mercy of God to the very people who had tried to chain him in the tombs, who had left him alone and howling. (Interestingly, Jesus does *not* charge him to be silent, a problem for enthusiastic proponents of the "messianic secret" approach to Mark.) In 2:1-12 the proof of the paralytic's forgiveness and healing is that he walks. Here the proof of the demoniac's deliverance is that he does what Jesus commands him to do. He proclaims in the ten cities of eastern Palestine under the Selucid king (the Decapolis) what Jesus did for him. The story closes with a typical Markan ending, the response of the onlookers, who were "amazed" (*ethaumazon,* they marveled, they wondered). Verses 18-20 provide a distinctively Markan close to the exorcism and inaugurate a mission to the Gentiles, a matter of particular interest to Mark's audience.

This is another particularly rich passage to preach, although, oddly enough, it is omitted from the Year B lectionary. How simple it is to show how "Jesus saves" the whole person by comparing the state of the man in vv. 2-5 with what he becomes after his encounter with the Lord in vv. 15,

18-20. At least four points suggest themselves for homiletical exposition. In this pericope Jesus crosses boundaries to make people whole. Ethnic boundaries are set aside in the reign of God. Jesus comes not to the "well" but to the "sick" (2:17), to those the majority population has marginalized and forgotten. Second, the pericope suggests we must recognize that, when they come to Jesus, people do change. How many people have we consigned to be zombies, to a living death, because we will not allow that they might be different? (This is a particularly potent point with regard to our attitudes toward the addicted and the mentally ill.) Are we unwilling to give those whom God has delivered from their personal demons (addictions, depression, prejudice, prison time) a second chance?

Third, the narrative confronts us with our own priorities. Are we more interested in "business as usual" (our pigs) than we are in the power of God to deliver our disordered lives and the ones of those around us? Do we celebrate God's power to liberate, or do we cower in fear before it because God might ask *us* to change? Finally, the Jesus who delivers is also the Jesus who sends. If we are honest, we admit that we are the ones who have been exorcised. In any given congregation, there are people who have been delivered from the "demons" of loneliness, grief, sin, doubt, confusion, prejudice, and fear. And to us Jesus says, "Go home to your friends, and tell them how much the Lord has done for you, and what mercy he has shown you." The charge to "go home and tell" is, in fact, the great Easter challenge. In Mark 16:7, the young man at the tomb charges the women to tell the disciples and Peter to go to Galilee, to return home to their ordinary circumstances, to meet Jesus. There, at home, their kingdom work begins. The story of the exorcism of the demoniac provides a powerful beginning for a sermon on local evangelism.

For Further Reading

E. S. Johnson, "Mark 5:1-20: The Other Side," *IBS* 20 (1998): 50–74.

5:21-43

Mark is carefully constructing a picture of Jesus as the vehicle of God's power. That power has been demonstrated over the natural world (4:35-41) and over the spiritual world (5:1-20). Now it is brought to bear on the human realm in its totality. Mark does this by combining two stories about people from opposite ends of the social spectrum: the family of a leader of the synagogue (5:21-24a, 25-43) and an anonymous and unclean woman from the crowd (5:24b-34). As is characteristic of his style, Mark intercalates the two, fitting the woman's healing into the other narrative; Jesus interrupts a mercy to do a mercy. Achtemeier thinks Mark combined the stories because they both had female sufferers, both employ the number twelve, and both use a vocabulary that includes "faith," "fear," "daughter," and "save."[9]

The setting of the two stories is the same. The sea crossing serves as the narrative link to what has gone on previously. Jesus and the disciples "had crossed again . . . back to the other side," and "a great crowd gathered around him" (v. 21), Jesus is back on the west side of the lake, back in Jewish territory, back where he is known and popular. In this great crowd by the sea (*thalassan*) are both Jairus and the woman. (For the sake of clarity, I treat the two narratives separately below.)

5:24b-34

Mark stresses that the crowd around Jesus was large and "pushed in against him" (*sunethlibon*). A woman with a gynecological disorder was in the crowd. Her suffering is vividly described in vv. 25-26; she had suffered bleeding for twelve years (fibroid tumors?) and spent all her savings on the first-century equivalent of gynecologists. Most women are hardly enamored of modern medicine in this field; we can well imagine the indignities of first-century treatment! But she has not improved, only grown worse. The nature of her complaint is not only messy and embarrassing, it is alienating. Leviticus 15:19-30 describes the law's reaction to a women with "a discharge of blood"; it separates her from the community because it makes her and anyone she comes in contact with "unclean" and "defiled." Mark's candor tells us not only that she had suffered physically for twelve years, but that she had been ostracized from the community, from ordinary human contact (and sexual contact if she were married), and from the worshipping life of Israel. No wonder she summons her courage to approach Jesus!

Verses 27-29 describe the woman's approach to Jesus and its effect. It was commonly believed at the time that great personalities had the power to heal (see Acts 5:15 or 19:12 for other New Testament examples), and that since their clothing was an extension of themselves, it too held power. Mark has already established Jesus' fame in the region, so we are not surprised that the woman knows of him and decides (with what fear and trepidation?) to approach him. Immediately upon touching Jesus "she knew in her body that she had been healed" (*egno to somati hoti iatai*). Only here in Mark is *iaomai* used for "heal" (the usual verb is *sozo* "to heal" and "to save"), perhaps for the force of the passive (a Divine passive again, or simply the correct form of a *mai* verb?).

Mark's description of the response to the healing is almost as dramatic as his description of the disease itself. Jesus knows that power (*dunamis,* used in the LXX primarily of God) "had gone out" from him (the past participle says it is no longer happening). He knows what has happened to himself and asks who has touched his clothes. For the second time in this series of miracle accounts, the disciples are sharp with Jesus (4:38; 5:31). The disciples simply repeat what we already know; they are in the midst of a large, milling crowd. Anybody could have touched Jesus and gone away. This intensifies the drama of the healed woman's confession in v. 33. It is she, the unclean and outcast, and not his disciples who responds in faith to Jesus. She comes "in fear and trembling," prostrates herself before Jesus, and tells him the truth about what has happened. She knows she has broken both social and religious taboos to approach Jesus at all, much less to touch the rabbi and thereby make him unclean. She probably expects a rebuke.

But this is not Jesus' view of the matter at all. His first word to her is not of condemnation but of inclusion—"daughter" (*thugater*), an affectionate word of address that establishes her identity as a daughter of Abraham and a member of Jesus' new family (3:34-35). Her healing is the direct result of her faith. The word the NRSV translates as "well" is a form of *sozo* that means both "to heal" and "to save." It is a delicious pun. Her faith has healed and saved her, made her a whole person by healing her body, and, because she is "clean," returned her to the worshipping community of Israel. And by her faith, she is also made part of Jesus' community. Jesus gives her a blessing ("go in peace") and sends her on her way.

In her commentary in the *New Interpreter's Bible,* Pheme Perkins summarizes the narrative this way:

> The exchange between Jesus and the woman removes any suggestion that Jesus' clothes were endowed with magical power, nor does Jesus condemn her for attempted "theft" of his power. Jesus does not possess a magic force that accounts for his ability to heal. Instead, healing reflects the presence of God's saving power . . . and Jesus' saving and healing presence demonstrates that the kingdom of God is near.[10]

This is a most extraordinary story. It depicts Jesus in a remarkable relationship to a woman. An anonymous woman approached him and was not turned away even when, by all rights and religious precepts, she could have been. No one would fault a rabbi for refusing contact with an "unclean" woman. The narrative provides evidence not only that there were women in the crowds around Jesus, but that some of their stories were remembered, and some of them became exemplary figures in early church tradition.

An interesting point for reflection is the difference in the way Jesus responds to an "interruption" (remember he is on the way to heal Jairus's daughter) and the way most of us do. There is no hint in the account that he is annoyed when an anonymous woman delays his work for an important man in the community. How often are what we deem interruptions really opportunities to reach out to others and, as in this case, to bring them into the family? How often might they really be opportunities to be further molded by God?

Another powerful preaching point is that in spite of her "fear and trembling," the woman *twice* approaches Jesus, once for physical healing (about which we are led to feel her compulsion) and once for no other reason than that she *knows* what Jesus has done for her and has the moral courage to make it publicly known. For this reason, she becomes a model of faith. And, in fact, she demonstrates to Jairus, who must have been waiting impatiently during the exchange, the faith that he must have to effect his own miracle.[11] (And, parenthetically, by her action and public confession after her healing, she makes her faith known and functions, in fact, as a "preacher.")

For Further Reading

Mary Ann Beavis, "Women as Models of Faith in Mark," *BTB* 18 (1988): 3–9.

Maria J. Selvidge, *Woman, Cult and Miracle Recital: A Redaction-Critical Investigation on Mark 5:24-34* (Lewisburg, Pa.: Bucknell Univ. Press, 1990).

5:22-24a, 35-43

Verses 22-24a set the stage for the miracle that actually transpires in vv. 35-43. Apparently working his way through the crowd around Jesus, a "leader of the synagogue" (*archisunagogos*, an "administrator" in modern parlance, and probably not a spiritual figure) comes to Jesus and falls at his feet in repeated supplication on behalf of his seriously ill "little daughter" (diminutives are characteristic of Mark's style; see 5:41-42; 6:22, 28; 7:27-28; and so forth). Jairus knows Jesus' reputation as a healer; he even knows how he heals by the laying on of hands (v. 23, 1:31; 3:5). I think Mark intends the hearer/reader to be sympathetically disposed toward this official, this distraught parent who braves the indignities of a crowd in order to seek help for a female child. In a world that valued sons over daughters, men over women, that in itself tells us something about the man. (And he is also proof that not all Jews were against Jesus.) The text of Mark says simply "and he went with him" (*kai apelthen met' autou*, v. 24). This is usually taken to mean that Jesus went with Jairus, but it could equally well mean that Jairus continued to accompany Jesus, who might or might not at this point have decided to help him. In any case, imagine the anxiety of the father when Jesus stops to deal with the hemorrhaging woman (vv. 24b-34).

As the narrative progresses, it looks as though the detour to heal the woman has made Jesus "too late" for the little girl. People come from

Jarius's house to report that his daughter is dead (v. 35). There is no need to plead with Jesus any longer. Notice in v. 36 that Jesus exhibits no unusual prescience; he "overhears" (although other ancient sources record variously that he "ignores" or "hears") this report and charges the father, "Do not fear, only believe" ("Do not fear" was the message to the disciples in the storm-tossed boat, 4:49), which is the key to the meaning of the account. Of the disciples who are with him, Jesus chooses only Peter, James, and John to accompany him. They continue as the "chosen few" or the "inner circle" who have closer intimacy with Jesus throughout Mark's Gospel (9:2, 23; 13:3; 14:33).

Mark does not relate what happens to the crowd around Jesus, only that when they reach Jairus's house, the professional mourners have already arrived and begun their work (v. 38). What others take for death, Jesus knows is something else; death is not the final reality that it seems. He communicates this by declaring, "the child is not dead but sleeping." "Sleeping" (*katheudei*) is a tender metaphor for death in Paul's writing, because he too knows it has been overcome (see 1 Thess. 4:13-15; 5:10; 1 Cor. 15:6, 51). Ignoring the jeering laughter and having separated from the "commotion," Jesus takes the parents of the girl, together with Peter, James, and John, and goes to her. He both touches the child and speaks to her. As is characteristic, Mark retains Jesus' words in Aramaic but translates them for his non-Aramaic speaking audience (v. 41). Morna Hooker points out that the Aramaic literally means, "Lamb, get up," which is a sweet mode of address for a child, but also reinforces the position of those who wish to see this story as an allegory of resurrection.[12] To the utter astonishment of the five witnesses, "immediately" (Mark's favorite word) the girl gets up and begins to walk. Jesus first charges the adults not to tell what has happened. The command to give the child something to eat reveals a practical side to Jesus and also serves as proof that the child is well. She can walk and take nourishment.

The charge to secrecy in v. 43 is perplexing. The leper was similarly charged (1:44), but the demoniac was told to go and tell (5:19). Here, there is already an "audience" in the house who will see that the "dead" child has been raised. Perhaps Mark's point is that resurrection should not be declared to those who are disposed to disbelieve. (We were previously told that the onlookers laughed when Jesus said the child was not dead, v. 40.) Or perhaps Jesus wants to delay the crisis that will inevitably occur when the full extent of his authority is known. I am afraid I have no ingenious solution to offer.

This text, usually including 24b-34, appears in the post-Pentecost "Ordinary Time" cycle and, as such, offers an opportunity to reflect again on the mystery of resurrection. Many preachers do this by means of an allegory in which death is the sleep that leads to eternal life. In v. 23, the father asks for healing/salvation (*sothe* from *sozo*) *and* life (*zoe*) for his daughter. It is what God the divine parent wants for all his children. A fine sermon can also be built on the theme "called by name," with connections made to the call stories in Mark 1 and to Mary of Magdala's experience in the garden of resurrection in John 20. Certainly in terms of the life of prayer, if we see the father as supplicator, we also see the result of his persistence (cf. Luke 18:1-8).

This might also be a good place for nonlectionary preachers to consider a cycle of sermons on "Jesus and Women in Mark." A four-sermon series can be built around the four healing miracles Jesus does for women: Peter's mother-in-law (1:29-31), Jairus's daughter, the hemorrhaging woman, and the Syrophoenician woman (7:24-30). In each account some difficulty or risk is taken in securing Jesus' help. In two accounts the woman comes to Jesus on her own and in two his help is sought for her. Mark depicts the women as exemplars of faith. (For greater detail on this subject, consult the article by Mary Ann Beavis listed in "For Further Reading" immediately preceding the commentary on this pericope.)

Summary
4:35—5:43

Mark arranges this block of four miracle stories in his continuing narrative to make clear what the title of 1:1 had declared: Jesus is the Christ, the Son of God. As such, Jesus is the authoritative teacher (4:1-34) who exhibits the power of God by exerting his authority over the natural world, the spirit world, the human body, and finally over life and death itself (4:35—5:43). Homiletically, we see Jesus as lord of every situation, especially those that seem hopeless.

What Mark is doing in this block of material would not have been unfamiliar to a Greco-Roman audience:

> The accounts inscribed at shrines like Epidauros demonstrate to the unbelieving that the gods . . . had healing powers. Some scholars think that collections of Jesus' miracles played a similar role. They served as demonstrations that God's divine power was in Jesus, the Son of God. The miracle itself provokes the question of Jesus' identity and awe over the power he exercises.[13]

In the narrative itself as well as in Mark's audience, some believe Jesus, trust in, and follow him (5:18-20, 23-23, 33-34), but some are perplexed (4:41), and some are openly contemptuous (5:40). Interestingly, in terms of the larger structure of Mark's Gospel, the block of miracles that show Jesus as the authoritative teacher and the series of miracles demonstrating the extent of Jesus' authority are framed by texts in which those who should have known him best and responded most positively to him exhibit no understanding (3:31-35; 6:1-6).

One final issue in this block of material calls for comment: the conjunction of the concepts of "faith" and "fear," pairings of which occur in 4:40 and 5:33-34, 36 (and are implied situationally in 2:5; 5:15; 6:50; 9:23; 10:32; and 16:8). The faith/fear connection is most clear in the healing miracles. While fear is associated with unbelief in outsiders, it signals lack of understanding among Jesus' disciples. And fear is the main characteristic of Jesus' opponents in Mark's passion narrative. Undoubtedly the matter of faith and fear was of existential concern to Mark's original audience. It certainly was to the biblical writers generally, since the most frequently repeated imperative in scripture and the most frequent word from heaven to earth is "fear not." Mark's Gospel depicts faith not so much as intellectual assent to propositions, but as an attitude of expectant trust in Jesus regardless of the circumstances. When the disciples falter, it is because they have not trusted Jesus enough. In the face of fear, Jesus calls his followers to faith and hope.

For Further Reading

Elizabeth S. Malbon, "Fallible Followers: Women and Men in the Gospel of Mark," *Semeia* 28 (1983): 29–48.

Bonnie Thurston, "Faith and Fear in Mark's Gospel," *The Bible Today* 23 (1985): 305–10.

5

The Ministry around Capernaum
Mark 6:1—8:21

Introduction

I admit at the outset that my division of material at this point is somewhat arbitrary and diverges from my tendency to present blocks of material according to literary type. Mark 6:1—8:21 presents a second view of the Galilean ministry of Jesus (the first was in 1:16—3:35). Mark 6:1 indicates a clear shift of geographical location in the narrative and introduces a new unit of material that includes miracles (6:30-44, 45-52, 53-56; 7:24-30, 31-37; 8:1-10) and controversy dialogues (7:1-23). The following section, 8:22—10:52, is clearly marked off by an inclusion formed by the healings of two blind men, with parallels in the intervening material that focuses on discipleship. While there are two feeding stories in this unit (6:30-44; 8:1-10), they do not seem to mark off a section of material unified by literary type or theme and, in any case, exclude 6:1-29.

Other students of Mark's Gospel have divided the material quite differently. J. D. Kingsbury suggests that 1:14—8:26 is the middle of the Gospel (with 8:27—16:8 as the end section).[1] His divisions are based on a pattern of growing opposition to Jesus; 1:14—8:26 is the first cycle of conflicts. Paul Achtemeier suggests that 6:45—8:26 is the second of a set of two parallel miracle catenae. The first is 4:35—6:44. Each contains a sea miracle, three healings, and a feeding miracle. He explains that the two cycles were formed in the early church against the background of traditions about Moses and were part of a liturgy of epiphanic Eucharist. Within that larger pattern, the function of miracles in the Hellenistic world was "epiphanic," so that in these two cycles Jesus is depicted as the one in whom divine power is at work.[2]

Perhaps the most detailed working out of a structure for this material appears in Hugh Humphrey's recent book, *He is Risen! A New Reading of Mark's Gospel*.[3] He argues that the lens through which to view Mark's Gospel is that of the Jewish wisdom tradition and that, in Mark, Jesus is the "righteous man" described in the Wisdom of Solomon. Humphrey thinks the large-scale structure of the Gospel is concentric, and he offers detailed structural analyses of subsections of Mark. Mark 6:30—8:21 is Humphrey's third major section of the Gospel; its function is to give the reader the opportunity to make the association of Jesus and the wisdom of God.[4] Formally, Humphrey thinks this section is an extended chiasm worked out as follows:

A	6:30-31	Jesus alone with disciples
B	6:32-34	boat journey, people come to Jesus, he responds
C	6:35-44	feeding of five thousand
D	6:45-52	miracle on sea done privately for disciples
E	6:53-56	response to Jesus, who heals many
F	7:1-23	controversy with Pharisees over eating "bread"
E1	7:24-30	response to Jesus, who exorcises a woman's daughter
D1	7:31-37	miracle on sea done privately
C1	8:1-10	feeding of four thousand
B1	8:11-13	boat, Pharisees come to Jesus, he responds
A1	8:14-21	Jesus alone with disciples

Humphrey explains that in this section of the Gospel Jesus exhibits the characteristics of wisdom found in Wisdom of Solomon 6–8. In "Mark's presentation *Jesus himself* is the 'sign from heaven,' *God's Wisdom come to Israel* to show compassion upon a people without a shepherd by feeding them abundantly with the bread of understanding."[5]

Obviously there are a number of ways to view this section of Mark's Gospel. One final point is noteworthy. In both Mark's and John's Gospels, the sequence of the narrative of feeding the five thousand, walking on the water, and the healings at Gennesaret are identical (Mark 6:30-56; John 6:1-25), suggesting that this unit of material was put together early in the tradition and maintained consistently across it. It is a group of stories of key significance to the early Christians.

6:1-6a

The early church was as puzzled as we are by the lack of positive response to Jesus from his own people and from eyewitnesses of his miracles. This rejection at Nazareth follows a section of the Gospel in which Jesus has done great miracles precisely to show that mighty works alone do not automatically produce faith. Perhaps because of this rejection in Galilee, the narrative in Mark 6:6b—9:50 shows Jesus engaged in ministry in a wider area beyond Capernaum.[6] Having returned to the western shores of the lake (5:21), Jesus makes the roughly twenty-five-mile journey to

Nazareth, which we know from Matthew's Gospel is his "hometown" (although the Greek word *patrida* literally means "birthplace," "native place," or "country"). Verse 1 says the disciples "followed him," the technical language of discipleship, which, with regard to the disciples, is found only here and at 2:15. That the disciples accompany Jesus suggests this is an evangelistic tour or a mission, not just a family visit.

Verses 2-3 depict the "home people's" response to Jesus and vv. 4-6 Jesus' response to them. Verse 2 stresses again Jesus' role as teacher within the Jewish tradition. The synagogue assembly who hear his teaching are "astounded" and, in Markan terms, they ask the right questions: Where did Jesus get his wisdom and power (*dunameis* is used of God in the LXX)? But their proposed answers are all wrong. They know Jesus. He is a carpenter (*tekton* in Greek is used for any artisan in stone, metal, or wood, thus a worker on a building, a person of considerable skill).[7] He is the "son of Mary." This is an unusual and ambiguous turn of phrase, since Jewish men are usually called after their fathers. It can mean that Jesus was the son of a widow, that he was an illegitimate son, or that his mother's lineage was superior to his father's.[8] Does it reflect small-town rumors about Jesus' birth? Certainly Mark would not have intended a slur against Jesus, but whether he meant to suggest that only God is the father of Jesus or to preserve a doctrine of the virgin birth is unclear. (For a discussion of the siblings of Jesus see the previous discussion of 3:19b-21, 31-35.) The point is that the people feel they know Jesus too well to be stirred by the reports of his actions. Mark says the hometown people "stumbled" (*eskandalizonto*, literally a rock on which one trips or stumbles) or "took offense" at him (cf. John 1:11; Rom. 9:33; 1 Pet. 2:8).

Jesus' verbal response is widely attested in early Christianity. It is also found in the Gospel of Thomas #35 and P. Oxyrhynchus I. 31–36 (cf. also Luke 4:23). Jesus reflects theologically on the simple truth that the locals "can't see the forest for the trees." Because faith is requisite to a cure (see 2:5; 5:34; 7:24-30; 9:24), Jesus is able to perform no "deed of power" (*dunamin*) there, although he does heal by his typical method, the laying on of hands. Those who should have known him best and recognized him for what he was were "clueless." In an ironic ending, Mark has Jesus respond to the people the way they usually respond to him; he was amazed (*ethaumasen*) by their lack of belief or trust (*apistia*).

The essential point of the narrative for preaching is faith/belief or lack thereof. By their failure to allow that Jesus could be anything other than who they *thought* he was, the locals blocked what Jesus wanted to do for them. Jesus does not force anyone. Even he cannot work in us without our invitation. Jesus freely offers us his invitation, but we must respond. Are there people that we "sell short" because we *think* we know them? Or are there people who may have changed that we "miss" because we chain them firmly to what they were? (see notes on 5:1-20 above). How many eager young Christians who have gone away for their educations are thwarted when they return to their home congregations because they are still treated as "the Smith child" or "little Susie"?

6:6b-13

Is it as a result of his own inability to reach people in his home country that Jesus sends out the Twelve to do what heretofore Mark has shown Jesus doing? Verse 6b reports that "he went about among the villages teaching" (Mark's characteristic picture of Jesus), but he sends (*apostellein*) the Twelve out to do "mighty works," in fact, the "typical activities" of Jesus depicted in 1:16-39: exorcism, vv. 7, 13; preaching repentance, v. 12; healing, v. 13.

Verses 8-11 are the "marching orders" for the Twelve. Matthew gives a greatly expanded version of these instructions in chapter 10 of his Gospel. Verses 8-9 concern physical or material aspects of the mission. The Twelve are to take no bread, bag, or money. Of course, if they take no provisions, they have no need for a knapsack (*peran*). The "staff" (*rabdos*) was what we would call a "walking stick." This "stripped down" travel is an image of the urgency of the task and suggests that the Twelve are to depend upon God for their sustenance, which will come through the hospitality of those they serve. They were allowed to wear sandals, but not "two tunics." Perhaps the idea is that they are not allowed the outside cloak that served as a covering at night.

Verses 10-11 are instructions on how to behave, "missionary manners." The Twelve (who function as apostles, "those sent") are to stay in the first home they enter, that is, not to shift from house to house seeking better accommodations for themselves. If they are not welcomed, they are to "shake off the dust that is on [their] feet as a testimony against them." Morna Hooker explains this action.

> Shaking the dust from the feet was a symbolic action normally per-
> formed by a Jew who had been abroad on his re-entry into Palestine:
> foreign dust must not contaminate Jewish soil.... Such an action on the
> part of the disciples was clearly meant to indicate that the village or
> town which had rejected them was no longer to be regarded as part of
> the Jewish nation.[9]

In view of the images of the urgency of the mission and of Jesus' own rejection in Nazareth, the action certainly has ominous overtones.

Mark begins the report of this mission in vv. 12-13 and picks it up again in v. 30. In the intervening narrative the martyrdom of John the Baptist is related, which allows for passage of time. The Twelve go out to proclaim the message of John and Jesus (cf. 1:4, 14-15; obviously they cannot preach the full Gospel until after the death and resurrection of Jesus), perform exorcisms, and cure the sick (v. 13). Oil was used as a medicine in the Greco-Roman world. Anointing with oil may, in fact, reflect later church tradition (see James 5:14; Isa. 1:6). Mark depicts the Twelve as having the same compassion that Jesus did, another indication that the followers of Jesus are not always failures. Disciples of Jesus are to do what Jesus does.

The text appears in the lectionary in the post-Pentecost Ordinary Time and is an appropriate choice for commissioning ceremonies for most ministries. The text makes clear that mission is initiated and empowered by Jesus (v. 7). We do not choose our call, and our own abilities do not make us adequate to the task. We are the "object," not the "subject"; we are "called," "sent," and "given." If the staff, bread, bag, money, sandals, and tunics can be seen as symbols of material culture, and if these are in some sense instructions for missionaries, then they make it clear that missionaries are to live as the persons to whom they are sent live. They are to receive as gift and accept the people (cultures) to whom they are sent; they are not to "export" culture. Those who are called to mission are called to the humility of the one who set aside the "culture" of heaven and emptied himself to take on human flesh (see Phil. 2:6-11).

6:14-29

Mark introduced John the Baptist at the outset of the Gospel (1:4-8) to link Jesus with Israel's past. In this pericope, John's martyrdom foretells Jesus' fate. Mark alluded to the arrest of John at the outset of Jesus' Galilean ministry (1:14); now he completes the story of John. The John material is inserted here to give a sense of the passage of time during the mission of the Twelve. Mark undoubtedly knew John's story from oral tradition, as John was a well-known figure. His end is related in Josephus *Antiquities* XVIII. 5.2, an account that is substantially the same as the synoptic record.

In vv. 14-16, Mark weaves the Baptist material into the mission account (6:6b-13, 30) by reporting that Herod had heard of the mission and of Jesus. The verses are a public prelude to a similar scene with the disciples in 8:27-30. The Twelve have been sent on a mission to further John's work of repentance (cf. 1:4; 6:12). Verses 14-16 rehearse the popular view of Jesus (and provide other answers to the questions raised at 4:41; 6:2-3). Some think Jesus is John raised from the dead, which leads to the account of the Baptist's martyrdom. Others think he is Elijah or one of the prophets "of old," a gentle reminder that it was popularly thought that prophecy had ended in Israel. (These are the same answers the disciples give Jesus in 8:27-28.) For the second time Mark repeats "Herod heard of it."[10] Herod Antipas (4 B.C.–A.D. 39) thinks Jesus is John (whom he beheaded) raised from the dead, an odd conclusion since Herodians were usually aligned with Sadducees, who denied resurrection. The association of John and Jesus was apparently widely held.

Verses 17-29 tell the horrifying story of John's martyrdom. Herod arrested John, who had denounced his immoral marriage to Herodias, his (Herod's) sister-in-law. Herod had left his legal wife for her (see Lev. 18:16; 20:21). Herodias (who is to be recognized as a latter-day Jezebel; cf. 1 Kings 19:2; 21:4ff.) took this especially badly and "nursed a grudge" or "cherished wrath" (*eneichen*) against John, whom Herod, to his credit, protected because he knew him to be "righteous and holy" (v. 20). Herod did not understand the message of John but "liked to listen to him." (One wonders if Herod enjoyed sermons of John like those recorded in Matt. 3:7-12 or Luke 3:7-17! When, in imitation of the Romans, Herod kept his birthday as a feast day, Herodias seized her chance for revenge.)

Roman banquets routinely closed with dancing or a coarse pantomime. If, indeed, a Herodian princess danced at such a dinner, it is bitter evidence of how corrupt the Herodians had become. What father would allow his daughter (or step-daughter) to dance for drunken men? But the dancing pleases this father, who promises on an oath (*omosen*, v. 23; cf. Matt. 5:33-37) to give her whatever she asks for, "even half of my kingdom." Herod hereby oversteps himself; as a puppet king, he had no kingdom to offer. This dutiful daughter consults her mother on what to ask for. Herodias "immediately with haste" (*euthus meta spoude*)—the girl is to act in haste lest Herod change his mind—wants the head of John the Baptist on a platter. The request "deeply grieved" (*perilupos*: the word used to describe Jesus in Gethsemane, 14.34) Herod, but he cared more for his "honor," his standing with his guests, than for the life of an innocent man. (In this his behavior is parallel to that of Pilate in 15:1-15.) He issues the order, and the gruesome gift is brought to the girl, who presents it to her mother. So much for a pretty picture of biblical family values!

This is the only account in Mark's Gospel not directly about Jesus. It is related here not just as an "interlude" in the mission of the Twelve, but to foreshadow the fate of Jesus and to indicate that his mission will go on in spite of official opposition to it. Verse 29, in particular, anticipates Jesus' death and burial (cf. 15:42ff.). Mark could hardly have made the John/Jesus parallel clearer. Both John and Jesus are martyred by rulers who recognize their goodness but are too weak, too influenced by popular opinion, to act on their behalf. But official opposition cannot stop God's plan of salvation (a message not lost on Mark's community, which suffered Roman persecution). As the proverb goes, the church flowers from the blood of its martyrs.

For Further Reading

Jerome Murphy-O'Connor, "John the Baptist and Jesus: History and Hypothesis," *NTS* 36 (1990): 359–74.

Robert L. Webb, *John the Baptizer and Prophet,* JSNTSup 62 (Sheffield: JSOT Press, 1991).

6:30-44

This pericope picks up the account of the mission of the Twelve begun in 6:6b-13. It has two parts: vv. 30-32, Jesus' response to the mission, and vv. 34-44, the feeding of the five thousand, with v. 33 as the link. At the center of chapter 6 are two very different banquets. One is hosted by King Herod and one by King Jesus; their juxtaposition invites comparisons.

The vocabulary of v. 30 is typically Markan, except for the word "apostles," which appears only here (and in some manuscripts in 3:14). In 6:7 Jesus called and sent out "the Twelve." Mark is more concerned with discipleship in general than with what, in later church development, became a small and authoritative group within the larger family of believers. What the Twelve report to Jesus was given in substance in 6:12-13. Jesus is a practical teacher. He knows that in addition to the daily pressures of the ministry (v. 31b), they must be weary from their travel and its intense public activity (even if, in the flush of success, they do not recognize it). Jesus invites the disciples to "come away privately" or "alone" (*kat idian,* thus highlighting Mark's tendency to separate "disciples" from the "crowd," cf. 1:35; 3:9-10, 20) and "rest." Only in Mark's Gospel does Jesus consecrate a time of rest and recreation. Again using a boat as refuge, Jesus and the disciples attempt to withdraw to a "deserted place" (literally a desert, *eremon,* "lonely" or "uninhabited" place, so the word introduces again the theme of "desert spirituality"; cf. 1:4, 12, 35).

But now Jesus and the disciples bear the burden of notoriety; they are recognized by many people "from all the towns" who apparently hurry around the shore of the Sea of Galilee and provide a less-than-welcome reception (v. 33). If the winds were headwinds against the boat, this is quite possible. (In interpreting the disciples' response in vv. 35-36, recall that they arrive already weary from active ministry.) Jesus' response to the crowd is not irritation but compassion. The Greek word for "compassion" here is *esplagchnisthe,* from *splagna,* literally "guts" or "entrails." But *splagna* is the Greek word used for the Hebrew *rahim* or "womb." It is an image used in Hebrew scripture to describe God's compassion, the compassion of a mother. Jesus is so moved because the crowd are like "sheep without a shepherd," an image of aimlessness and wandering (see Num. 27:17; 1 Kings 22:17; Ezek. 34:2, 5). Note that Jesus' first response to the people was that he began to teach. Teaching is Jesus' compassionate response to the directionless crowd (and, of course, it is Mark's favorite description of Jesus).

At this point (v. 34) the miracle story proper begins. As it unfolds, the interpreter should keep in mind Hebrew scriptural parallels. Moses instructs and feeds a multitude in the wilderness, and both Elijah and Elisha effect feeding miracles (1 Kings 17:8-16; 2 Kings 4:42-44). Again, the point of the miracles in Mark is christological; they reveal something about Jesus. The presence of miracles in Mark's Gospel is to remind the hearer/reader of the continuing power and authority of Jesus as a teacher.[11] This one also tells us something about the shortsightedness of Jesus' disciples. They have, in effect, been cheated out of their rest. The teaching has gone on for some time; the day is well advanced, and the disciples want Jesus to send the people away to forage for their supper (vv. 35-36).

From the point of view of the disciples, Jesus adds insult to injury by asking *them* to feed the people. In the context of the chapter, we are to understand this as a further charge in mission (cf. 6:7-13). But the sharp response of the disciples reveals their shortsightedness. In v. 37 they behave exactly like people who are "stressed out" by overwork (recall v. 31). Two hundred denarii was roughly a laborer's wage for two hundred days of work. Obviously the disciples do not carry that kind of money! (They were charged not to do so in 6:8.) But they do carry provisions. The five loaves (probably small, round barley loaves) and two fish (dried or salted fish) are probably the meal intended for their "retreat day."

Beginning at vv. 39-40 all the indications are that this is not the usual picnic. Jesus literally "commanded them all to recline" (*epetaxen autois anaklithenai pantas*). "Reclining" was the position for dining at a banquet. Only Mark tells us they reclined on "green grass," which, if not an eyewitness detail, at least tells us this event occurred in spring after the winter rains when there is green grass in Galilee. And so, in a picture of orderliness, the "great crowd" reclined in ranks. The image is that of the order of the Mosaic camp in the wilderness (see Exod. 18:21). Taking the provisions at hand and looking up to heaven (the normal Jewish posture of prayer), Jesus performs the essential eucharistic actions: he takes, blesses, breaks (cf. Mark 14:22-23; 1 Cor. 11:23-26), and then gives the provisions *to the disciples* to distribute. It is the job of Jesus' disciples to feed those who are "like sheep without a shepherd." (I think this "feeding" is to be understood literally and metaphorically. See, for example, John's explanation of this miracle in John 6:25-65.)

Verses 42-44 describe the result of the miracle. There was enough to go around. Five thousand men (and who knows how many women and children) got not only "some" but enough to be "filled" or "satisfied." And the disciples took up twelve baskets (I would not make overly much of this number) full of leftovers, more than they began with. (See Ezek. 24:23-31; Isa. 25:6-9.) The miracle is in the leftovers! This abundance is an image of divine bounty. And a messianic expectation is also depicted. It was popularly held that, when the Messiah came, he would host a great banquet for Israel, and only the Messiah could host it. Certainly this must have entered the minds of some in the crowd and later in Mark's community. Here the inclusive fellowship meals that were part of Jesus' ministry become an image of the kingdom he inaugurates.

One common line of interpretation of the miracle suggests that what "really happened" is that Jesus got the assembled multitude to share. When people saw the disciples pull out five loaves and two fish, they began to offer the bits and pieces they, too, were carrying, and in the sharing there was enough to go around. This interpretation destroys what Mark is doing with the story. He is comparing the kingdoms of this world (Herod) with "the kingdom of our Lord, and of his Christ." Provision of food in the wilderness is a mark of God's saving grace. Jesus is doing the work of God. That, in itself, provides fruitful sermon material.

Two other points in the account are homiletically fruitful. First, a fine sermon can be built around vv. 30-32. In an overworked, stressed out, and consequently burned-out world (and church!) it is important to highlight those places in scripture where Jesus invites, in fact, commands his followers to withdraw and to rest. Solitude and rest are not "icing" or "extras." They are the very environment from which fruitful ministry grows. Verses 35-37 are stark reminders of what happens when they are ignored; Jesus' disciples can find themselves at odds with what he wants them to do. And that is the second point for another sermon. If people are hungry, Jesus expects his disciples to do something about it: "*you* give them something to eat" (v. 37). If what we provide is not to be the spiritual equivalent of "junk food," then we must have deepened ourselves through the "withdrawal" described in v. 31. But it is more serious than this. We are not only the ones commanded to feed, but we are the ones who are "taken, blest, broken, and given" *to* feed. Sometimes we, like the disciples, are called to meet serious, human needs at just the point we find ourselves at the very "end of our ropes" physically and spiritually. And precisely then we *become* the body of Christ, as in our brokenness, we are blest and given to others.

6:45-52

The miracle of walking on water follows quickly upon the previous one. Verses 45-46 both "finish" the previous narrative and introduce the miracle in vv. 47-52. As soon as the feeding miracle is complete, Jesus attempts once again to provide the disciples with respite from active ministry (see 6:30-32). He sent the crowd away and "made" or "compelled" (*enagkasen*, the word implies the disciples were unwilling) the disciples to get into the boat and cross the sea ahead of him. Although the destination is much discussed in the commentaries, it is generally assumed that they made for Bethsaida on the east side of the Sea of Galilee. Then Jesus takes the advice he offers others and goes "up on the mountain" (like Moses? Elijah?) to pray. (One wonders if he is not tired of both the crowd and his recalcitrant disciples!)

Since the five thousand were fed late in the day (6:35), "when evening came" (v. 47) must imply nighttime. Verses 47 and 48 are heavy with symbolism. It is dark (an image of lack of understanding); the boat (an image of Jesus' community, the church?) is "at sea" and struggling (*basanizomenous*, literally "tortured" or "straining") with adversity ("an adverse wind"). And Jesus is not "with them"; he is "alone on the land." When the disciples are separated from Jesus, they flounder. Notice there is no indication that the disciples in the boat called out to Jesus or invoked his (or God's) aid. Early in the morning (v. 48, the fourth watch of the Roman night and perhaps in partial light), he comes toward them, walking on the sea. He does not intend to stop. He has not been invited to do so (remember the conclusions from 6:1-6a). And, in any case, the disciples do not recognize Jesus. In fact, "they thought it was a ghost" (v. 49), and in Jewish superstition, a spirit in the night brought disaster. No wonder they are terrified when they see this "ghost."

Verse 50b is crucial for understanding the account. Jesus, apparently perceiving the terror of the disciples, speaks first to them: "take heart" (*tharseite*, an imperative meaning "cheer up" or "courage"). In Mark's Gospel, the words of Jesus (his teaching) always take primacy over miracles. The reason they are to take heart? "It is I" (*ego eimi*). In Hebrew scripture the one who says this is God (Exod. 3:14; 6:6). The same phrase is the great Johannine declaration of Jesus. Because Jesus "is who he is," his disciples must not fear. When Jesus joins them in the boat, the wind ceases, and they are "utterly astounded" (*existemi*, "baffled" or "puzzled").

If the story ended here, the interpretation would be reasonably straightforward. Without Jesus, the church is in danger of being overwhelmed by darkness and storm. But in the hour of darkest need (Neronian persecution?), Jesus comes as a "real presence," and courage returns. The account does not end at v. 51, however; Mark adds v. 52, which somehow links the feeding miracle and the walking on water. The matter of their hearts being hardened harkens back to 4:10-12 and the discussion of lack of understanding. I think that Bratcher and Nida are correct when they note: "What the Gospel writer implies is that they did not understand the implications of the miracle."[12] Our problem is the translation of *peporomene*, to harden or to petrify. When "used of 'heart' it means 'to grow (or, make) dull,' 'blind,' obtuse.'"[13] "*Hardened* indicates primarily a state of being resulting from a process, not a specific process requiring the identification of the particular agent. The Greek has reference to the condition of the hearts, not the process by which they became hardened."[14]

Mark indicates that the disciples should by now have understood that Jesus had power from God over natural things. They have, after all, already experienced his stilling of the storm (4:35-41, and the previous miracles, 5:1-20, 21-43). But it is still possible to miss the meaning through lack of faith (see Rom. 11:7, 25; 2 Cor. 3:14; Eph. 4:18).

Two other theological difficulties in this passage, while they may not affect our congregations' hearing of them, are significant. Because this is one of the few places in Mark's Gospel where Jesus is not depicted as being fully human, where Jesus acts "outside humanity," is this a "Docetic Jesus" (that is, one who only *seems* to be human, but is in fact a divine being)? And, second, is this not a "useless miracle"? The disciples are in no real danger. Therefore is not Jesus' action here just thaumaturgy? In the context of Mark's Gospel, we must remember the previous "sea miracle" at 4:35-41. Both here (by the ability to walk on it) and there (by the ability to calm it), Mark's point is Jesus' control of the sea (and only God can control the sea, which in the ancient Near East was frequently a metaphor for chaos). Mark is only secondarily interested in Jesus' display of power. His primary interest is Jesus' word and the declaration of Jesus' identity (v. 50), and (perhaps) secondarily, assisting the disciples (which is probably the point that most preachers will stress in the account).

Three other points may be of interest for preaching. The first two are found in vv. 45-46 (which parallel 6:30-31). It is important to know "when to stop," when to end an event and "dismiss the crowd," and when to withdraw ourselves. It takes considerable art to do what Jesus does when he calls the assembly to an end and, simultaneously, "takes care of" his followers' needs. Furthermore, if we are unable to judge our own degree of exhaustion and burnout, it is important to be obedient to those who recognize in us what we do not see in ourselves (our spouses? our ecclesiastical superiors? our congregations?). We learn from Jesus not only to "go up on the mountain to pray," but to encourage others to do so when they need respite. Finally, it is noteworthy that there is no inkling in this account that the disciples even asked or expected God (or Jesus) to help them in their difficulty. And when Jesus does appear (and the implication is that happens after they have struggled all night, vv. 47-48), they do not recognize him and are afraid. We, like those disciples, must learn to ask for and expect greater things from God than we normally do. We must outgrow our "hardened hearts." In life's storms, we disciples must learn to expect our Deliverer to appear, but according to his timetable.

For Further Reading

P. J. Madden, *Jesus' Walking on the Sea: An Investigation of the Origin of the Narrative Account* (New York: de Gruyter, 1997).

6:53-56

This brief passage is a Markan summary and continues the evangelist's picture of the fevered activity around Jesus and the disciples. (In the lectionaries, this passage is usually appended to another account.) Although Markan geography is often hazy, it seems evident that the disciples and Jesus once more crossed the Sea of Galilee from east to west (or perhaps they had to change course in mid-journey since the wind was against them?) and made land at Gennesaret, a fertile plain south of Capernaum. Their retirement was only a brief interlude between two crowds (6:33; 6:54-55). (This suggests that a retreat for prayer is for improved, empowered ministry, not for escape.) As Mark has indicated before, people recognize Jesus and come to him not to beg him to teach (which is what he views as his purpose, 1:38-39; 6:34), but to gain his assistance as a healer. The idea is that the crowds press in on Jesus, even reaching out to touch his clothes. A comparison of 5:27-30 and 6:56 gives some indication of how exhausting this must have been for Jesus.

Mark says that all who touched "even the fringe of his cloak" were healed. (*Kraspedon,* used only here in Mark, means the "edge" or "border," but specifically the "tassel"—in Hebrew, *cicith,* worn by pious Jews on the four corners of their cloaks, cf. Matt. 23:5.)[15] The word used for "healed" is *esozonto,* Mark's usual word for "healed," which also means "saved." It did, of course, save people to heal them when their sicknesses meant not only physical distress but ritual uncleanness and marginalization from the religious community (see 1:40-45; 5:25-34).

Mark depicts Jesus as the one who appears in the drama and storms of life and also in the midst of ordinary people in their daily lives and practical needs. It is more than a little sobering to me to note that what the disciples, those who were supposedly closest to Jesus, miss (6:47-52) seems manifestly clear to common people and peasants (6:54-56). This is not the first instance of the disciples (or his family) not "knowing" Jesus (4:41 or 6:1-6a, for example) when the crowds clearly recognize (*epiginosko*) him (3:7-12; 6:33, 54). What do we clergy, we preachers, "miss" that others see?

Although it is probably not of homiletical significance, it is possible that Mark 6:52-53 appears as a fragment in 7Q5 of the Dead Sea Scrolls. If the fragment is Markan, it would mean that Mark's Gospel is considerably earlier than is generally thought. But scholarly opinion on the matter is divided.[16]

7:1-23

Chapter 7 opens with a long controversy account; the passage has attracted a great deal of attention from scholars interested in tradition history and Mark's redactional work. The number of parallelisms and repeated phrases suggests that the text is a Markan collection of previously independent sayings. As it stands canonically, the passage has three sections, determined by noting those to whom Jesus speaks: vv. 1-13, with the Pharisees and scribes; vv. 14-15, to the crowd; vv. 17-23, Jesus gives private instruction to the disciples (see 4:10; Schuyler Brown refers to chapter 7 as another public parable with a private explanation).[17] Thus, as Elisabeth Struthers Malbon has noted, 7:1-23 illustrates three types of relations with Jesus. First, those who argue with him from "authority" (the Pharisees and scribes); second, those who will listen (the crowd); and finally those who ask questions (the disciples).[18]

Unfortunately, the passage is usually broken up in the lectionaries. Studying it in its entirety is important for understanding Mark's reason for preserving the account. The controversy over eating without washing is the particular instance that raises the larger and more important question of where Jesus stands with regard to the oral law, the "tradition of the elders" (v. 3). The "tradition of the elders" were the interpretations, rules, and procedures that had grown up around the written law, oral commentary on the written Torah, and application of it to real life situations. The Pharisees were the "good guys" of Judaism of their day; they wanted to help people live Torah. We think of them as "bad" because of their antagonistic position in the narrative vis-à-vis Jesus. The Pharisees held that both the written law and the oral traditions were gifts from God and of equal value. Here they want to know if Jesus shares their views (v. 5). In this passage, the Pharisees are defined by their concern for ceremonial purity (vv. 1-4) and for the sacredness of vows (vv. 10-13).

At 7:1 Mark picks up the theme of official opposition to Jesus. Mark does not indicate where the controversy takes place. He does say that the Pharisees and scribes had come from Jerusalem (increasingly seen in Mark's Gospel as the center of opposition to Jesus). They are apparently on a fact-finding mission, and it does not take them long to see the "fact" that Jesus' disciples eat without washing. The word for "defiled" in v. 2 is *koinais,* from *koinos,* meaning literally "common" or "communal." It is a Jewish technical term. The issue at hand is not cleanliness or hygiene, but ceremonial purity, the kind of ceremonial "cleanness" that was nearly impossible for ordinary people to achieve. Verses 3 and 4 are a Markan aside, an explanation of Jewish customs for an audience (possibly Roman?) unfamiliar with such matters. (There are several interesting textual and technical matters in these verses that can be pursued in the longer commentaries.)[19]

Assuming that a rabbi is responsible for his disciples, the Pharisees and scribes ask Jesus about his disciples' behavior. The word in v. 5, which the NRSV translates "live," is actually *peripatousin*, "walk," a metaphor that Paul also frequently employs to describe "usual procedure," "the way one does things," "how one lives." Jesus' response is anything but irenic. He calls his questioners "hypocrites," literally "dissemblers" (the word was originally used in reference to stage actors) and quotes scripture to the scriptural experts. Verses 6b-7 are a quotation from Isa. 29:13 in the LXX version. This leads to the supposition that the verses are Markan, since Jesus in Palestine would hardly quote Greek scriptures to scholars from Jerusalem. At issue is not only the contrast between the commands of God and human traditions, but the relationship between inner motivation and outward behavior (a subject treated extensively in Matt. 5:21-48). Verse 8 makes crystal clear Jesus' view of the "human traditions." His point is that human tradition can conflict with the intention of the law. Verses 9-13 provide a specific example of the general point.

Jesus accuses the Pharisees and scribes of elevating human tradition over express commands of God. In v. 10 he quotes the Decalogue (Exod. 20:12; Deut. 5:16) and Mosaic ordinance (Exod. 21:17) as "commandment of God." Verses 11-12 are the way "human tradition" evades them. "Corban" (used only here in the New Testament) comes from the Hebrew *korbanas*, literally an offering or a gift consecrated to God. (Note that Mark provides another explanation for his hearers/readers in vv. 3-4.) Jesus accuses the Pharisees and scribes of withholding resources that should be used to care for parents by verbally declaring them "corban," but then retaining them for private use. The natural duty and responsibility enshrined in the law, which should have first claim, is set aside for a human tradition. Thus the "word of God" is made "void" (*akuroo*, also used only here in Mark and meaning "annulled" or "invalidated") "through your tradition." And, adding insult to injury, Jesus asserts "you do many things like this" (v. 13b).

The conflict here is about interpretation of Torah. Jesus upholds the primacy of the Torah over any human interpretation of it, precisely because Mosaic law is God's Word. (Would that the Word were always so absolutely clear, requiring no interpretation!) The principle is that obedience to one commandment should not be used to nullify another. To enlarge the focus from the particular issues of ceremonial cleanliness, use of resources, and vows to what Jesus asserts is to say that religious customs (or "duties") should not take precedence over the fundamental requirement of love. But as in the earlier conflicts with religious leaders, the underlying conflict is about authority. Jesus assumes his right to pass judgment on interpretation of the law and on the Pharisees and scribes. In fact, his position echoed the common Jewish view that "God had given the people of Israel in the Torah his universal, final revelation through Moses at Sinai. All the later words of the prophets . . . were expositions of this Torah."[20]

Unlike earlier conflicts between Jesus and the scribes and Pharisees, in this account Mark does not describe the response of Jesus' interlocutors. In fact, they simply drop out of the narrative when Jesus turns to the crowd in v. 14 to radicalize and broaden still further the context of the discussion. But this silence is telling. In an article on the rhetoric of the Gospels, Jerome Neyrey points out that, first, silence is an admission of defeat and, second, if one loses a debate in public, one is shamed. Mark uses this rhetorical device to showcase the cleverness of Jesus. But this very cleverness increases the antagonism between Jesus and the religious authorities precisely because he confronts, accuses, and shames them publicly.[21]

Verses 14b and 15 may be an originally independent saying, inserted here by Mark to devastating effect since it is uttered within earshot of the fact-finders from Jerusalem. That Jesus calls the crowd "again" suggests it is part of his standard practice to speak thus to crowds. He prefaces the saying itself with a solemn charge to "listen" and to "understand" (cf. 4:3, 9). Verse 15 is a very short implied parable that comments on the matter of ceremonial defilement. As Gundry notes, Jesus moves from how to eat to what to eat.[22] The saying demonstrates that moral uncleanliness is far more serious than ritual. What has "come out of" the Pharisees and scribes is, in this case, an unbecoming readiness to criticize fellow Jews and to use their implied criticism as a way to entrap Jesus. They exhibit the "evil thoughts" ("evil designs or plans"), "deceit," perhaps "envy," and certainly "foolishness" of vv. 21-22. (Verse 16 is omitted in many translations. It does not occur in the Alexandrian family of texts and is thought by scholars to be a scribal gloss intended to make this teaching end like the parable in 4:9.)

As was Jesus' pattern in chapter 4, here (v. 17) he leaves the crowd and enters a house (cf. 4:10, 34). Again in this setting (the setting familiar to Mark's house churches?), Jesus' disciples ask him about the meaning of the parable. Verses 18-19 explain its first part ("going in") and vv. 20-23 its second ("come out"). Somewhat startled by their lack of understanding, Jesus explains that things that enter a person (foods) do not defile[23] but pass through the normal bodily processes and are excreted. In v. 19b Mark provides the third gloss for his audience, explaining that the effect of this teaching was to set aside what came to be called "kosher" food laws. This might well have been an important issue for Mark's own community. It certainly was an issue in Romans 14 (cf. Peter's experience in Acts 10–11 and discussions of food and table fellowship in 1 Corinthians). What defiles is what issues forth from a person's heart, not what she or he eats. Verses 21b-22 provide examples in the form of a characteristic Greco-Roman vice list, a catalogue of moral failings used to teach "don'ts" (see Gal. 5:19-21a). It has twelve vices, six singular and six plural. In view of the form, I wonder if vv. 20-23 are not an early Christian interpretation of the word of Jesus in v. 15. It is, however, characteristic of Jesus to be as concerned for inner motivation as for external action. (See the "antitheses" in the Sermon on the Mount in Matthew 5.) In any case, the interpretation given here both calls into question the necessity for dietary laws and criticizes defiling or impure impulses.

Mark 7:1-23 is a crucial text. First, it provides insights into Mark's original audience. We see Mark explaining Jewish practices, beliefs, and Hebrew expressions (vv. 3-4, 11b, 19b), which suggests his audience is not familiar with them. The setting for explanation, "in the house," parallels the setting of Mark's community in house churches. And we know from Paul's letter to the Romans that matters of food and eating were of particular concern to the Roman church. Is Mark here reassuring a Gentile audience that believing in Jesus does not require adopting Jewish cultic food practices? In the passage, "Jesus powerfully puts down the Pharisees and some of the scribes from Jerusalem on a question of cultic purity" and "authoritatively pronounces all foods clean despite cultic laws to the contrary."[24] The effect is further to alienate Jesus from the Jewish leaders.

Second, the passage reintroduces the tension between Jesus and Israel's religious authorities. Kingsbury has suggested that Mark's portrayal of the religious leaders is not so much historical as polemical; he thinks Mark expects the hearer/reader to see them as a composite character opposed to Jesus.[25] While I hold the historicity of the account, I agree with Kingsbury that the underlying issue is authority. Certainly, in terms of narrative movement in Mark, we see the conflict with authorities heightening. It begins with oblique criticism (2:1-12), moves to open questioning (2:23-28; 3:22-30), and finally to plotting (3:6), which culminates in condemning Jesus to death (14:53ff.). Here the "ante" is upped significantly as the emphasis shifts from interpretation of the law to the validity of the law itself. The real point of the passage is Jesus' power and authority. Because of who he is, Jesus has the authority to change or set aside commandments. For Mark, at least, it seems that the era of the law's sovereignty has passed. This leads in the narrative directly to miracles done for those *outside* Judaism (7:24—8:10).

How do we preach this passage in churches that have long since given up concern with Jewish purity laws? Several possibilities present themselves. Probably the most common approach focuses on vv. 6-13 and the matter of hypocrisy. We all need to be reminded to "walk our talk." Additionally, vv. 1-8 raise the issue of legalism. Almost every congregation has a percentage of members who think Christianity is a matter of legal rectitude of some sort, of properly observing the "do's and don'ts." This provides yet another opportunity to disabuse members of that serious but very common error. Juxtaposing the opening of the text and its closing, I personally am taken by the image of the "Pharisees and some of the scribes who had come from Jerusalem" apparently to "fact find," but more accurately to "find fault." Instead of self-examination, of being sure that what they said they believed and what they did was consistent, they go looking *within their own community* for the faults of others. It is always easier to see the mote in another's eye while ignoring the log in one's own (see Matt. 7:1-5). As the desert father Abbot Moses remarked, "They who are conscious of their own sins have no eyes for the sins of their neighbor."[26] An inward attitude of evil intention and slander defiles me, but it also creates havoc in my community.

7:24-30

Mark's narrative logic is quite clear. Jesus' miracle for the Syrophoenician woman follows immediately upon his dispensing of categories of clean and unclean. There is clearly an implied comparison between the way the scribes and Pharisees have come to Jesus (7:1-23) and the way this woman comes (7:25-26). As Anderson's commentary notes, the evangelist has set forth Jesus' emphatic declaration that "the old way of the law is passé." The story of the Syrophoenician woman "suggests that only on the basis of new insights from outside the pale of Judaism does faith arise."[27]

Since feeding the five thousand, Jesus seems to be skirting Galilee, perhaps to avoid confrontations like the one just related. Tyre was a Gentile city on the Mediterranean (and if, as some manuscript traditions suggest, the reference is to "Tyre and Sidon," then all of Phoenicia is implied). Is Jesus trying to lead his disciples to a "seaside holiday" (recall 6:31, 45-46, 53-56)? There is no mention of disciples in this account. Verse 24 certainly suggests that Jesus seeks again in vain to distance himself from the crowds by being inside (6:31, 45-46). Verses 25 and 26b give an unusually full introduction to the woman. Jesus' reputation has already reached as far north as Tyre. A woman (mentioned alone without a husband, so she is either a widow or has never married) has a "little daughter" (a Markan diminutive) with "an unclean spirit." The woman was a "Gentile" (so the NRSV translates *hellenis,* literally "Greek"), understood to be someone of any nationality who was not Jewish; her nationality is Phoenician from Syria. She is a "born loser" on three counts: she is a woman in a man's world (and a single mother), the wrong religion, and the wrong race, since "Syrophoenician" was an unsavory racial term. In addition, she has the double liability of a female child who is demon possessed.

Mark depicts her approach to Jesus sympathetically. She prostrates herself (*prosepesen*) at his feet and begs (*erota,* "makes a request") on behalf of her daughter. She is the first Gentile in the Gospel to ask something of Jesus, "to cast the demon out of her daughter" (v. 26). The response of Jesus in v. 27 is disturbing and, in spite of many ingenious attempts to soften it, remains so. Jesus says, in effect, that he cannot feed the "dogs" (literally "little dogs," another diminutive, the Gentiles), until the "children" (the Jews) are fed first. The word for fed is the same as that in 6:42 and means "fully satisfied" (cf. also 7:27 with Rom. 1:16; Acts 13:46, 18:6). We see here, unvarnished, the contempt of the first-century Jew for the non-Jew and apparently utter disregard for the feelings of a distraught mother. Beyond this it is fruitless to speculate about Jesus' behavior. We cannot see the exchange, so we have no visual cues and, as F. F. Bruce so sensibly notes, a "written record can preserve the spoken words; it cannot convey the tone of voice in which they were said."[28] Surprisingly, the woman responds by agreeing with Jesus. "Lord" (contra NRSV's "Sir"), she replies, even dogs accept the children's table scraps (v. 28).

I have read many interpretations of this exchange. I think it presents an honest, if unsettling, picture of Jesus. He is weary. He has been buffeted by crowds and attacked by religious leaders. He has tried to "get away from it all" only to be sought out in the home in which he has taken refuge by one more person with one more demand on him. Who could blame him for responding sharply? Jesus was, after all, human. Mark's is no Docetic Jesus. What makes him "Lordly" in my view is his recognition of the wisdom and faith-filled-ness of the woman's response. He has been "hoisted on his own petard," and he knows it. His response is not a great show of macho self-justification but the long-distance exorcism of the little girl. "For that saying," for reminding Jesus of who he is and what he teaches, the woman is rewarded by having her request granted (v. 29).

Unlike the Pharisees and scribes, who at the outset of the chapter come with authority and power, the Syrophoenician comes to Jesus empty-handed but with knowledge of what he has done. She does not seek confrontation but is ready to accept whatever Jesus offers. In contrast to legalism, she exhibits the faith that waits on God. And what she ultimately receives is the desire of her heart. I agree with Sharon Ringe that this text is at core a remembered incident in his life when Jesus "was caught with his compassion down."[29] And yet in response to one who comes to him in faith, in the engagement with her, *he* is freed to heal, to move beyond what, on the surface of it, seems to be racism. In my view, the Syrophoenician woman teaches Jesus a valuable lesson. The narrative ends with both ennobled. And it certainly must have spoken to Mark's original audience and their struggle with the relationship of Jews to Gentiles in the church.

As a text to address the evils of racism, few Gospel narratives surpass this one. To develop such a sermon, time should be spent uncovering the implications of geography (v. 24) and of the designations of the woman

(v. 26). Alternatively, the Syrophoenician woman can be held up as more than a foil to the Jewish officials; she is a sterling example of faith (even though the word does not occur here). Her approach of faith is altruistic (it is on behalf of her daughter), persistent (it does not turn away at the first rebuff, cf. Luke 18:1-8, another "pushy woman" account!), and inventive (she uses a negative response to her advantage). This "uppity woman" is an example of faith; she exhibits the courage of those who have little to lose and can act on behalf of others for the sake of wholeness and liberation.[30]

For Further Reading

T. A. Burkill, "The Historical Development of the Story of the Syro-Phoenician Woman," *NovT* 9, 2 (1967): 161–77.

Hisako Kinukawa, *Women and Jesus in Mark* (Maryknoll, N.Y.: Orbis, 1994), chapter 3, "The Syrophoenician Woman."

P. Porkorny, "From a Puppy to a Child: Some Problems of Contemporary Exegesis Demonstrated from Mk 7:24-30, Mt 15:21-28," *NTS* 41 (1995): 321–27.

7:31-37

To properly interpret this miracle account, it is important to remember that "deaf and dumb" is also a metaphor for the inability to hear and understand (a theme to be raised again in 8:11-21) and to communicate with the world around one. Mark's geography in v. 31 seems especially garbled. A map of Palestine under the Herods shows clearly that Sidon is north of Tyre (not on the way to the Sea of Galilee) and the Decapolis is north and west of the Sea. Perhaps Jesus went north to Sidon, then west into the Decapolis before heading south to the Sea? Perhaps Mark wants to emphasize that Jesus took a circuitous route in order to keep clear of crowds and controversy? Certainly it is clear that Jesus is in Gentile territory.

The pericope is a classic miracle account: the description of the problem is followed by the healing, its proof, and the response of the onlookers. Jesus cannot escape his reputation. "They" (unspecified by Mark) bring him a deaf man with a speech impediment (*mogilalon,* a LXX word used only here in the New Testament) and beg Jesus "to lay his hand on him" (v. 32). "To lay the hands on" is both a metaphor for healing and a description of how Jesus has healed heretofore (1:31; 5:23, 41). Verses 33-34 describe the healing. Jesus performs it in private, away from the crowd, in another attempt to prevent "publicity" (cf. 7:36). He uses techniques well-attested among wonder-workers of the day. For example, saliva appears frequently in healing accounts of the time (in Tacitus's *History* IV.81, Vespasian so cured a blind man in Alexandria). Jesus looks up to heaven, the standard Jewish posture for prayer, and thereby indicates the source of the healing. Mark characteristically describes the emotions of Jesus. Here he recounts that Jesus "sighed." Was this in compassion for the man? In human weariness? Or should it be translated "groaned," thereby indicating the difficulty of the miracle? Again, it is characteristic of Mark to retain the Aramaic (cf. 5:41); *ephphatha* is a Greek transliteration of *phathah,* the causative for "open."

Verse 35 relates the healing in language reminiscent of Isa. 35:5-6. It literally says that the "bonds of his tongue" (*ho desmos tes glosses autou*) were released, hinting of demon possession. The command to silence echoes that in Jairus's story (which exhibits many parallels to this one). But it seems that the more Jesus commands silence, the more he is proclaimed. Verses 36-37 are, in fact, a portrait in miniature of the responses to Jesus to this point in Mark's Gospel. The latter verse bespeaks a universal approbation of Jesus that we know was not the case. "Astounded beyond measure" (*huperperissos,* another hapax legomena) is an extremely strong reaction, so strong, in fact, that it has led some scholars to suggest that v. 37 was originally the conclusion for a number of miracle stories.

The text is best preached in the context of the ministry of Jesus at this point. It is part of a series of stories that depict active, almost frenetic ministry. It comes in the context of Jesus' withdrawing from Jewish territory into a Gentile region and follows directly on a pericope in which his own view of those to whom he has been sent is widened. It provides another example of the contrast between the enthusiastic approval of the people versus the suspicion of the religious authorities. And finally, it provides testimony to Jesus' messiahship (Isaiah says the ears of the deaf will be unstopped and the "tongue of the speechless sing for joy," 35:5-6) and to his identification with Wisdom ("for wisdom opened the mouths of those who were mute, and made the tongues of infants speak clearly," Wis. of Sol. 10:21). Here the ears are opened to understand and the tongue released from its chains in anticipation of the confession of Jesus in Mark 8:27-30. Perhaps the best gloss on the central verse of the text, 7:36, is from Prudentius's Hymn 9:

> Deafened ears, of sound unconscious, every passage blocked and closed,
> At the word of Christ responding, all the portals opened wide,
> Hear with joy friendly voices and the softly whispered speech.
> Every sickness now surrenders, every listlessness departs,
> Tongues long bound by chains of silence are unloosed and speak aright.[31]

Another approach to a sermon on this text could focus on the matter of listening in Mark's Gospel (and in our society). The command to hear or to listen frames Jesus' kingdom teaching (4:3, 9). He teaches that understanding the Word requires hearing (4:23-25), and careful hearing results in deeper understanding. In a world filled with words, we might note that God has given us two ears but only one mouth, which suggests we should listen twice as much as we speak. In this text the connection between hearing and right speech is clear in v. 35. When ears are opened by Jesus, the resulting speech is plain (clear or accurate).

8:1-21

In order to understand Mark's interest in this material, it is best to read and study the large unit 8:1-21. The lectionaries tend to omit 8:1-10, perhaps because of its similarity to the earlier feeding of the five thousand (6:30-44). Because of the apparent duplication, this text has been the focus of much attention. Some scholars think it is a "doublet," a second account of the same event narrated earlier, although one from another source. I tend to doubt this simply because "pairs" or "doubles" seem characteristic of Markan style; he includes two sea miracles, two healings of blind persons, two healings of children, and so forth. Other scholars understand 8:1-10 to be part of the second of two cycles of material (4:35—6:44 and 6:45—8:10, or 6:35—7:37 and 8:1-26). Saint Augustine noted in the fifth century that this second feeding story depicts Jesus as the Bread of Life for the Gentiles. I find this a helpful comment. In terms of Mark's construction, Jesus is in Galilee in 6:30-44 among what 7:27 called "the children." Following his pivotal encounter with the Syrophoenician woman (7:24-30), Mark has Jesus in Gentile areas among "the dogs." Austin Farrar thinks this represents a Eucharist among Jews and then Gentiles. He notes parallels both in 2 Kings 4:42-44 and in the life of Moses, who feeds the Hebrews manna and quail (Exod. 16) and a "mixed multitude" quail (Num. 11).[32]

Mark does not designate where the feeding miracle itself takes place, but since in 7:21 Jesus is in "the region of the Decapolis," it is safe to assume the miracle takes place there but not far from the sea (cf. 7:10, 13-14). Again, around Jesus there is a great crowd with nothing to eat (v. 1). Jesus summons his disciples (who have been absent from the narrative since 7:17). As in the earlier feeding, Jesus has compassion on the crowd that has been with him for three days, but the disciples doubt they can "feed these people with bread here in the desert" (v. 4, more Markan "desert spirituality"). It seems odd that the disciples have no recollection of the earlier feeding nor of the fact that God, through Moses, provided bread for his people in the desert. Verse 6 echoes 6:41 and the eucharistic actions of taking, giving thanks, breaking, and giving (cf. 1 Cor. 11:23-26). Again, the disciples distribute the bread, and later "a few small fish" are handled in the same way. As in the earlier account, the great crowd eats and is filled, although here a total of four thousand people (not just men) are fed (v. 9). The miracle begins with seven loaves and ends with seven baskets full of broken pieces left over. (The *spurides* here is larger than the *kophinoi* of chapter 6.) Jesus dismisses the people and sets out by boat with his disciples. Textual corruptions in v. 10 make the destination uncertain. The best reading is "Dalmanutha," but it is not clear where that is.

The notes on 6:30-44 may help in preparing to preach this text. I am struck by how frequently I see parallels to the disciples' attitude (and how frequently I behave as they do). How often we neglect to expect God to act *soon after* God has supplied a need (or effected a miracle) in our lives! Hooker thinks this is Mark's purpose in including the second feeding story, "to underline the stupidity and incomprehension of the disciples."[33] (More on that momentarily.) That same incomprehension is evident in the Pharisees in 8:11-13.

As is typical of Mark, the Pharisees in 8:11 appear abruptly (and in Gentile territory?). Mark says explicitly that they came, began to argue (*suzetein,* to debate, to dispute), and asked for a sign "to test him." The word "test," *peirazontes,* implies to test with bad intent; it is the word used in 1:13 when Satan "tempts" Jesus. The Pharisees knew that great spiritual leaders like Moses and Elijah were proven authentic by their sign acts. Deuteronomy 13:1-3 suggests that a sign from heaven is the "guarantee" or "accreditation" of a prophet. The problem is not so much the request (although what more telling sign could Jesus give than he has just given as he, like Moses, fed the people in the wilderness?) as its motivation (see 7:21-23). Mark communicates something of Jesus' emotional response with the opening phrase of v. 12, "he sighed deeply in his spirit." It might also be translated "he groaned inwardly."

The question "why does this generation ask for a sign?" is significant in view of the fact that Jewish apocalyptic literature of the period depicted the last generation before the apocalypse to be faithless. Faith is not faith if it must ask for proof. A solemn negative Hebraism precedes Jesus' refusal to supply what we know would be *yet another* sign (v. 12). But why does he refuse, particularly since he has done all manner of miracles up to this point? First, this request is much like the temptation recorded in Luke 4:9-12 and Matt. 4:5-7. The Pharisees are, in effect, putting the Lord to a test. Jesus knows who he is (see 1:10-22) and has no need to provide special proofs to those with malicious motives. This is the second reason for his refusal. The request is not sincere; it does not seek faith but seeks to "argue" and "test." Just as there can be no "deed of power" without faith (6:5), there is no proof for those who have already decided. Therefore, Jesus withdraws from these tempters by the familiar means of crossing the sea in a boat (v. 13) This is a stock device in the Markan narrative (see 3:9-10; 5:18, 21; 6:45, 53; 8:10).

The pericope raises an important issue for modern apologetics. It reminds, in the words of Heb. 11:1, that faith is "the conviction of things not seen." Faith is an act of will, not a proposition to be proven by logic or demonstrated in the laboratory. No amount of evidence, or in this case a further sign, will be convincing to a person whose mind is already made up. Those who are not moved by the preaching of the Gospel and the spiritual truths of the kingdom are unlikely to be convinced by a physical sign. To receive what Jesus has to offer, one must approach him with the openness of the Syrophoenician woman (7:24-30).

The astonishing incomprehension of those around Jesus continues in 8:14-21. At the center of the Gospel is an account in which Jesus' own disciples fail to understand what he says and does. In many ways this account parallels the response to the "teaching in parables" in chapter 4 (cf. especially the words of Jesus in 4:10-13, and notice how similar his rhetoric is to what appears here and to Mark's comment in 4:33-34). Once in the boat and crossing the sea, the disciples discover they have forgotten to bring bread (v. 14). The conversation that ensues is a classic example of speaking at cross-purposes. The disciples speak about physical bread; for Jesus, bread is the metaphor for a greater truth. (This sort of exchange is much more common in John's Gospel; see, for example, John 3.) Even in their concern for material things, the disciples have quickly forgotten what Jesus can do (that is, provide bread). They have forgotten that he provides not only enough, but abundance ("leftovers").

The request for bread seems to suggest to Jesus the metaphor of leaven in v. 15. As a rabbi or teacher, leaven is for Jesus a symbol of evil and an image of how the evil of a few can infect and affect the many. Leaven is akin to the hardening of the heart that prevents spiritual insight. Jesus may be thinking of the exchange he has just had with the Pharisees from Jerusalem. But the disciples (v. 16) only understand the material connection (bread and leaven), not what Jesus suggests by means of it. In vv. 17-21 he first chides them severely in the language of the prophets (vv. 17-18; see Isa. 6:9-10; Jer. 5:21; Ezek. 12:2) and then by means of Socratic questioning tries to draw them toward understanding (vv. 19-21). The reminder of the effects of these two spiritually revealing miracles is intended to underline both that they reveal the truth about (and identity of) Jesus and that they depict the abundance of the kingdom of God. Tellingly, the pericope closes with the question of Jesus, "Do you not yet understand?" (v. 21). The hearers/readers of the Gospel are far from certain that the disciples do, in fact, understand. Their incomprehension will be at the center of the next major block of Mark (8:22—10:52).

It is important to remember why Mark stresses the incomprehension or blindness of the disciples. As Morna Hooker remarked about this passage:

> Miracles and parables have a parallel function in Mark. To those who have eyes to see and ears to hear, both miracles and parables demonstrate the power of the Kingdom of God. But those without ears hear only the parables and do not understand the secret of the Kingdom (4:11f.), while those without eyes see only amazing acts, so that to them no sign from heaven is given.[34]

The disciples' lack of understanding serves as a foil for the hearer/reader whose understanding is Mark's real concern. But in terms of the narrative, the disciples *cannot* yet understand. Real understanding comes on the other side of suffering and the cross. And this is precisely Jesus' primary message in 8:22—10:52, as well as the reason why Mark's narrative moves so inexorably toward the cross.

Things the disciples fail to understand suggest the preaching points. They fail to understand that Jesus is the "one loaf for Jews and Gentiles."[35] The sermon can stress the inclusive love of Jesus for all people, his ability to "feed" everyone. The disciples also fail to understand Jesus' warning in v. 15 about the dangers of uniting spiritual (Pharisees) and political (Herod) power (a point the American religious right might do well to ponder). In what circumstances even (or especially) in the church do issues of power overshadow what should be spiritual matters? Verses 14-21 also provide a wonderful opportunity to provide instruction on "how to read the Bible," because they demonstrate what happens when metaphor (bread/leaven) is taken literally. The disciples (those closest to Jesus, his students) fail to grasp the crucial message of his actions because they cannot go beyond their own literal-mindedness. The verses are an object lesson on the dangers of literalism.

For Further Reading

Norman A. Beck, "Reclaiming a Biblical Text: The Mark 8:14-21 Discussion about Bread in the Boat," *CBQ* 42 (1981): 49–56.

David Hawkin, "The Incomprehension of the Disciples in the Marcan Redaction," *JBL* 91 (1972): 491–500.

J. B. Tyson, "The Blindness of the Disciples in Mark," *JBL* 80 (1961): 261–68.

Summary

Although 6:1—8:21 may appear to be a random collection of material, its effect is quite powerful. First, the unit is especially revealing of Mark's techniques as a narrator, and it provides a remarkable amount of information about his original audience. Second, it brings together all the main themes that have been suggested earlier in the Gospel. Let me elaborate on this second point. First, the Gospel began with the ministry of John the Baptist as preparation for "the one who is more powerful" and "is coming after" (1:7). John's ministry and preaching prepared the way for Jesus, whose miracles attest to his power. In 6:14-29 the end of the Baptist's life and ministry continues to be closely connected to that of Jesus as it foreshadows the Master's own end. Second, earlier in the Gospel, Jesus is described by Mark as a teacher in parables and a worker of miracles. Jesus continues to do both in this section of the Gospel. In fact, insofar as the miracles in Mark's Gospel are christological, intended to witness to Jesus' identity, perhaps the most revealing miracles to date appear in this section, the two feeding accounts (6:20-43; 8:1-21). Mark portrays Jesus as the teacher whose miracles attest to his authority. Third, it is the authoritative teaching and action of Jesus that continues to draw him into conflict with the religious leaders, particularly the Pharisees and scribes. In this section of the Gospel, the hostility between the two groups is not even thinly veiled. Jesus responds with "both pistols blazing" to the attack in 7:1-23 and simply walks away from the "ridiculous" request in 7:11-13 (an action which itself is insulting to the Pharisees).

Fourth, the disciples have figured as important characters since the beginning of the Gospel (1:16-20; 3:13-19), both as foils to Jesus and as points of identification for the hearer/reader of the Gospel. They are, again, depicted as uncomprehending (4:10-12, 33-34; 8:14-21) and even sharp with Jesus (5:38; 6:35-36; 8:4). But they are not completely ineffective. The depiction of the mission of the Twelve (6:6b-13, 30) suggests that Mark's view of the disciples must not be dismissed too easily. The disciples *have* left much behind for Jesus; they *do* follow. And with Jesus' authority they accomplish the very things that he himself does. But they do not understand all that they experience. In this, I tend to sympathize with them. Jesus is so different from what they have seen of religious authority and from what they have come to expect. They need further instruction on discipleship, and they will receive it in the next section of the Gospel.

Finally, and perhaps most poignantly, those nearest to Jesus, his family and those of his home area, continue to misunderstand him (3:31-35; 6:1-6a). Those scenes are perhaps the saddest example of what happens when premature conclusions are drawn about what is apparently "known." Lots of people in Mark's Gospel cannot (or refuse to) see the forest for the trees. And no one in the Gospel really "sees" until he or she gazes upon the "tree of the Cross."

6

The Journey to Jerusalem and Discipleship Teaching

Mark 8:22—10:52

Introduction

Almost all commentators understand this section of the gospel to be not only the spatial but also the ideological center of Mark. Accounts of the healing of two blind men (8:22-26 and 10:46-52) form an inclusion within which Mark situates three passion predictions. In each case, the disciples misunderstand Jesus, thus giving him the opportunity to provide more teaching on the nature of discipleship. The following narrative pattern is repeated three times:[1]

Geographical Reference	8:27; 9:30; 10:1
Passion Prediction	8:31; 9:31; 10:33
Disciples' Misunderstanding	8:32; 9:34; 10:35
Further Teaching	8:34; 9:35; 10:42

Everything in this unit of material is related either to the meaning of Jesus' messiahship or the meaning of being his disciple. "The rule of discipleship is: Jesus. As Jesus was, so the disciple must be."[2] Between the healings of the two blind men, the narrative is cast as a journey, being "on the way." On this journey, the disciples "follow" Jesus. "Follow" is both Mark's technical term for discipleship and an indication of motion. By means of the narrative, Mark suggests that we learn the meaning of Jesus and of being his disciple "on the way."

Another of Mark's purposes in this section is to link the sufferings of Christians with the suffering of Jesus. He accomplishes this by emphasizing the passion of Jesus that was foreshadowed in Mark's presentation of the ministry of John the Baptist, especially the narrative of 6:14-20. John preached, was delivered up, and was martyred. This is what Jesus predicts for himself. This passion material is directly related to the discipleship theme. If the disciples are to follow Jesus, and Jesus suffers, then the disciples should expect suffering to be their lot as well. "What does it then mean to follow Jesus? It means to drop in behind him, to be ready to go to the cross as he did, to write oneself off in terms of any kind of importance, privilege or right, and to spend one's time only in the service of the needs of others."[3]

Because this section of the gospel is so crucial to Mark's purposes, the preacher would do well to consult discussions of the whole section before preaching any pericope in it.

For Further Reading

Ernest Best, *Disciples and Discipleship* (Edinburgh: T & T Clark, 1986), especially chapters 1 and 7. (See note 2.)

Norman Perrin's discussion in *What Is Redaction Criticism?* (Philadelphia: Fortress Press, 1969). (See note 1.)

Robert C. Tannehill's article, "The Disciples in Mark: The Function of a Narrative Role," first published in *JR* 57 (1977): 386–405, and reprinted in William Telford, ed., *The Interpretation of Mark* (Edinburgh: T. & T. Clark, 1995), 169–95.

8:22-26

As Pheme Perkins notes, this account is the second of three miracles that deal with the senses (7:31-37; 8:22-26; 10:46-52) and that indicate Jesus is fulfilling the prophecy of Isa. 35:5-6.[4] This text and 7:32-37, with which it shares both vocabulary and content, is peculiarly Markan. In both pericopae, Jesus is depicted as are other Jewish and Hellenistic healers of the time; he heals by means of saliva and the laying on of hands. The healing is set in Bethsaida on the northeast side of the Sea of Galilee and in the Tetrarchy of Philip, a logical place from which to move to Caesarea Philippi, which is theologically important to the following account. The blind man is brought to Jesus (as was the paralytic in 2:1-12) to be touched/healed, although the narrative does not say by whom.

Jesus takes the blind man by the hand (a characteristic gesture, cf. 5:41) and leads him out of the village, perhaps in search of privacy and quiet in which to heal. At the time, spittle was generally thought to have healing powers. Jesus "put saliva on his eyes" (v. 23), but this application gives the blind man only partial sight (v. 24; the Greek of this verse is quite awkward). The second laying on of hands (v. 25) is unique in Jesus' ministry, but it completes the healing and restores the blind man's sight. Jesus sends the man home (cf. 5:19) with the charge (depending upon the manuscript tradition of the text consulted) either not to go to the village and/or not to tell anyone in the village, in either case another example of the "messianic secret."

Some commentators divide Mark at this point. They argue that this text is the consummation and close of the first half of Jesus' public ministry;

8:27—10:45 represents "the way of the cross" in which the theme of suffering becomes prominent. Those commentators who make much of the fact that in this text Jesus seems unable to heal the man the "first time around" miss the subtlety with which Mark makes his point. In my view, this pericope introduces a new block of material (8:22—10:52) characterized both by passion predictions (the suffering theme) *and* discipleship teaching (see introduction above). The gradual restoration of this blind man's sight is intended to suggest the gradual opening of the disciples' eyes, their slow coming to "see," to understand the nature of Jesus' messiahship and their own discipleship. Thus the text is programmatic for what follows.

In preaching the text, it would be appropriate to note that some come to the kingdom abruptly and some come by degrees. (One might, for example, compare and contrast the "enlightenment" of the Beloved Disciple, Peter, Mary Magdalene, and Thomas in John 20.) Alternatively, the preacher may wish to stress that Jesus is not satisfied with second best. To a blind person, even imperfectly restored sight is a great improvement. But it is not good enough for Jesus, who continues to work until sight is clearly restored. Jesus works in human lives until grace is complete.

8:27-30

Peter's confession, his lack of understanding of "Messiah" as it applies to Jesus (8:31-33), leads to Jesus' first passion prediction (8:34—9:1). Many commentators see 8:27-33 as one complex narrative with four themes: the messianic identity of Jesus; the secrecy motif (what we have been calling the "messianic secret"); the messianic mystery of Jesus; and the incomprehension of the disciples.[5] According to Mark, from Bethsaida (8:22) Jesus and the disciples travel to Caesarea Philippi, which is also in the tetrarchy of Philip. That this is the location of Peter's confession is significant. First, it is Jesus' furthest journey from Jerusalem, which for Mark represents opposition to him and to his message. Second, Caesarea Philippi is the site of ancient Paneas, a city with both a place to worship Pan (as the name suggests) and, later, a temple to Augustus. Thus in Caesarea Philippi both the forces of nature and of political power were worshipped. The reader is to understand that Jesus' messiahship will take precedence over both. Finally, the area was racially mixed. To confess Jesus there is to confess him Messiah for all people (cf. 7:24-30).

In v. 27 Jesus takes the initiative by asking the general question, "Who do people say that I am?" The disciples apparently called out answers: John the Baptist (who is now martyred, cf. 6:14-15), Elijah (who was associated with the coming of the Messiah), one of the prophets (whose messages Jesus' own certainly resembles). Whether we are to see these responses as evidence of the disciples' obtuseness or whether we are to excuse them since they did not hear the voice at 1:11, the text indicates that Jesus is not interested in hearsay, in what the general opinion is. He wants to know what *they* now think. Jesus' query is timely. He must see the "handwriting on the wall"; opposition to him by the religious leaders has hardly been veiled. Jesus must know his time to instruct the disciples is limited. Here Jesus, whom Mark prefers to call "teacher," ascertains how advanced—or backward—his students are. "But who do *you* [the "you" in Greek is emphatic] say that I am?" he inquires.

Peter calls out the correct answer, "You are the Messiah." Mark's gospel uses the term seven times, three occurrences of which are in the sayings of Jesus, although he never uses the title of himself. "Messiah" (the Greek translation of the Hebrew is "Christ") literally means "anointed one." Although in Judaism prophets, priests, and kings are anointed, popular thought in the period associated the Messiah with political and national aims. The Messiah would liberate Israel from the Romans. As the immediately following pericope indicates, Peter knows the correct answer but does not understand what it means. Jesus has further teaching to do.

Again in v. 30 we find the "messianic secret," the charge not to proclaim the truth about Jesus. While Jesus does not deny the title, he does not want it broadcast, probably because in popular thinking Messiah was associated with "King of Israel," which is both an inadequate understanding of Jesus and opens him to charges of sedition. As later chapters of Mark indicate, the trial of Jesus revolves around the title "king." Jesus silences the disciples ("them," v. 30) to avoid both dissemination of false information and a precipitous final conflict with the authorities.

8:31—9:1

Jesus' first passion prediction proceeds seamlessly from the previous pericope and is considered by many the watershed of the gospel. In terms of the narrative, Jesus is responding to the inadequate understanding of his disciples by further teaching. In terms of Mark's larger, christological purpose, the text serves to show that Jesus foresaw and accepted his suffering. And the text must also have spoken eloquently to the suffering Christians in Mark's original audience.

The title "Son of Man" has received much attention, because it is used eighty-one times in the gospels and is always found on the lips of Jesus. (Interestingly, it is *not* found in the early church's confessions *about* Jesus.) Most commentators connect the title to the figure in Daniel 7. In that association, it is variously interpreted as (1) a collective term for a remnant of faithful Jews who in Maccabean times resisted Hellenistic forces, were vindicated by God, and received their own country; (2) a term for a figure (a shepherd or a king) who brings with himself a company of people; or (3) a third-person self-designation. While in its origins the term is ambiguous, here Jesus connects it with his own predicted suffering, death, and resurrection (see Isa. 52:13—53:12) and with authority (see 2:10, 28). This is the first of three such predictions (9:31; 10:33-34); each is more detailed than the previous one. The disciples never "get it," even though Mark comments that Jesus "said all this quite openly."

Peter's response to Jesus in v. 32 continues the Markan picture of the disciples as sharp with Jesus (see, for example, 4:38), and it indicates that Peter has not understood his own use of Messiah. Apparently the Messiah is a triumphant figure in Peter's view, one not subject to suffering and death. Peter is "satan" (v. 33, understood not as a proper noun but as the "adversary"), because he presents Jesus with the same temptation faced at the beginning of his public ministry—to assume political, revolutionary power (see Matt. 4:8-10 and cf. Matt. 16). Mark's Jesus understands that the cross is part of his divine destiny. ("Cross" is used five times in this section of the gospel: 8:31; 9:9, 12, 31; 10:33, 45.) If the disciples "believed that he was the Messiah, they must know what kind of Messiah he was; if they were still minded to follow him, they must realize clearly what kind of leader they were following, and what lay at the end of the road he was pursuing."[6] As is the case throughout this section of the gospel, the disciples' incomprehension gives Jesus opportunity for further teaching. But note in v. 34 that he calls "*the crowd* with his disciples." The teaching that follows in 8:34b—9:1 is for the multitudes, for everyone (and certainly for Mark's original, persecuted audience).

Verse 34b is one of the most misused verses in the New Testament. It does *not* mean stoically accepting the difficulties that come unbidden in life, as in "arthritis is my cross to bear" or "my mother-in-law is my cross to bear." To "take up the cross" is voluntary. It is a choice, not something that comes because of circumstances beyond one's control or that is forced upon one; and it is always, as v. 35 makes clear, for Jesus' sake and out of fealty to him. In v. 34 *thelei* implies resolve, desire, resolution, not passive acceptance. The word "deny" (*aparnesastho*) is the same word used of Peter's denial at 14:72. It is good to remember that people who carried crosses in Jesus' day (and in that of Mark's first audience) were people on their way to a gruesome execution—their own. To "take up the cross" is to choose death.

Verse 35 provides the reason for such a choice: "for my sake, and for the sake of the gospel," Jesus says. This phrase is especially important to Mark, whose audience faced dire consequences for being Christian. The point is not a sort of negative, even masochistic, self-abandonment; the point is loyalty to Jesus. In the first of two rhetorical questions, v. 36 compares "world" (*kosmos*) and "soul" (*psuche*). Of what value is the material and temporary if the spiritual and permanent is "forfeited" (*zemiothenai*, to lose by way of penalty)? Verse 37 is a metaphorical way of saying the loss is irrevocable. Nothing a person can do will save his or her life if it is spent in pursuit of the wrong goals.

Jesus again uses "Son of Man" in v. 38; this time the figure becomes a judge. (Cf. Dan. 7:10, 13-14 and Rom. 1:16. The Q form of the saying is found in Matt. 10:33 and Luke 12:9.) If one "is ashamed of" (that is, denies) Jesus in the present age, in the age to come, that one will be denied.

The introductory phrase in 9:1, "and he said to them," suggests that what follows may originally have been a separate saying. "Truly I say" occurs thirteen times in Mark to introduce solemn announcements. What follows is remarkably ambiguous. By placing the saying here, Mark seems to want to associate the Son of Man with the coming of the kingdom. Or it may be that the announcement is meant to suggest that where Jesus is, the kingdom has already drawn near in his words and deeds. Or it has been suggested that 9:1 is intended to introduce the transfiguration account that follows. Peter, James, and John saw the kingdom in its power when they witnessed Jesus transfigured.

In preaching the text, it is imperative to correct its common misuse. Crosses are not passively accepted; they are actively chosen "for Jesus' sake." The sacredness of human life is clearly in focus here (vv. 36-37), as is judgment (8:38; 9:1). A concern for what one "gives one's life" to or for is in evidence. It would be appropriate to use Jesus' teaching in vv. 34-37 in connection with any of the Pauline statements about the atonement.

For Further Reading

Lewis Hay, "The Son-of-God Christology in Mark," *JBR* 32 (1964): 106–14.

David Rhoads, "Losing Life for Others in the Face of Death: Mark's Standards of Judgment," *Int* 47 (1993): 358–69.

9:2-13

The account of the transfiguration of Jesus is one of the most interesting and perplexing pieces of the synoptic tradition. It has been interpreted variously as a theologizing of the preceding passion prediction showing how suffering is glory,[7] a misplaced resurrection appearance (although it does not exhibit the literary characteristics of that form), a fulfillment of 9:1, and an anticipation of the parousia. In Mark's mind it is certainly connected to Peter's confession in 8:29 and serves as a special attempt to alleviate the blindness of those who will become the leaders of the Jerusalem congregation (Peter, James, and John). After the dark shadow cast by the first passion prediction, something of the light of the Messiah's ultimate glory is seen here. Without denying that the account has much in common with Greek theophanies, in light of 2 Pet. 1:16-18, I tend to read the text as a historical event interpreted through the lens of Hebrew scripture, especially Ps. 43:3.

The pericope falls into two parts: the transfiguration itself (vv. 2-8) and a conversation with the three disciples on the way down the mountain (vv. 9-13). As is frequently the case in Mark, a geographical shift signals the beginning of a new pericope. The reference to six days in v. 2 narratively links passion prediction with transfiguration.[8] Mt. Tabor, Mt. Hermon, and Mt. Meiron have been suggested as locations of the event, although the fact that mountains provide typical spots for theophanies is the more important point (see, for example, Exod. 19; 1 Kings 19:11-18; Isa. 40:9; Ezek. 40:2). Here begins both the constriction of numbers of persons around Jesus (he is first seen with crowds; then disciples; then the Twelve; then Peter, James, and John; and finally, he dies alone on the cross) and a focus on his "inner circle" (see 5:37; 14:33). Jesus takes Peter, James, and John "apart, by themselves" (privately, a Markan redundancy); his work is now done in smaller and smaller groups as he concentrates his teaching on the disciples.

The word "transfigured" (*metemorothe*) is in the aorist passive and is a "Divine passive," an oblique way to indicate that God is the "doer"; here God transfigures Jesus. The word has strong roots in Jewish apocalyptic and is a late Greek technical term for a change of form, "a change outwardly visible in its effects."[9] Here, momentarily, Jesus exchanges human form for his "glorious body" (see *1 Enoch* 62:15-16 and 2 Cor. 3:18). Verse 3 is a stammering attempt to describe this change using a metaphor (whiteness) associated with heavenly beings in Jewish apocalyptic (see, for example, Dan. 10:5). The figures of Moses and Elijah are also suggestive.[10] They symbolize both those who have suffered at the hands of God's people and those who did not die in an ordinary way. (Deut. 34:5-6; 2 Kings 2:11). They "both were rejected by Israel and vindicated by God, as Jesus will be."[11] Moses represents the lawgiver and authority figure (Deut. 18:15) and Elijah the prophets. Elijah was expected to return before the Messiah came (Mal. 4:5-6). They are "two figures who best represent the human capacity to 'see God.'"[12] In a midrash (a rabbinic explanation) of Psalm 43, Moses, Elijah, and the Messiah appear together. That Jesus appears with Moses and Elijah is, for Mark, proof that he is the Messiah. Gundry calls this pericope "visual and auditory evidence that Jesus is God's son."[13]

As he was in the previous unit of material (8:27—9:1), Peter is singled out for special attention. He addresses Jesus the way followers address a teacher ("rabbi," cf. 10:51; 11:21; 14:45) and offers to build three "dwellings." *Skene,* used only here in Mark, literally means "tents" or temporary dwellings. Some scholars think the word suggests the Feast of

Booths, a time of intense nationalism. Again Peter does not understand Jesus' messiahship; he seems to want Jesus to lead the people to freedom (like Moses) and to deliver them from their enemies (like Elijah). Or, more simply, perhaps as is characteristic of his impulsive personality, Peter wants to prolong an experience that v. 8 suggests is meant to be temporary. But disciples cannot "stay on the mountain"; they must return to the world and there suffer with and for their Lord.

Verses 7-8 focus on Jesus' divine sonship and on the word he brings. Again, as at his baptism (1:9-11), a heavenly voice reveals Jesus' true identity (see Ps. 2:7 and perhaps Gen. 22:2). Here it is made explicit that God's authority is behind the teaching of Jesus. Mark's emphasis is on the word Jesus brings, to which his disciples are to listen. Clouds are a characteristic feature of theophany (Exod. 16:10; Num. 9:15-22; Isa. 4:5), and in Exodus they are also symbols of God's presence to protect and guide.

Verse 8 is probably the end of the original narrative. Verses 9-13 are problematic. Luke omits them, which has led scholars to suggest that his is the earliest version of the event. In Mark's gospel the verses serve as an "appendix" to the transfiguration; vv. 9-10 deal with resurrection and vv. 11-13 with the figure of Elijah. Verse 9 serves to set a time limit on the messianic secret; the secret of Jesus' identity is to be kept only until he rises from the dead. The suggestion is that the truth of Jesus will be made known in his death and resurrection. Verse 10 is consistent with what we know of the disciples via Peter; they did not associate resurrection with the Son of Man because, in their view, the Messiah could not suffer and die.

Verses 11-13 pick up the Baptist theme (since he also was associated with Elijah) as "they" (presumably Peter, James, and John) ask about the interpretation of Mal. 4:5-6. Jesus' answer, though veiled, is that Elijah, understood as harbinger of the Messiah, came in the person of John the Baptist. He was treated as Elijah; Herodias was his Jezebel (1 Kings 19:2, 10). Elijah, John the Baptist, and Jesus all suffered for their leadership. The fate of John foreshadows the fate of Jesus.

The transfiguration text is not a simple one to preach. If nothing else, it reminds us that there are no easy answers to life's mysteries. Jesus raises as many questions as he answers; in Mark's gospel he is not the "super problem-solver." Finally, we must let the text rest in the realm of mystery, but "enlightened mystery." As the Canon of the Feast of the Transfiguration in the Orthodox liturgy declares, "How mighty and fearful is the vision that was seen today! The visible sun shone from heaven, but from the earth there shone upon Mount Tabor the spiritual Sun of Righteousness, past all compare."

I think it is most helpful to approach the text in the context of the overarching structure of Mark's gospel. Mark's story rests on three theophanic pillars: the baptism, the transfiguration, and the resurrection of Jesus. It is at these points that the reader is told explicitly what those in the narrative do not know about Jesus. The transfiguration is a christological text par excellence. The preacher should not be sidetracked by "what really happened" or what Peter's response means. In studying this text, one of my students once remarked that the Bible was like a child passing on a parent's message. Its writers did the best they could without understanding the whole thing; some of the message may have been scrambled along the way, but the gist is there.[14] "This is God's Son," is the gist of the text; "listen to him," it proclaims.

For Further Reading

Herbert Basser, "The Jewish Roots of the Transfiguration," *BR* 14 (1998): 30–35.

Ernest Best, "The Markan Redaction of the Transfiguration," in *Disciples and Discipleship* (Edinburgh: T. & T. Clark, 1986), chap. 12.

Walter Liefeld, "Transfiguration," in *DJG*, 834–41.

Jerome Murphy O'Connor, "What Really Happened at the Transfiguration?" *BR* 3 (1987): 8–21.

9:14-29

Narratively, the attention now shifts to what went on with the larger group of disciples in Jesus' absence. This section of Mark contains no other "mighty work," and this account is unusually detailed, so we should examine carefully its two primary parts: vv. 14-19, the disciples' failure; and vv. 20-27, the father's faith.

Like Moses when he came down from Mt. Sinai, Jesus also meets disbelief and disorder when he comes down from the Mount of Transfiguration. His other disciples, a crowd, and some scribes are arguing. The argument seems to be a result of the disciples' failure to heal. In a crisis, all they can do is talk; this argumentative spirit demonstrates lack of faith. Jesus' appearance has changed, a change immediately recognizable (v. 15, herein is another parallel to Moses). Jesus seeks to discover the cause of the confusion (v. 16) in another text in which he takes initiative as a questioner.

Verses 19-27 occur only in Mark and deal primarily with faith in crisis (a special concern of Mark's original audience). Jesus' outburst against the disciples (v. 19) is because of their faithlessness. An argumentative spirit and disbelief stand in the way of a cure. As in earlier Markan accounts, the spirit world recognizes Jesus (1:24), who turns to engage the father (whom we now know as the speaker in vv. 17-18, which describes what appears to be epilepsy). The father's approach to Jesus is tentative ("if you are able to do anything"), and it is just this tentativeness that concerns Jesus, who throws the issue back on the father (v. 23). If he can believe, the power of God will be made operative.

In a burst of both insight and honesty, the father replies, "I believe; help my unbelief!" (v. 24). In response (before a crowd forms, a veiled reference to the messianic secret?), Jesus permanently exorcises the unclean spirit ("never enter him again"). It is worth noting, however, that v. 26 suggests things get worse before they improve, so much worse that people think the youth has died. Characteristically, Jesus takes him by the hand and raises him, symbolically bringing another child back from the dead (cf. 1:31; 5:41-42). Whether or not vv. 28-29 are a post-Markan addition, they focus again on the issue of faith. Characteristically, Jesus gives the disciples special instruction in the house, privately and away from the crowds (see 4:10, 34).

The disciples, Jesus explains, were unable to cast out the demon because of their lack of prayer (and some manuscripts add "fasting"). Prayer to God is an expression of faith in God (here compared to an argumentative attitude). This faith is not cheap; it comes by disciplined behavior. The alternatives presented here are futile contentiousness, which indicates lack of trust or faith that God will act, and trust in spite of moments of unbelief (v. 24). No explanation of why faithful prayer seems not to be answered, no program of "how to" is presented by Jesus, but only an indication of the importance of belief and faith (even in the face of what may seem a worsening situation).

The text is an especially potent one for a teaching sermon on the spiritual life. The "dumb spirit" (vv. 17-18) can be seen as a metaphor for all that would keep us from trust in God, all that would lead us to "grind our teeth" or "be rigid" instead of calling out to God, reaching for God. The three causes for the disciples' failure to exorcise that spirit—their argumentativeness, their lack of faith, and their lack of discipline in prayer—are spiritual difficulties of our age as well. In a crisis, all the disciples can do is talk. The exorcism/healing as a whole suggests the "active" alternatives of trust and prayer. Within the larger context of Mark 8:22—10:52 the emphasis is clearly on the faith that must characterize discipleship. As Ralph Martin notes in his preaching commentary on Mark, "in its original setting [the account] referred to Jesus, the man of faith who is claiming the confidence to see the boy healed on the ground that he trusts his heavenly Father to work through him. We get a fresh insight into Jesus' own life of trust here, and it calls us to share his faith in the limitless energy of God to touch and heal human lives."[15]

For Further Reading
Paul J. Achtemeier, "Miracles and the Historical Jesus: Mark 9:14-29," *CBQ* 37 (1975): 473–91.

Gregory Sterling, "Jesus as Exorcist," *CBQ* 55 (1993): 467–93.

9:30-37
This is the second passion prediction account in this section of Mark's gospel. As the first (8:27—9:1), it follows the pattern of geographical reference (vv. 30, 33), prediction (v. 31), misunderstanding (vv. 32, 34), and further teaching on discipleship (vv. 36-37). Narratively it initiates the last journey through Galilee and the last visit to Capernaum (and thus the beginning of the movement to Jerusalem) and is characterized by private teachings to the disciples.

Verse 30 opens with an image of a peripatetic school of private instruction to the disciples. Jesus does not want these teachings widely disseminated. The prediction itself (v. 31) is the least detailed (and perhaps the most primitive) of the three. Jesus "is to be betrayed"; the present tense suggests inevitability, and the word "betrayed" (*paradidotai*) carries the connotations of both divine necessity and martyrdom. (The same word was used in connection with the martyrdom of John the Baptist.) Once again, the disciples fail to understand. But why are they "afraid to ask him" (v. 32)? Is it because of the strong response Peter's rebuke engendered (8:32ff.)? Or is there some internal fear that recognizes that, as disciples, they are somehow implicated in the passion?

The trip through Galilee (again, Jesus' ministry is depicted as itinerant, cf. 8:27; 9:24; 10:17, 32, 52) ends at Capernaum, where "in the house" (cf. 8:27), privately, Jesus quizzes the disciples on their travel conversation. In these passion predictions/discipleship teachings Jesus takes the initiative with his questions (8:27; 9:16), an interesting reversal, since in the Jewish world of the time disciples usually asked their teachers questions. We are, I think, to understand that Jesus knew very well what they were talking about and needed to address just those attitudes that had been expressed. Even the disciples are depicted as having some understanding. Is it that knowing they will have a kingdom, they are discussing their place in it, arguing about who will be greatest? Their conversation has focused on the question of status and identity within the group, and even they know that this is unworthy of them.

Verse 35 should not be passed over quickly. Mark indicates that Jesus takes the official, authoritative position of a teacher; "he sat down" (cf. Matt. 5:1-2). And he calls not the disciples (a larger group of men and women who traveled with him) but "the Twelve," the inner circle who followed him in the last days of his public ministry. Whoever wants to be first in the kingdom, he explains, must be last of all and servant of all. The word "servant" here is *diakonos,* not *doulos,* slave. It is a somewhat "softer" term, one that appears throughout the New Testament in the context of official ministry, but it still clearly shows leaders their "place."

What Morna Hooker calls an "acted parable" (vv. 36-37) illustrates the saying. Following two instances of argumentativeness and querulousness (9:14, 34), Jesus points out that "instead of worrying about their own positions, they should be concerned for the weakest and most humble member of the community," typified by the child.[16] Roman Palestine is not post-Enlightenment Europe, with its romantic cult of the innocence and importance of children. Children were at the low end of the social ladder; only slaves were below them. The child serves as a "visual aid" of both lowliness and powerlessness as well as of the trustfulness and simplicity that deeply understands God's kingdom. (Hence another connection to the previous pericope, 9:14-29.) Verse 37 summarizes the exchange by focusing on the upside-down quality of the kingdom and on Christology (two of the important preaching points in the text). Jesus identifies with the child, the representative of those who are poor, needy, and without status. In welcoming such a one, disciples welcome Jesus. To welcome "in his name" is to welcome with all the unconditional love and openness of Jesus himself. Discipleship includes such hospitality ("welcoming") as well as the specific care of orphans (see Jas. 1:27). Instead of concern for their own status, disciples of Jesus should be concerned for the weakest members of the community, should offer them hospitality in the broadest sense of that term. The primitive Christology here emphasizes the Christ as the one whom God has sent. In welcoming Jesus, disciples welcome God.

For Further Reading

U. C. Von Wahlde, "Mark 9:33-50: Discipleship: The Authority that Serves," *Biblische Zeitschrift* 29 (1985).

9:38-40

These verses represent the kind of dispute that must have arisen in Mark's community. Narratively, it looks back at the exorcism in 9:14-29 and is linked to 8:33-37 by references to the name of Jesus (8:37, 39, 41). I presume that "John" is the John of the "inner circle," Peter, James, and John. It is his only solo appearance, and here he represents exclusivism and conformity. His remark to Jesus reflects a sectarian spirit that would seek to exclude those not in his own group.

Jesus' response in vv. 39-41 set forth a principle for church life. Those who do miracles or great works (*dunamin*) in Jesus' name cannot be opposed to him. (We are expected to remember here 9:14-29 and the faith that facilitates miracles.) Only active opposition to Jesus and his followers seems of concern. Verse 41 is omitted by Matthew and Luke in their account of the exchange. In Mark, Jesus is showing the disciples how to represent him after his death. The teaching is intrinsically connected to 9:37 (and recall Matt. 25:31-46, especially v. 40, "just as you did it to one of the least of these who are members of my family, you did it to me") and is the only place in Mark's gospel where "Christ" is used as a proper name. (And note that all the benevolent or charitable activity in the text—exorcism or "giving a cup of water"—is done "in my name," that is, under the authority and example of Jesus.) Instead of seeking to exclude others, disciples of Jesus are to accept service *from* those they might have chosen to exclude! Verse 41 depicts Jesus' followers not in the "power" position (with the authority to exclude), but in the "weak" position as recipients of water, a necessity of life.

T. W. Manson remarked that this verse shows that there is "no closed shop in the kingdom." Today the text serves as a potent reminder of the need for the various branches of the Christian family tree to acknowledge one another. It is a good starting point for a sermon on ecumenism. And it warns us not only against sectarianism, but against that more general human tendency to draw the circle of fellowship far too narrowly, to try to secure our own position by excluding others. It asks us to be willing to accept the "charity" of others, much as Jesus accepted a drink of water from the Samaritan woman in John 4 or anointing from the woman in 14:3-9.

9:42-50

At this point Mark inserts a rather miscellaneous collection of sayings to continue the discipleship teaching of the previous pericope. The sayings focus on discipleship in relation to internal things and continue to illustrate what it means to follow Jesus. The structural principle of vv. 42-48 is an "if/then" statement, followed by an explanatory comment, introduced by "it would be better." The verses are linked by a "catchword" (German *stichwort*) principle, repetitions of forms of "stumbling block."

Verse 42 is the negative statement of an idea stated positively at 9:37. It follows from the teaching against exclusion and sectarianism in 9:38-41. "Little ones," then, are to be understood as either the "child" of 9:36-37 or, more generally, as a follower of Jesus. The warning is against leading others astray. A "stumbling block" (*skandalise,* from whence the English "scandal") is literally something one falls on, a trap or hindrance placed in another's way. A millstone (literally *mulos onikos*) was so large that it was normally turned by a donkey in harness.

Verses 44 and 46, which are identical with v. 48, are missing in the best manuscript traditions. Verses 43-48 deal with stumbling blocks "from within," in relation to one's self. The hand, the foot, and the eye are metaphors for those faults and shortcomings that are very close to us, so close that they are depicted as parts of our own bodies. If hand or foot or eye cause hindrance to the way of Jesus (to discipleship), they should be removed. The word translated "hell" in vv. 43, 45, and 47 of the NRSV is *Gehenna*. The Hinnom Valley was a ravine running southwest of Jerusalem. It served as the town dump; thus the images of worm and fire (see Isa. 66:24, LXX). Gehenna was also traditionally understood to be the place of Moloch worship and thus was a symbol of punishment to come. The point is that it is better to reside in a garbage dump or even in a place of idolatry (!) than to allow forces within (or attached to) ourselves to lead us astray.

There are many variant readings of vv. 49-50 that, in my view, are to serve as summary of the whole chapter. Verse 49 is something of a puzzle. (Perhaps for this reason Matthew omits it.) Salt makes palatable and preserves; it was used both as a seasoning and as medicine. Similarly, fire both refines and purifies. Is the idea that the purification process (persecution? trial?) can either destroy or preserve? The Twelve or disciples of Jesus are to be salt to the larger community. Mark's first readers would have understood that salt was not pure, but mixed with other things (sand, for instance). If the saline quality of the mixture is too low, it cannot season or cure. The question is, if the disciples of Jesus lose their "saltiness," how will the world be "flavored" (or "healed" if salt is understood as a medicine)? F. F. Bruce points out that the "figure of insipid salt appears in the words of the rabbis, with reference . . . to Israel's role as the salt or purifying agency among the nations."[17] The implication is that the disciples of Jesus have a similar (or at least a particular) function. "They may be intended to have a preserving and purifying effect on their fellows or to add zest to the life of the community or to be a force for peace."[18] The final two verses of the chapter remind the followers of Jesus to maintain peacefully (versus the argumentativeness of vv. 14, 34) their own, distinct character. (If the phrase *exhete en eautois* in v. 50 is translated "have salt among yourselves" rather than "have salt in yourselves" [as per the NRSV] the reference might be to eating salt together as an expression of table fellowship, of peaceful relationships again, versus the sectarian spirit of vv. 38-41.)

It is significant that salt is always a small quantity in relation to the work it is to do. Only a small amount of salt flavors a stew. But try a can of salt-free soup some day and see what a difference only a small amount makes! The image of salt presumes both that there will be relatively few real followers of Jesus in the world and that those few will make a huge difference to the whole. In this section of the gospel, discipleship is of particular interest. The image of it here is startlingly realistic and must have provided comfort to Mark's small, beleaguered community.

In chapter 9 as a whole, Jesus' most dire warnings are directed at religious leaders and his own disciples, in short, at those who should "know better." But those who should know better are argumentative rather than faithful, self-seeking rather than humbly childlike, exclusive rather than inclusive in attitude, and in danger of being "diluted," of losing their "saltiness" or distinctness. More teaching is required.

10:1-12

The change of venue in 10:1 signals a new segment of material. The peripatetic character of Jesus' ministry continues (cf. 9:30), but the journey to Jerusalem seems now to have begun. (Remember that in Mark, Jerusalem is a symbol of opposition to Jesus.) The theme of discipleship continues, now in relation to external things like marriage (vv. 2-12), children (vv. 13-16), and possessions (vv. 17-31). In his commentary on Mark, Hugh Anderson suggests that the arrangement of material is reminiscent of the *haustafeln* (household codes) that regulated life in the Greco-Roman family and addressed wives, husbands, children, fathers, slaves, and masters (see, for example, Col. 3:18—4:1 or Eph. 5:21—6:9).[19] It is significant that Jesus is now in "the region of Judea and beyond the Jordan." This is Herod's jurisdiction—Herod who was tricked into executing John the Baptist for his views on divorce and remarriage.

Characteristically in Mark, when crowds gather, Jesus teaches (2:13; 4:1-2; 6:34; 11:17; 12:35). The Pharisees represent those who do not come to Jesus with a desire to be taught, but with the desire to test him (cf. 7:1-23). The issue at hand is not the legal right to divorce, which, on the basis of Deut. 24:1-4, is assumed. Since in Jewish Palestine women could not sue for divorce, many scholars think this pericope reflects the controversy between church and synagogue as it was played out in the early Gentile church. The preacher should note that divorce was very common in the Roman world and that, within Judaism itself, there were two schools of thought on the matter. The followers of Shammai held the strict view that divorce should be sought only for infidelity. The followers of Hillel held a more lenient interpretation and allowed divorce for a variety of reasons.

As is often characteristic of his response to questioners, in v. 3 Jesus turns the question back on this questioners, who reply according to "party line" (v. 4). Jesus' own answer (vv. 6-9) takes a very different approach. The law, he says, was shaped for those for whom it was written; it is concessionary. But what God *wills* is not what the law *allows*. The purpose of Deut. 24:1-4 was to ameliorate the harsh consequences of divorce. Verses 6-7 remind the crowd of God's intentions for marriage before it was blotted by human sin (see Gen 1:27; 2:24; 5:2). The principle Jesus lays down in vv. 5-9 is actually stricter than that of the rabbis.[20] Rather than ruling out divorce, he elevates marriage—and this suggests what the homilist ought to stress in preaching the text.

Verse 10 reflects again the Markan theme of special instruction to the disciples (4:10, 34; 7:17; 9:28; 10:23; 13:3) that often occurs "in the house." Matthew abridges and Luke omits vv. 10-12, which some think are a later addition to Mark. Since in Judaism there were no procedures for a wife to initiate divorce, these verses are seen as either reflecting the circumstances of Mark's Roman audience or as further evidence of Jesus' remarkably enlightened view of women. In either case, vv. 11-12 should be read in light of women's lack of legal rights and Jesus' high view of marriage.

In our own day this text should be preached with great pastoral sensitivity. We must be careful not to add further pain and guilt to those already wounded by divorce. Perhaps it is best to preach the text in the context of the theme of discipleship that dominates Mark 8:22—10:52. The general principle of discipleship that can be extracted from the specific example of marriage is that one who follows Jesus must not look for concessions. Discipleship (like marriage) is an all-or-nothing proposition.

For Further Reading

F. F. Bruce, *The Hard Sayings of Jesus* (Downers Grove: InterVarsity, 1983), chap. 12, "Divorce and Remarriage."

Robert Stein, "Divorce," *DJG*, 192–99.

Although not about Mark's text, Ben Witherington's "Matthew 5:32 and 19:9—Exception or Exceptional Situation?" *NTS* 31 (1985): 571–76, sheds light on the issue.

10:13-16

While it continues the Markan picture of the disciples as insensitive and status conscious (cf. 9:33-37; some see this text as a variant or doublet of 9:36-37), this pericope stands in stark contrast to the adult skepticism in the previous account. People ("the crowds" of 10:1?) bring children to Jesus in the understanding that even simple contact with him confers blessing (v. 13). Verse 14 is the only account in the Gospels in which Jesus is described as being "indignant" (*eganaktesen*—angry, aroused, indignant, vexed). Recall that in 9:33-37 Jesus used children to represent the lowly or "underdogs." Here, again, the kingdom (or reign) of God is theirs because of their attitude of dependence and receptiveness. It is not the receiving of the child (although Jesus certainly does so) but of the kingdom that is finally the focus.

Verse 15 is widely accepted as a genuine saying of Jesus. It implies that trustful simplicity and openness to the "gift" quality of life characterizes citizens of the kingdom. While *hos paidion* can be read "as one receives a child" rather than "as a little child" (NRSV), the idea that the kingdom is God's gift is focal. This grace/gift is demonstrated in v. 16 as Jesus complies with the desire of the people in v. 13 and freely blesses the children they bring. Once again, the disciples' expectations (and Mark's original audience's? and our own?) are radically reversed.

While ecclesiologically the text has been used to support the practice of infant baptism, that was probably not Mark's intent in fashioning and inserting it here. Two other avenues of approach to preaching the text in a more Markan context suggest themselves. First, the preacher can explore what it means to receive the kingdom as a child would do so. This is probably the most common exposition of the text. But it is also possible to focus on the "people who were bringing little children." If we understand ourselves to be the "people" or the "crowd" who listen to Jesus, the question becomes, "Who are the 'little' ones whom we need to bring to Jesus, knowing (because he has blessed us) that he will take them in his arms and bless them?" From this point of view, the text can be used effectively either as an evangelistic or a missions-emphasis sermon.

For Further Reading

Ernest Best, *Disciples and Discipleship* (Edinburgh: T. & T. Clark, 1986), chap. 6, "Mark 10:13-16: The Child as Model Recipient."

10:17-31

The unit of material that begins with the approach of the wealthy man to Jesus continues Mark's discipleship teaching and, in its context, suggests that not only possessions, but the pride and self-sufficiency that they engender, hinder entrance into the kingdom. The unit is made up of four discrete pieces: Jesus' encounter with the wealthy man (vv. 17-22), Jesus' more general remarks on wealth (vv. 23-27), Jesus' promise to his disciples (vv. 28-30), and a concluding saying (v. 31).

Again, Mark puts Jesus in the context of a journey (9:30; 10:1). Here in v. 17 he is "setting out," as we know, toward Jerusalem. In this context, the wealthy man is every man or woman who wants to know how to "inherit eternal life." Since almost no one runs in the hot Palestinian sun, we are led to expect that the man's question is urgent. The adjective "good" (*agathe*) appears only infrequently in personal references in the LXX; the Psalms only use it for God. Jesus' attitude in v. 18 is that of a good Jew; he believes that only God is good. This probably authentic saying of Jesus ("no one else was likely to put into his mouth words which seemed to cast doubt on his goodness"[21]) was problematic to the church as it sorted out its Christology. But Mark is only interested to show Jesus shifting the focus from himself to God. In responding to the wealthy man, Jesus enumerates only the second part of the Decalogue (Exod. 20:12-16; Deut. 5:16-20), which deals with duty toward the neighbor.

The wealthy man feels that since he was a youth (since he was twelve or thirteen), he has kept "all these." Certainly the rabbis thought it was possible to keep the whole law (Paul felt he had, Phil. 3:6). Certainly in matters of ritual purity and external conformity, the man's riches would have allowed him to be completely compliant. It is important to note that Jesus does not contradict the man. I think we are to take at face value Mark's notation: Jesus "loved him." Jesus saw great possibility in a man who was concerned to keep the law and to have eternal life, and so he issues the same call to him that earlier disciples received (1:17, 18, 20; 2:14). But Jesus also knows what this particular man lacks. The request in v. 21 is for *this* man's spiritual problem; it is not to be understood as a general rule for discipleship, although some, like St. Francis of Assisi or, closer to our own time, Charles de Foucauld, were so called. (It is Matt. 6:19-21 that raises the issue in general terms; cf. Matt. 19:21, which is a counsel for "perfection.")

And this particular man cannot respond. He was "shocked" (*stugnasas*, literally "becoming gloomy," used only here in Mark) and "grieving" (*lupoumenos*, literally "sorrowing," "sad," "distressed"), possibly because he understood his wealth had allowed him to keep the law, certainly because he was attached to his wealth. Attachment is at the spiritual root of his problem, as are his priorities. The man apparently has greater desire for his possessions than for eternal life. The man's response in v. 22 leads both to Jesus' general remarks (vv. 23-27) and to Peter's (the representative disciple) implied question (v. 28).

"Looked around" (*periblephamenos*, v. 23) is one of Mark's ways of introducing special sayings of Jesus (3:5, 34). Notice Jesus does not say it is impossible for the rich to enter the kingdom, but it is hard (*pos duskolos*, "with what difficulty"). Some manuscripts of Mark reverse vv. 24 and 25. In any case, the disciples' perplexity is because they undoubtedly assume (as did many Jews) that wealth was a sign of God's favor; they certainly know it made it possible both to perform religious duties and to avoid ritual defilement. In v. 24b Jesus again broadens the scope of his reflection, noting it is hard for *all* to enter the kingdom. The proverbial saying in v. 25 may well show Jesus' sense of humor. Both Matthew and Luke place it in the same context in their Gospels (Matt. 19:24; Luke 18:25). Whether or not, as some suggest, a particular low gate into the city of Jerusalem is in view, or whether there has been a misunderstanding between two Greek words (*kamilos*, "cable," and *kamelos*, "camel"), this hyperbolic expression is not lost on the disciples, v. 26 (cf. Matt. 7:14).

Note, however, that the disciples do make the connection between the kingdom and salvation. "To be saved" is to enter the kingdom. And entrance always comes as a gift. Salvation is always by God's grace. (See Gen. 18:14; Jer. 32:17 for Hebrew scriptural examples. Cf. Luke 12:32. And, of course, this is the cornerstone of the Pauline gospel.) By implication here, only God makes discipleship possible. And willingness to accept the gift of salvation is closely tied to the example of "little children" in 10:13-16.

Peter's remark (v. 28) returns to the original situation (vv. 17-22), but Jesus' response broadens the context beyond wealth to include family relationships. Robert Gundry thinks Mark 10:29 has the Tenth Commandment as its background. A "household," he suggests, is everything that belongs to a person. The list in v. 29 is presented in an "ascending scale of economic value in agrarian culture."[22] Verse 30 offers the followers of Jesus wonderful compensations but exhibits no "rose-colored view" of the cost of discipleship. Mark's original audience would have been well aware of the "persecutions" alluded to (which both Matthew and Luke omit in their versions of the event). The language of v. 30 is eschatological and leads to the eschatological principle of reversal in v. 31.

"The first will be last and the last will be first" is a piece of folk wisdom used by Jesus in different contexts in Matthew, Mark, and Luke. Here in Mark it seems to suggest that the disciples, because they have given up much to follow Jesus, should not, therefore, assume they will be first in his kingdom. In his very interesting commentary on Mark from the point of view of Mahayana Buddhism, John Keenan notes that the disciples must abandon not only wealth, self, and family for the sake of the good news, but also "the very hope of rewards." "There is no quid pro quo here, as if one earns the result by the performance of an act of renunciation. To abandon things in the context of self is merely to strengthen one's sense of self and will in no wise avoid self-clinging. This is why those who think themselves to be first, to be already disciples and followers of Christ, will be last."[23] "To possess eternal life is to abandon all attempts to possess anything. It is that insight into emptiness that allows one to follow the commandments, not as a means to earn eternal life, but as conventional paths of practice which point beyond those paths to the silent mystery of God."[24]

As the lectionaries indicate (or allow), Mark 10:17-31 is best preached as a unit of material. Only in that approach is it clear that much more than wealth or material possessions is at issue. If only 10:17-22 (or even 27) are treated, it is much too easy to rationalize "I'm never going to be really wealthy, so this passage has nothing to say to me." In fact, the passage asks that we consider what are our greatest obstacles to entering the kingdom. To what do we cling that we should be willing to let go of?

Perhaps, as vv. 28-31 suggest, it may be our sense of ourselves as disciples of Jesus! Do we think that by our various renunciations or our acceptance of persecution for Jesus and for the sake of the gospel we have "earned" the kingdom/salvation? If so, we may find "in the age to come" that we were very much mistaken. The sermon that plumbs the spiritual depths of this passage goes well beyond the matter of wealth and possessions.

For Further Reading

Ernest Best, "The Camel and the Needle's Eye (Mk 10:25)," in *Disciples and Discipleship* (Edinburgh: T. & T. Clark, 1986), 17–30.

Robert H. Gundry, "Mark 10:29: Order in the List," *CBQ* 59 (1997): 465–75.

Excursus on Structure

It has occurred to me that in this carefully constructed section of the gospel, the story of the rich man parallels that of Peter's confession. Just as Jesus was interested in what the disciples and Peter in particular thought of him (8:29), here he is interested in what this particular man needs to do to enter the kingdom. Some commentators see the rich man as wrong in his priorities, flattery, and superficiality, but I tend to take seriously v. 21; Jesus "loved him." The wealthy man is one who has done the right things but who cannot go the whole route of the radical demands of discipleship. Each of us has these obstacles. This unit of material is asking us to examine them. The unit fits the passion prediction/discipleship teaching of the section, which can be seen to have the following structure:

Blind man healed	8:22-26
Question of personal understanding	8:27-30
Passion prediction unit	8:27-9:1
Passion prediction unit	9:30-37
Question of personal understanding	10:17-31
Passion prediction unit	10:32-45
Blind man healed	10:46-52

Such a structure sets off 10:32-45 as of particular interest, and it brings together the various themes of this section of the gospel.

10:32-45

This passage is the third passion prediction unit in this section of Mark, and like the previous two, it follows the pattern of geographical reference (v. 32), prediction (vv. 33-34), misunderstanding (vv. 35-37), and further teaching (vv. 38-45). The journey of discipleship continues (8:27; 9:9, 30; 10:1, 17), but for the first time Mark reveals that Jesus is going to Jerusalem, with all that location implies. Heretofore Jerusalem has sent "spies" to "check up on" Jesus; now he is journeying toward the headquarters of opposition to his message. In v. 32 Jesus leads, and those who follow (that is, disciples) are both amazed and afraid, as well they might be.[25] Is Mark's implication that they have some inkling of what "going up to Jerusalem" means?

Once again, Jesus calls the Twelve aside for special teaching, this time "what was to happen to him." The prediction itself in vv. 33-34 is much more detailed than the two previous. It outlines what will follow in chapters 14 through 16 of Mark's Gospel. The fact that Jesus says "*we* are going up to Jerusalem" implicates the Twelve (and "those who followed" generally?) in Jesus' own fate. John the Baptist preached, was "delivered up," and killed; Jesus, who followed John, preaches, and is to be delivered up and killed; the disciples who follow Jesus may expect the same treatment.

Against this background, the request of James and John in v. 35 seems particularly obtuse. Disciples of Jesus still misunderstand Jesus' message. In 8:32-33 Peter failed to grasp it. Now the two others in Jesus' "inner circle" do the same. Certainly the Transfiguration, where Peter, James, and John saw Jesus in glory (9:2-13) stands behind this account. James and John seem to be asking on the basis of what they remember from that event, but they are also representative of all those who do not understand God's will and way in Jesus. As opposed to being child*like*, the unconditional request made in v. 35 seems child*ish*. (It is so embarrassing that Matthew's account of the event has the mother of James and John ask the question, cf. Matt. 20:20-28.) Seats to the right and left of the monarch were, in an oriental court, seats of honor, seats that symbolized special dignity. "Glory" is a metaphor for "kingly power" (cf. Luke 23:42). In James and John we see the human aspiration to dignity and power, which is contrary to the way of Jesus' kingdom and to the will of God.

Jesus knows his own fate (vv. 33-34) and thus knows that James and John "do not know what [they] are asking" (v. 38). His response in vv. 38-40 is highly metaphorical and allusive. The figure of the cup is complex. In Hebrew scripture, "cup" can symbolize joy and salvation (Pss. 16:5; 23:5; 116:13) or suffering and punishment (Pss. 11:6; 75:8; Isa. 51:17, 22; Jer. 25:15, 17). In Mark's gospel, the "cup" appears in the context of great suffering in Jesus' Gethsemane prayer (14:36). "Cup" is also a Jewish expression for a share in someone else's fate. The baptism that Jesus accepted was not just the water baptism of John the Baptist, but the baptism of fire to which John alluded (1:8). To accept baptism (or "deep water," used in ancient literature for "flood" or "getting soaked"; Ps. 42:7; Isa. 43:2) is to accept God's way of suffering.

Verse 39 reiterates metaphorically the straightforward prediction of vv. 33-34. Some scholars think James's and John's assent prefigures the martyrdom of James under Herod Agrippa about A.D. 44 (Acts 12:2) and John's death before the destruction of Jerusalem (A.D. 70). It is recounted by Papias, who quotes Philip of Side. In v. 40, Jesus does not reject the position James and John assign to him, but does explain that the assignment of positions of honor is not his role. Even Jesus cannot usurp God's authority (see also 14:36; Acts 1:7). Rather than read a kind of fatalism into v. 40, I think it is to be taken as an indication of Jesus' understanding of his relation to God and of the inevitability of God's benevolent purposes, even in the face of apparent suffering and failure.

The other ten apostles are angry with James and John (v. 41), but Mark's gospel does not say why. Did James and John "get the drop on them" and ask first for what they, too, wanted? In view of their characterization to this point in the gospel, I am slow to assume that the ten understand Jesus when James and John do not. Jesus' response in v. 42 is a clear and accurate picture of the manners and behavior of earthly lords and rulers, of which the Greco-Roman world was full. His kingdom is intended to subvert that pattern. The "but" at the beginning of v. 43 rhetorically signals that reversal. Verses 43 and 44 provide another answer to the question raised at 9:34 and a variation on the theme of 9:35. Greatness in the kingdom is measured by servanthood and "firstness" in terms of the willingness to give up rights, in fact to become like a slave (*doulos*), who has none.

What Jesus asks of those who follow him (v. 32) is nothing less than what he himself did. He came to serve (which John dramatically depicts in the foot washing in chapter 13 of his gospel) and "to give his life as a ransom for many" (v. 45). This is the first explanation Mark gives of the significance of the death of Jesus, and it is an important verse for the theology of atonement. The word for "life" here is *psuchen,* meaning "his complete self." Mark uses the word variously to mean earthly life itself (8:35), the inner life of a person, his or her feelings and emotions (12:30), and the life that transcends earthly existence (8:36; 37).[26] The idea is that Jesus came to give the entire essence of his being "on behalf of" (*anti,* which can be translated simply "for" or "on behalf of" or "in place of") as the "ransom for many."

"Ransom" (*lutron*) appears only here in Mark, though, is used elsewhere in the New Testament. It means the "price of release" or "what is given to gain release." In Greek documents at the time of the New Testament, the word appears in the context of money paid for the release or manumission of slaves (so the term is especially appropriate in view of v. 44). Mark 14:24 communicates a similar idea (as does 1 Cor. 6:20). Jesus does this "for many." In English, the phrase suggests exclusion, "for many, but not for all." As Morna Hooker points out, "in Semitic thought, the emphasis is more likely to be inclusive: the contrast is not between the many who are saved and others who are not, but between the many and the one who acts on their behalf."[27]

Mark 10:32-45 serves as a summary of the themes of passion and discipleship that dominate this section of the gospel. Disciples are those who, although perhaps uncomprehendingly, follow Jesus, and who follow with amazement and fear. They are to do as their master has done. Not only are they, like him, to be servant (or slaves) "of all" (v. 44), but they are implicated in his suffering and death. Mark undoubtedly shaped this material to serve as instruction for the early church. In our day, it can be fruitfully preached not only to explain in very personal terms the atonement and its cost, but to address the question, "What must we do (or avoid doing) to see that our lives conform to Jesus' (and the kingdom's) view of greatness?"

10:46-52

The account of blind Bartimaeus closes the bracket around the passion prediction/discipleship teaching section of Mark's gospel, which opened with the healing of a blind man in 8:22-26. To understand this final healing miracle in Mark's Gospel, it is important to understand that blindness is a symbol for ignorance as well as a literal, physical condition. Understood in this light, Bartimaeus's request in v. 51b is in sharp and ironic contrast to that of James and John in 10:35-37. Ironically, the sighted are blind and the blind sighted. We are to understand that it is faith that leads the blind man to ask for sight.

Jericho was an ancient city about fifteen miles northeast of Jerusalem and on the pilgrim route up to the Temple, so it was a good place to beg from spiritually inspired travelers. The pericope opens with a rather confused description of such coming and going. Mark characteristically retains the Aramaic (Bartimaeus) and translates it for his Greek readers, "son of Timaeus." The designation "Jesus of Nazareth" has not been used since 1:24 to identify Jesus. Bartimaeus couples it with the messianic title "Son of David." He is the first (and perhaps only individual) person to use a messianic title for Jesus. His cry presages the "triumphal entry" into Jerusalem, which follows in chapter 11, as he is the first human in the narrative who correctly and openly identifies Jesus. Jesus' self-designation as "Son of Man" in 8:27—10:45 becomes "Son of David" in 10:46—12:44. As Vernon Robbins notes, this story links the Son of God tradition with Son of David activity in Jerusalem.[28]

Bartimaeus is not the first person to be discouraged from approaching Jesus (2:2-4; 5:24-27; 10:13). It is unclear whether the "many" who "sternly ordered him to be quiet" (v. 48) are Jesus' disciples (v. 46). If so, their attempt may be to prevent the trouble for Jesus that accepting a messianic title would entail, or perhaps they are simply persons embarrassed by the blind beggar's unruly behavior (or, as we so often are, uncomfortable in the face of a severe handicap). But like the Syrophoenician woman in chapter 7, Bartimaeus is not to be silenced; he sees more than the sighted and cries out "even more loudly" (v. 48). Jesus responds to the cry, stops, and summons Bartimaeus. Verse 50, which describes Bartimaeus's approach, is fascinating. Certainly his leaving behind the cloak (the *himation* or outer garment that was often the only night covering the poor had—which is why the Torah forbade it to be taken in pledge) and springing up is an image of his eagerness to get to Jesus. But it also symbolizes the renunciation that following Jesus requires (cf. 10:28-31). If his occupation is begging, and generous people put their offerings on the cloak, then it represents leaving behind the symbol of his occupation just as James, John, and Levi did (1:18, 20; 2:14). Perhaps most generally, leaving behind the cloak represents abandoning what hinders approach to Jesus. Ironically, the one who has nothing finds this easier than the one who has "many possessions" (10:17-22).

In response to Bartimaeus's approach, Jesus offers him the "blank check" for which James and John asked in v. 35. Bartimaeus, who gives Jesus the title of greatest reverence that he knew (*rabbouni*, another Aramaic word used only here and in John 20:16, when Mary Magdalene recognizes Jesus after the resurrection), asks for the "hardest thing." He wants not just temporary alms, but restoration of sight. As he has done before, Jesus links faith and healing (2:5; 5:37, 36; 7:29; 9:14-29). In v. 52a the word translated "well" (*sozo*) is also the root word for "saved" (see Isa. 6:9-10 for another connection of salvation and "spiritual vision"). "Immediately" (Mark's favorite word, with over forty occurrences in the gospel) the blind man not only sees, but follows Jesus "on the way." He becomes a disciple as he uses his sight to follow. He is another instance of the healed becoming disciples of Jesus (1:29-31; 5:18) and of faith from unexpected quarters (7:24-30; 9:14-27).

In his study *Other Followers of Jesus: Minor Characters as Major Figures in Mark's Gospel*, Joel Williams points out that, as a narrator, Mark encourages the reader to identify with minor characters in his gospel. Bartimaeus's forms of address to Jesus indicate his insight into Jesus' identity. With the gift of physical sight, he follows Jesus. Following Bartimaeus, Williams notes, Mark presents a series of minor characters whose actions display the very values Jesus has tried to teach (12:28-34, 41, 44; 14:3-9). If readers are to identify only with the disciples (as we tend to do at the beginning of Mark's gospel), then they can maintain distance from the expectations of Jesus. In this section of Mark, the disciples do not "get it," and so readers can excuse themselves for their ignorance and lack of response to the demands of discipleship.[29] As a corrective, Mark introduces these minor characters.

As Earl S. Johnson Jr. had pointed out some years prior to Williams's study, Mark 10:46-52 focuses on the persistent faith and confidence that Bartimaeus must have for Jesus to heal him, and this in the context of the blindness of Jesus' disciples. Markan miracles that have faith as the key factor are "designed to assist the Christian as he or she struggles with doubt and unbelief." "Bartimaeus serves as a prototype of the true disciples and provides a model for the Christian who needs to know what it means to see and be saved. After he receives the gift of sight, he follows Jesus on the way."[30]

The focus in the pericope is on faith rather than healing, so the sermon should address faith issues. Certainly behind the text stands Isa. 35:5, which alludes to the identity of Jesus. It is common for Mark to commend faith from unlikely persons, and that may provide entrée for the sermon. Here a "nobody on the road of life" takes the initiative to cry out to Jesus, who responds with three things that every human being needs: recognition, restoration to productive life, and purpose, which in this case is to become a disciple, a follower of Jesus.

For Further Reading

Paul J. Achtemeier, "And He Followed Him . . ." *Semeia* 11 (1978): 115–45.

Mary Ann Beavis, "From the Margin to the Way: A Feminist Reading of the Story of Bartimaeus," *Journal of Feminist Studies in Religion* 1 (1998): 19–39.

Earl S. Johnson Jr., "Mark 10:46-52: Blind Bartimaeus," *CBQ* 40 (1978): 191–204.

Vernon K. Robbins, "The Healing of Blind Bartimaeus (10:46-52) in Marcan Theology," *JBL* 92 (1973): 224–43.

Joel F. Williams, *Other Followers of Jesus: Minor Characters as Major Figures in Mark's Gospel*, JSNTSup 102 (Sheffield: JSOT Press, 1994), chap. 4, "The Characterization of Blind Bartimaeus in Mark 10:46-52."

Summary

Mark 8:22—10:52 exhibits careful structuring, with special attention to the role of disciples and to suffering in the life of Jesus. Thus it relates the approaching passion of Jesus to two problems in Mark's church: that of persecution and martyrdom (8:34-38) and that of the desire for status and domination (9:33-37 and 10:35-45).[31] When we read 10:46-52, we encounter a man who takes the initiative to come to Jesus and who confesses his identity and follows him. In short, we encounter one who understands who Jesus is and what his message means. Narratively, then, the way is prepared; the time is ripe for Jesus to go to Jerusalem with its inevitable violence.

At this point, it is very clear that there is no discipleship without suffering. For Mark, Jesus' suffering is the key to the meaning of his life. And so it will be for his disciples. But before the climactic scene of Jesus' crucifixion, Mark provides one more block of Jesus' teaching, chapters 11 through 13.

7

The Ministry around Jerusalem
Mark 11–13

Introduction

As noted at the end of the previous chapter, the confession of blind Bartimaeus in Mark 10:46-52 is the narrative preparation for Jesus' entry into Jerusalem. Chapters 1–8 of the Gospel occur in and around Galilee. In 8–10 Jesus and his disciples are presented as constantly traveling; discipleship is learned "on the way." Chapters 11–16 occur in and around Jerusalem, particularly in the temple precincts. The ministry of Jesus in Jerusalem is a great Markan irony. For most Jews in first-century Palestine, going to Jerusalem meant going to meet God, going to a holy place, the Second Temple, the locus of God's presence with God's people. For Jesus, going to Jerusalem is going to a place of religious corruption, personal rejection, and death. The reader has known since 10:32-33 that Jerusalem is the place of Jesus' death—ironically, his "going to God."

Many commentators have noted that chapters 11–16 of Mark are clearly set off as Jesus' final week in Jerusalem. The schema is as follows:

Sun.	Entry into Jerusalem	11:1-11
Mon.	Fig Tree/Temple	11:12-19
Tue.	Discourses	11:20—13:37
Wed.	Anointing/Betrayal	14:1-11
Thu.	Passover Prep./Last Supper	14:12-72
	Gethsemane/Arrest/Trial	
Fri.	Trial/Condemnation/Crucifixion	15:1-41
Sat.	Jesus in the Tomb	15:42-47
Sun.	Resurrection	16:1-8

Chapters 11 to 13 represent the "Sunday through Tuesday" section of the week.[1] The material falls into five large sections as follows:

Triumphal Entry	11:1-11
Fig Tree and Temple Cleansing	11:12-25
Discourses	11:27—13:37
Controversy Dialogues	11:27—12:44
Apocalyptic Discourse	13:1-37

Since the symbol of the temple and conflict with the Jewish leadership dominate chapters 11 to 13, I introduce the material with a word about the temple now and close it with a note on Jesus and the Jewish leadership. The temple that Jesus and the disciples approached was Herod's temple, or the Second Temple. It was not nearly as large or splendid as Solomon's but had recently been refurbished by Herod the Great (37–4 B.C.), thus the disciple's remark in 13:1. For Israel, the temple symbolized God's presence with the people, Israel's cultic life, and the forgiveness of sins. For Mark, the temple symbolized Israel itself. Perhaps for this reason, Mark's Jesus is extremely critical of the temple. He generally attacks the groups he encounters there. As I intend to show presently, in this context, Jesus' remarks in 12:41-44 are more critical of the temple than they are commendatory of the widow; with 12:38-40, the passage is an attack on the temple system. Jesus' criticism culminates in 13:2 with a prediction of the Temple's destruction.

In a very helpful article on the temple theme in Mark, John Paul Heil argues that the audience of Mark's Gospel is being led by the evangelist to replace temple practice with doing what Jesus has asked of disciples.[2] Temple is replaced by discipleship. Similarly, in her book on Mark 11, Sharyn Dowd argues that Mark is commending a spirituality that shifts the devotional focus of believers from the temple as a place to prayer as a practice.[3] It seems clear that Mark's Gospel is moving toward supplanting the temple, which makes both historical and theological sense if the Gospel is written during the Jewish War or at about the time of the destruction of Jerusalem in A.D. 70.

One final general issue is of note. There are more quotations of and allusions to Hebrew scripture in Mark 11–16 than in 1–10. In his article on the subject, Howard C. Kee notes fifty-seven quotations and 160 allusions in the section.[4] Both Jewish scriptural traditions and commonplaces of religious thought in Jesus' world seem more important in the final week of Jesus' life (as the tradition preserved it and as Mark depicts it). Mark gravitates toward eschatological passages and usually quotes the LXX, often blending two unrelated passages (what Kee calls "merged quotations"[5]), which are synthesized in such a way that a new assertion is made. By this means Mark is especially keen to depict suffering as part of the divine plan and a precondition for the age of fulfillment. When preaching from Mark 11–13, then, it is particularly important to check scriptural quotations and allusions, for as Kee's article demonstrates, Mark is consciously appealing to scripture, which he understands to be fulfilled in Jesus.

11:1-11

In Mark's Gospel, 11:1-11 opens a new section that describes Jesus' final days in Jerusalem. Traditionally the text is understood in light of Zech. 9:9 (quoted in Matt. 21:5 and John 12:15), but it also reflects triumphal-entry traditions in the Greco-Roman world, especially the "epiphany procession," which featured the presence of a deity who received hymnic acclamation and included both the entry itself and a subsequent sacrifice.[6] Behind the messianic figure of Jesus, here Mark may also have intended to introduce the figure of God as a "Divine Warrior" (see, for example, Zech. 14).

The Mount of Olives (v. 1), which in Jewish tradition was associated with the coming of the Messiah (but also with Israel's defeat, cf. 2 Sam. 15:13-30), is east of Jerusalem and would, indeed, be the route into the city from Jericho (10:46). The fact that Mark reverses the geographical order of the villages (from Jericho one comes to Bethany before Bethphage) suggests his lack of personal acquaintance with the area. (Recall the "scrambled geography" of chapters 6 to 8.) Verses 2 to 6 focus on finding a colt and have a great many scriptural associations. Num. 19:2; Deut. 21:3; and 1 Sam. 6:7 all speak of unused animals for religious purposes, although Zech. 9:9 is most often cited in connection with the verses. Some commentators think the verses represent a "minor miracle" story in that Jesus seems to have supernatural knowledge of the animal's location and is able to ride an unbroken animal. The great detail about where the animal is found (v. 4) suggests eyewitness tradition. (Was Peter one of the "two disciples" of v. 1, Mark's source?) Note that the colt is being borrowed, not stolen (v. 3), a point important to the bystanders in vv. 5-6. Jesus' use of the designation "the Lord" in v. 3 is the term's loftiest use in Mark and is for some scholars evidence that Jesus is accepting messianic status. We might note, historically, that a king has the right and authority to commandeer an animal and that an "ass" (*polon*, "colt," "young donkey," "foal of an ass") was an appropriate mount for a Middle-Eastern king. Theologically, it is good to note that when Jesus speaks and is obeyed, things turn out well.

Verses 8-10 exhibit many features of Greco-Roman entrance processions as well as features from Zech. 14 (and perhaps observances during the Feast of Tabernacles). The NRSV helpfully translates *stibadas*, "leafy branches." Palm branches (which are mentioned in John 12:13) are native to Jericho but not Jerusalem, where branches from olive trees would be more likely. The point, of course, is that of smoothing the road as a matter of homage to a king (Isa. 40:3-5) and was a feature of Israel's festival processions (2 Kings 9:13; 1 Macc. 13:51). The fact that some people were "ahead" and some "following" (here used in a physical sense) suggests a long procession. "Hosanna" represents "the Aramaic *hosha'-na*, the Hebrew of Ps. 118:25 . . . 'save Thou now!', a petition addressed to God."[7] "Hosanna" is a cry of help to God or to the king. (See the Hallel, Ps. 118:25-26b, part of one of the praise songs sung at Passover.)

Similarly David is invoked in v. 10 because of the messianic kingdom promised to his son (2 Sam. 7:11-14). That his kingdom is "coming" means that it is no longer in the distant future; it is near or "on the way." It certainly seems to be the case that Jesus is accepting his public messianic role. Verse 11 is without parallel in Matthew or Luke. (It is John who tells us that Jesus stayed in Bethany with Mary, Martha, and Lazarus.) Note that Jesus goes first to the temple, the very heart of Israel, and then, because of the lateness of the hour, returns to Bethany. (And perhaps because of the crowds in the city, he was unable to secure lodging there.)

Scholarship is divided on whether for Mark this account is a story of failure or of confirmation of Jesus' identity. Is Mark depicting the disciples' belief that this is the grand entrance of the messianic king and a show of popular support for Jesus' messiahship? Certainly Passover time (14:1) was a time when the hopes of deliverance were strong, and for this reason there was a strong Roman military presence in Jerusalem at Passover season. And this raises a historical question. Why was there no official intervention in such a boisterous show of support for a new king? Some have argued that no official intervention suggests that no Roman official saw any threat that Jesus was a king. (Certainly there will be no reference to this "triumphal entry" at Jesus' trial.) Morna Hooker believes that this story is only superficially a "success story." For Mark, she argues, this begins a story of failure, "the failure of Israel and of her leaders to worship and serve God, and her failure to receive his Messiah."[8]

The "triumphal entry" of Jesus into Jerusalem is, of course, traditionally chosen by Protestants as the Gospel lesson for the Sunday before Easter. In fact, in Year B of the lectionaries, the first Gospel lesson is not this text but Mark's passion account. (In the Episcopal lectionary, Mark 11:1-11 is the Gospel that accompanies Proper 29 for the Sunday closest to 11/23). The problem with using this as the primary preaching text on the Sunday before Easter is that instead of seeing Jesus' time in Jerusalem as *bracketed* by victory (an earthly victory at the beginning and a heavenly victory at the end), most churchgoers who, alas, will not attend most of the Holy Week services (or belong to churches that do not hold such liturgies) miss the very real conflict and suffering through which final victory is won. And, as I have noted, this conflict and suffering are very much Mark's concern and are crucial to his understanding of Jesus.

In preaching the text we should take the historical ambiguity seriously. Certainly, Mark has narratively clearly alluded to messianic texts and figures. But was Jesus so received? Perhaps the most responsible preaching focuses on the fickleness of crowds. The crowds who cry, "Hosanna!" here will in a few short days cry, "Crucify!" The story that begins so well on such a high note ends quite wrongly, with a crucifixion rather than a coronation. Perhaps in contrast to the fickleness of the crowds, the preacher might lift up the obedience of the two disciples (v. 1) who, in following Jesus' instructions (vv. 2-3) to the letter, receive a happy outcome. In any case, if the text is chosen as the primary Gospel for the Sunday before Easter, it should be preached in full knowledge of the conflict and suffering that follows for Jesus and the disciples in the intervening days *before* the victory of resurrection.

11:12-25

It is extremely important to read and interpret Mark 11:12-25 as a single unit of thought; otherwise vv. 12-14 and 20-21 present an almost insurmountable christological problem: Jesus seems a "divine spoiled brat," more akin to the Jesus of the apocryphal Gospels than to what we have learned of him heretofore in Mark. Without its context, vv. 12-14 is a "miracle of destruction," and Jesus is entirely out of character. The block of material seems a clear Markan intercalation; the two parts of the fig tree episode (vv. 12-14 and 20-25/26) bracket the cleansing of the temple (vv. 15-19). Victor of Antioch, who was, so far as we know, in the fifth century the first commentator on Mark's Gospel, understood this material as a unit and suggested that Mark used the fig tree to set forth the judgment that was about to fall on Jerusalem. (Victor expects us to know that in Jeremiah 7 the fig tree was a symbol of Israel.) In my view this is still the best approach to the material.

In 11:12-14, Jesus and the disciples ("they") are apparently going from Bethany into Jerusalem (11:11). Beginning with v. 12, Mark supplies temporal references that allow us to trace Jesus' movements during the week (see the introduction to this chapter). As is characteristic of Mark, he provides a motivation for Jesus ("he was hungry") in v. 12 that shows us Jesus' very human side. Verse 13 says Jesus sees in the distance a fig tree "in leaf" which, indeed, it would have been in Passover season. When Jesus draws closer to it, he finds it without figs, "for it was not the season for figs," and he curses the tree (v. 14). The last phrase of v. 13 is extremely problematic. Why would Jesus curse a tree for not having figs when it was not the right time of year for figs?

F. F. Bruce quotes W. M. Christie, a Church of Scotland minister serving in Palestine, who observed that fig trees begin to leaf at the end of

March. At this time small knobs appear on the trees that, while not figs, are their early forerunners. Their appearance signals the coming of real figs about six weeks later. If foliage appears without any of these knobs (*taqsh* in Arabic), it is a sign that there will be no figs on the tree. "Since Jesus found 'nothing but leaves' . . . he knew that 'it was an absolutely hopeless, fruitless fig tree,' and said as much."[9] If Christie is correct, he gives a tidy, naturalistic explanation for the seemingly enigmatic words of Jesus.

Textual commentators, on the other hand, generally take one of two tacks to address the issue.[10] Either they explain that the text has been tampered with, or they resort to a symbolic explanation. Richard H. Hiers suggests in his article on the phrase that what we have in vv. 12-14 is an "acted out parable."[11] Hiers explains that the way Jesus entered Jerusalem suggests he was expecting the arrival of the messianic age. If Jesus entered Jerusalem with the expectation that the "age of blessedness" was about to begin, then he could expect fruit on a tree out of season, because in the messianic age, nature is always fruitful (Ezek. 36:35; 47:12). Jesus has accepted Bartimaeus's acclimation (10:48), entered Jerusalem in a messianic way (11:1-10; Zech. 9:9) and is thus in a messianic, "end of the ages" frame of mind when he approaches the tree. Alternatively, on the basis of Pliny's notation that the fig tree is the only tree whose leaf forms later than its fruit (*Historia naturalis* 16:49), Wendy Cotter thinks Mark presents Jesus' expectation of the tree in v. 13 as reasonable.[12] The phrase in v. 13d is a "backwards explanation," explaining not 13c but 13b. Cotter argues this syntactical explanation on the basis of 16:3b-4b, which she explains has a construction parallel to 11:13.

My own tendency is to follow a metaphorical line of interpretation and to understand the cursing of the fig tree as a "sign act" like that of the prophets (cf. the parable in Luke 13:6-9). This involves reading vv. 12-14 in the wider context of vv. 12-25. In Mark 11:15-19, then, Mark presents the episode of Jesus' cleansing the temple. Jesus and the disciples continue on their journey from Bethany into Jerusalem and go directly to the temple (v. 15). Jesus is interested in the temple, not the city per se, because of all the temple represents (see the introduction to this chapter). The temple's "sin" (if it can be so described) appears in vv. 15-16. First, it had become a center of trade. People came to the temple to make sacrifices, and the sacrificial animals had to be bought with temple currency. Since Roman money had the head of the emperor on it, it could not be used to purchase sacrificial animals or to pay the temple tax. Roman currency had to be exchanged for temple currency, making the temple not only a marketplace but a currency exchange. Part of Jesus' problem with this is that the outer court of the temple, the "Court of the Gentiles," was the only place in the temple compound where Gentiles could pray. Knowing this provides a link to 11:22-25, which deals with prayer.

Second, v. 16 suggests that the temple was also being used as a short-cut. *Berakoth* 9.5 of the Talmud expressly forbids the temple to be so used. The Greek phrase is *tis dienegke skeuos dia tou hierou* (literally, anyone should [or might] carry a vessel through the temple [or holy place]). The word *skeuos* (vessel) is also used specifically of temple vessels, leading some commentators to see Jesus as attacking the temple cult itself and not just misuses of the temple. The temple was intended as "a house of prayer for all the nations" (Isa. 56:7) but has been made "a den of robbers" (Jer. 7:11). This is an example of what Kee calls Mark's "merged quotations" (see the introduction to this chapter). The Court of the Gentiles was the place where "the nations" were to be included in Israel's worship life, but the marketplace atmosphere there had made it a robber's den. This suggests that the money exchange and animal sales were "shady." Mark's is the only Gospel to include the phrase "for all the nations" in the quotation from Isaiah. It is further evidence of his interest in a Gentile mission. Lightfoot comments as follows:

> even before the arrival of the messianic king the Gentiles had been allowed certain privileges upon the threshold of the temple, and of these the Jewish authorities . . . had allowed them to be robbed; must it not therefore be the first act of the messianic king on his arrival to restore to Gentiles at least those religious rights and privileges which ought already to be theirs, especially if, as would surely happen with the coming of Messiah, Jewish worship would now become a universal worship?[13]

Verse 18 makes clear that the controversies that follow (11:27—12:37) have their origin in Jesus' criticism of the temple. The verse is chilling, since it depicts those who were to function religiously on behalf of Israel as conspirators in murder. It also continues the picture of Jesus' popular appeal that was begun in 11:1-10. Like other pilgrims, only a few of whom could find lodging in Jerusalem when its population increased during Passover, Jesus is lodged outside the city (v. 19) in Bethany (v. 11, less than two miles from the temple mount over the Mount of Olives), to which he returns. I noted in the commentary on 11:1-11 the historical problem of the lack of official response to Jesus' triumphal entry into Jerusalem. There is a similar problem here. It seems odd that a disturbance like this in the temple is not addressed by the Romans, especially since the Antonia Fortress overlooked the temple.

The closing bracket of the intercalation, 11:20-25, explains the lesson of the fig tree (vv. 12-14) and is used as a means to introduce Jesus' teaching on prayer. Again in v. 20, Mark introduces a clear temporal reference (11:11, 12, 19). Returning to Jerusalem the day after the temple cleansing, the disciples ("they," v. 20) notice the tree Jesus cursed (v. 14) was "withered away to its roots," that is, completely destroyed. Once again, Peter serves as the "mouthpiece" for the disciples (8:29, 33; 10:28). Jesus' response in vv. 22-25 does not appear to be connected to the tree but to the issue of faith and answered prayer. Many commentators think that vv. 22-25 were originally an independent unit of material that Mark has inserted for his own purposes at this point. Verses 22-23 are often cited as an authentic saying of Jesus.

In her important study of this passage, Sharyn Dowd explains that Jesus' teaching on prayer follows the temple pericope because in the ancient world prayer was associated with places, with temples.[14] The problem for Mark's original audience after the destruction of the Jerusalem temple in A.D. 70 would have been, "if there is no temple, does the God of Israel still hear prayer?" Jesus' teaching stresses that faith and *attitude*, not location, is what is critical in prayer. The most important point comes first: "Have faith in God" (v. 22). Faith in prayer "moves mountains" (v. 23), which we are to take as a metaphor for the miraculous things faithful prayer can effect (cf., as well, Ps. 46:2). Jesus seems to be saying that prayer is answered in proportion to the conviction (the faithfulness) of the one who prays, although I think the unstated idea must be that faith moves mountains according to God's will. What God wills is always possible for God (even throwing mountains into the sea) and for the one who is in God's will.

There is, as well, a connection between this teaching on prayer and the eschatological/messianic theme in vv. 12-19. At this point, Jesus and his disciples are probably walking on the Mount of Olives. On the Day of the Lord, the Mount of Olives was to be the site of a violent earthquake (Zech. 14:4). "If Jesus had this . . . in mind on his way across the Mount of Olives, his meaning might have been, 'If you have sufficient faith in God, the Day of the Lord will come sooner than you think.'"[15]

The point about praying in God's will is important pastorally. If, for example, a man prays fervently and faithfully that his wife's diagnosis of breast cancer not be fatal, and if she dies, does that mean that he did not have faith enough to save her? Shall we add guilt to his grief? I know the matter is very complex. It may not be very consoling pastorally to imply that it was not God's will that someone be spared death from cancer. What does *that* say about God? Only what we already know: that God's ways are mysterious (Isa. 55:8-9).

It is probably the word "prayer" in v. 24 that leads Mark to introduce the saying of v. 25 at this point. "Standing" was the normal position of prayer (1 Kings 8:22; Luke 18:11, 13). In substance, v. 25 is the "residue" of the Lord's Prayer (Matt. 6:7-15) in Mark's Gospel, which does not record it. The point is that we cannot be in proper relationship to God in prayer unless we are in right relationship to others. Taken as a whole, then, vv. 22-25 make three assertions about prayer: it must not be half-hearted; it must be faithful and full of conviction; and it must exclude any uncharitableness toward others.[16] (Verse 26 is omitted. It is probably an insertion by early scribes to make Mark's text conform to Matt. 6:15.)

Seen as a whole, 11:12-25 is perhaps the crucial text for understanding the spirituality of Mark's Gospel. The cursing of the fig tree in vv. 12-14 is best understood as an "enacted parable," a metaphorical way in which Jesus is showing the fall of the temple. The reasons for the temple's destruction are set forth in vv. 15-19, in which Jesus' actions are again to be understood not only literally but metaphorically. As the Coming One, Jesus has the authority (which is at issue in 11:27-33) to destroy the temple (cf. 14:57-59). Lightfoot thinks that "the cleansing is, according to St. Mark, the great act of the Lord as the messianic king on His arrival at His Father's house."[17] Subsequently, Peter (who represents all the disciples) seems to misunderstand the meaning of the withered fig tree (v. 21), which gives Jesus further opportunity to teach (vv. 22-25). (Recall that this was the pattern of the three passion predictions in 8:22—10:52: misunderstanding followed by teaching.) His teaching is about prayer, because Mark understands that for disciples of Jesus, prayer takes the place of temple worship. Spiritually, disciples of Jesus abandon religious places and practices that have become corrupt. For them, Jesus commends faithful, wholehearted prayer offered in a condition of peace with others. The community of Jesus' disciples is a community of forgiveness.

This unit of material, though difficult and requiring quite a bit of explanation for most parishioners, is remarkably fruitful for preaching. It can be used to raise the issue of "righteous anger." How does the Christian define righteous anger? Indeed, how does he or she deal with anger at all? Usually not very well, I expect. (Anger is especially difficult for women, who are socialized not to feel it, much less express it.) Another gut feeling the text highlights is fear. Verse 18 suggests that the chief priests plot against Jesus out of their own fear (of loss of power?). Theologically the text raises the question of the relationship of temple worshippers (Jews) and followers of Jesus (Christians). However this issue is treated, the preacher must be exquisitely careful to avoid any hint of anti-Semitism. I would suggest that in vv. 15-19 the issue is not the temple itself but the uses to which it has been put by persons with ungodly motivations. This series of texts also cries out for a christological sermon that explains Jesus' odd behavior in vv. 12-14 and his only act of violence in Mark's Gospel, described in vv. 15-19. Finally, and this may be the most theologically difficult matter, the text can address Christian prayer. Since prayer itself has become the "house of prayer for all nations," what guarantees its efficacy? How do we deal with prayer which *seems* to go unanswered? (I say "seems" because "no" is an answer to prayer, although one we usually dislike.)

For Further Reading

Sharyn Dowd, *Prayer, Power, and the Problem of Suffering*, SBLDS 105 (Atlanta: Scholars, 1988).

Richard Hiers, "Not the Season for Figs," *JBL* 87 (1968): 394–400.

R. R. Lightfoot, *The Gospel Message of St. Mark* (Oxford: Oxford Univ. Press, 1962), chap. 5, "The Cleansing of the Temple in St. Mark's Gospel."

11:27—12:12

As Anderson's commentary notes, Mark has fused "the cleansing of the temple and the cursing of the fig tree together, and makes them the introduction to a new series of controversies with Judaism and its leaders."[18] (For more on this conflict, see the summary of this chapter.) Mark characteristically presents blocks of material of the same literary type (2:1-3, 6; 4:1-34; 4:35—5:43). Jesus' public ministry opened with a series of controversy stories (2:1—3:6), and it closes in a similar fashion (11:27—12:27). Although the lectionaries and most translations break the material into shorter units, Mark 11:27 through chapter 13 is one long day in which Jesus teaches within sight of the temple. He is approached by persons representing the major groups within Judaism: chief priests, scribes, and elders (11:27); Pharisees and Herodians (12:13—these two would, of course, normally have been enemies, but Jesus' power and popularity is such that enemies align against him); and Sadducees (12:18). As the miracles of 4:35—5:43 depict the extent of Jesus' authority in the world, the controversies of 11:27—12:37 depict his authority within Judaism. By this collation of controversy stories, Mark demonstrates how Jesus confounds all the official opposition to him and depicts Jesus as taking center stage in the central place of worship.

In his first encounter with officialdom, Jesus is questioned by scribes (the accredited teachers of Judaism), chief priests (Judaism's ruling hierarchy), and elders (the Sanhedrin), the three groups that constituted Jewish authority. They react to the temple cleansing, as well they might, by asking who gave the authority for it. The question in v. 28 is probably understood to be rhetorical, since they thought they *were* the authority figures (cf. John 2:18). Jesus refuses to take the bait and responds in rabbinical style with another question: "Was John's baptism from heaven (that is, from God) or of human origin?" (vv. 29-30). F. F. Bruce notes that Jesus is testing them "to see if they were capable of recognizing divine authority when they saw it."[19]

The question sparks a debate among the priests, scribes, and elders (vv. 31-32). They "argued with one another" (*dielogizonto,* literally "they were debating," which is the same word Mark used in 2:6, 8 when the scribes questioned Jesus' authority). If Jesus' interlocutors respond "from heaven," then John the Baptist, who had pointed to Jesus as one greater than himself, had the same source of authority that they, themselves, felt they had. If John's baptism is from heaven, then in opposing Jesus, they are opposing God. On the other hand, if John's baptism is from earth, then they stand opposed to the popular verdict, that John was, indeed, a prophet. So Jesus would be the greater one. The disingenuous answer they give Jesus is "we don't know" (v. 33a). To those who will not commit themselves to a truthful answer, Jesus refuses to respond directly. St. John Chrysostom notes that Jesus does not say "I do not know" (which is the dishonest answer of his opponents), but "I do not tell." Nevertheless, he does, in fact, "tell" in the parable that follows.

The parable in 12:1-11 certainly assumes knowledge of Isa. 5:1-7, the "song of the vineyard," in which God does everything possible for the vineyard (Israel), which nevertheless produces "wild grapes" and is destroyed.[20] It is addressed to "them," the priests, scribes, and elders of 11:27, who can hardly fail to understand the reference. In this extended comparison, the vineyard in vv. 1-9 is Israel, the owner is God, and the tenants must be Israel's leaders. The slaves sent to the tenants are the prophets, and we are certainly to understand the "son" (v. 6, the "only" or "beloved" son, *huion agapeton* as in 1:11) as Jesus himself. So the parable is not only an allegory of salvation history but another, albeit veiled, passion prediction of Jesus (which will be acted out in the passion narrative that follows in chapters 14–15). Verses 2-8 are a terrifying picture of how violence breeds more violence. The son is not only murdered, which is bad enough since he is legitimate heir of the vineyard, but he is cast out unburied, a particularly horrifying insult (see John 1:11). The point, however, is the tenants' failure to recognize the legitimate claim of the owner. Verses 10-11 are a verbatim quotation of Ps. 118:22-23, which was interpreted later by Christians as a messianic text and a picture of Jesus' rejection.

The Jewish authorities may not be straightforward, but they are not stupid. They realized that Jesus "had told this parable against them," v. 12 (cf. 4:11-13). Their response to Jesus is exactly as it was in 11:18 and 32 (are they perhaps some of the same people encountered there?); they want to get Jesus out of the way but are afraid to act directly because of his popularity with the crowd. Note that once again their motivation for action is fear. Mark's Gospel consistently sees faith and fear, not faith and unbelief, as opposites.[21] Those who exhibit faith receive a variety of blessings. Those who are fearful generally behave foolishly or, in this case, in an evil manner. Jesus has outmaneuvered his questioners. Round one goes to him. From here until the end of chapter 13, we see him responding to questions and teaching with authority.

The controversy dialogue (11:27-33) raises the very important question of religious or ecclesial authority. Where is true authority to be found today? In a religious hierarchy? In popular opinion or consensus? (Recall what happens in 15:1-15 when the "authority" bows to popular opinion.) Is it in personal opinion? What principles help us determine true authority today? F. F. Bruce's comment on 11:33 is worth pondering: "There are some people who will demand authority for truth itself, forgetting that truth is the highest authority."[22] Another sermon found in Jesus' parabolic response (12:1-11) would deal with the failure of stewardship of the church, which is representative of religious authority for us. If the priests, scribes, and elders represented God's tenants, then the church is God's tenant now. Like them, we can easily forget that we are tenants and not owners. How do we treat God's messengers? Are we a fruitful vineyard? What would it mean to be fruitful? Verse 9 and the quotations from the Psalms point to the fact that God's people must be open to new revelations in history. Are we open to the new ways God might use to communicate with us?

For Further Reading
J. Keller, "Jesus and the Critics," *Int* 40 (1986): 29–38.

12:13-17

Behind this controversy story stands an important issue for the Jewish community before the Jewish War of A.D. 66–70. Should they pay the poll tax? Imperial provinces of the Roman Empire paid a poll tax directly to the emperor. It was not a large tax, but it was a symbol of subjection to Rome, and the coins with which it was paid bore the image of the emperor. And, of course, this tax was in addition to other Roman taxes and the temple tax. Some sources estimate that as much as 40 percent of the very modest income of first-century Palestinian Jews was paid out in taxes. The question of paying taxes is of more import in Jerusalem than in Galilee, where taxes were paid to a Jewish tetrarch.

Jesus is approached by an odd duo, Pharisees and Herodians, sent by the chief priests, scribes, and elders. ("They" in v. 13 refers back to 12:1 and 11:27.) Pharisees were known for their intense loyalty to Judaism, and thus to the nation of Israel, and for their strong objection to any foreign rule.[23] Herodians, on the other hand, were a political party that supported Herod, whose power came from Rome.[24] Ordinarily these two groups would oppose each other, although Mark aligned them previously in 3:6.[25] Their alliance here signals both the threat that Jesus represented and the insincerity with which they approach him. They come, not to seek wise counsel, but "to trap him in what he said" (v. 13). "Trap" (*agreusosin*), used only here in the New Testament, is found in the papyri in the context of hunting and fishing.

Their question (vv. 14-15a) was not only a pressing one for observant Jews in the first century (see above) but is intended to impale Jesus on the horns of a dilemma. If he answers no (an answer pleasing to the Pharisees), then the Herodians can denounce him to Pilate as a revolutionary. If he says yes (an answer pleasing to the Herodians), then he loses popular support. (Mark probably also understood another point to be at issue here, that of the charge later to be brought against Jesus at his trial that he claimed to be a king.) Although this is clearly a trick question, Jesus' opponents do recognize his honesty and his refusal to pander to others when approaching difficult issues (v. 14). (Alternatively, Gundry notes "the greater the flattery, the greater Jesus' ability to see through it."[26]) The NRSV says Jesus shows "deference to no one," which, of course, is a characteristic of God, who shows no partiality (Acts 11:34; Rom. 2:11; Col. 3:25).

Jesus' response (vv. 15b-17) both takes into account their hypocrisy (*hypokrisis*, literally means "acting"[27]) and exhibits his characteristic rabbinic mode (cf. 11:29). That he asks for a denarius is interesting and adds an ambiguous note to the encounter. A denarius was a silver coin; common coinage was copper. Do they have to go and get one, or does Mark imply that they have one? And if they have one, they are really caught up short, both because it bears the head of the emperor (and a Latin inscription that reads "Tiberius Caesar Augustus, son of the divine Augustus"!) and because Jews were not to make "graven images" (Exod. 20:4), so having such a coin implies commerce with Rome. This is why, in v. 16, Jesus focuses on the image on the coin.

Jesus' verbal answer (v. 17) says, in effect, "the coin bears Caesar's image; it must be Caesar's," but it is a both/and answer rather than an either/or answer. On one level it recognizes the legitimate claims of government ("give to the emperor the things that are the emperor's"), but on the other it implies that *everything* is ultimately God's ("and to God the things that are God's"). What good Jew would be able to name anything that is outside the realm of God the Creator's sovereignty? (see Ps. 24:1). Interestingly, the Pharisees and Herodians had used the word for "pay" in v. 14 (*dounai*), but Jesus' response uses the word "give" (*apodote*, literally "give back" or "return"), which implies that what is offered to God was God's originally and is God's anyhow. (This is what Anglicans and Episcopalians say in the liturgy as their offerings are brought to the altar: "All things come of thee, O Lord, and of thine own do we give thee.") More subtly, Jesus tries to avoid a conflict of duties (which is the root of the "trick"). What he says is that one should try to fulfill any given duty in a way that is consistent with all the others. (Recall the controversy in 7:1-13.) Finally, then, 12:13-17 is a "pronouncement story" in which everything is subordinate to Jesus' declaration in v. 17. His questioners' response is amazement. "Even those who have come to trap him in his speech succumb to admiration of his person."[28]

In preaching the sermon on this text one should probably avoid the "obvious" comparison between political obligation and religious loyalty. That is to take the position of the Pharisees and Herodians in the text! (cf. Rom. 13:1-7; 1 Pet. 2:13-17). The more profound issue is the extent of God's "ownership" and obedience to God's requirements. Also significant is the recognition of his interlocutors that Jesus does not "regard people," that he does not answer questions with a view to currying favor with some particular group. An interesting sermon could be built around the comparison of our own decision making—so often influenced by our peer groups, political parties, places of employment, and so forth, and our concern with people-pleasing—with Jesus' singular focus on God (cf. Eph. 6:5-6).

For Further Reading

F. F. Bruce, "Render to Caesar," in *The Hard Sayings of Jesus* (Downers Grove: InterVarsity, 1983), 214–17.

C. H. Giblin, "'The Things of God' in the Question Concerning Tribute to Caesar," *CBQ* 33 (1971): 516–626.

12:18-27

This is Jesus' first encounter with the Sadducees, because they would not normally be found outside Jerusalem, where they were the temple aristocracy. Some scholars think the name "Sadducee" derives from "Zadok," the high priest of King David. They belonged to the hereditary, priestly families and were archconservatives. They accepted as authoritative only the written books of Moses and rejected the oral law (which defined the Pharisees and thus made the two groups opponents). They did not believe in resurrection (which makes their question here insincere), so they understood children to be the only source of immortality. Nor did they believe in angels or heavenly beings. When the temple was destroyed in A.D. 70, the Sadducees were replaced by the Pharisees as Judaism's "elite."[29] The mode of discourse in this encounter is thoroughly Jewish.

In vv. 19-23 the Sadducees present a hypothetical case. At root it is a question about Levirate marriage, the practice of brothers of a deceased man marrying his wife to keep her "in the family" and impregnating his wife to keep his name alive (Deut. 25:5-10). But there is a "twist" in this case; none of the seven brothers of the deceased succeeds in making her pregnant. (Is she barren? Is there a genetic defect in the male line that leads to infertility?) The key issue is childlessness, because a child would both keep the original husband's name, and thus person, alive and determine to whom the wife ultimately belonged.

Verses 24-27 are Jesus' response. His opening gambit raises the level of debate with a counterquestion (cf. 11:29; 12:15) not calculated to "win friends and influence people." He accuses the Sadducees of knowing neither the scripture (their sole source of authority, the Torah, which he quotes) nor the power of God (the two sources that became the basis of early Christian preaching). The Greek construction of v. 24 implies that the answer is yes; they are deceived. First, in v. 25 Jesus assumes resurrection (see the passion predictions in 8:31; 9:9, 31; 10:34) and corrects a materialistic view of it. In resurrection life, he explains, people will not engage in earthly relationships no matter how dear; they will be like the angels (that is, have different bodies and patterns of relationship; compare 1 Cor. 15:35-54), in whom, in any case, the Sadducees do not believe. Jesus is not concerned with issues like legitimacy and inheritance of property. As Morna Hooker notes, "what he is rejecting is . . . the notion that this social contract continues in the resurrection life."[30] Second, in v. 26 Jesus corrects the Sadducean disbelief in resurrection by quoting the Pentateuch (Exod. 3:6), which shows their ignorance of their own scripture. "The accusation is all the more telling in light of the fact that for the Sadducees, the Torah, the five books of Moses, was supremely *the* Scriptures, of greater authority than other Scriptures."[31] The present tense "rise" of v. 25 becomes the passive "are being raised" in v. 26, a "Divine passive"; God does the raising. Finally, in v. 27 Jesus teaches that relationship with God is not limited by time or material existence. God does not stop being the patriarchs' God just because they die. In whatever state human beings (or former humans!) find themselves, God is still living; God is still God. "Jesus grounds the resurrection in the nature of God, not in the nature of human being."[32]

The real issue here is not the poor woman (more on this momentarily) and her deceased husband's family, but whether the dead will be raised. Jesus comes down emphatically on the side of resurrection, which aligns him with the Pharisees with whom we often see him in conflict in the Synoptic Gospels. He argues for resurrection on the basis of the fact that there is new life to come (v. 26), that it will be a new order of existence (v. 25), and that what really matters is fellowship with God, which is sustained (by God's love) forever (v. 27).

In the early church this passage was frequently used to discourage second marriages. In our day it might well be preached with a focus on the woman in the Sadducees' example (vv. 19-23). How would this poor bereaved woman feel as she is passed as a sexual partner from brother to brother? She clearly has no say in the matter in the patriarchal family structure. One of the important implications of Jesus' response (vv. 24-27) is that women are not to be treated or used as possessions. Jesus rejects a view of women that makes them pawns in a male theological game, objects to be man-handled. That, with its contemporary implications, makes a powerful "family values" sermon.

Alternatively, the sermon focused on this text can herald the hope of resurrection. It can be used to correct a common mistake that, like these Sadducees, many Christians make: thinking of the future life, the resurrection life, as simply an extension of this one. The apostle Paul spoke to this issue in 1 Corinthians 15 with his metaphor of "earthly bodies" and "heavenly bodies." Jesus gives wonderful assurance that there *is* a resurrection life. He does not say we will not recognize our near and dear, or that personality will not continue in that life. He does suggest that there will be a new state of being in which our ties to one another will be different from what they are now. Belief in the resurrection of the dead is central to Christian doctrine (which is why it appears in our creeds) and a fundamental point of hope for Christian living. As Paul says, "If for this life only we have hoped in Christ, we are of all people most to be pitied" (1 Cor. 15:19). The reality of the resurrection should be preached and proclaimed much more frequently than it is in our day. Preaching on the resurrection provides good pastoral care to congregations.

For Further Reading

J. G. Janzen, "Resurrection and Hermeneutics: On Exodus 3:6 and Mark 12:26," *JSNT* 23 (1985): 43–58.

12:28-34

This pericope marks a subtle shift in material. From the combative questioners in 11:27—12:27, the narrative moves to a person whose question seems genuine. Mark does not make him an emissary of the chief priests, scribes, and elders, nor is there any "fishy" relationship between his role (scribe) and his question. That question is essentially like the one asked by the rich man in 10:17-28. Behind the question in 12:28 stands the fact that, by the first century, rabbis counted 613 individual statutes in the law and differentiated between those that were "heavy" and those that were "light." So it was no small matter to decide if there were one basic principle in the law.

Jesus' response in vv. 29-31 begins with the Shema, the Jewish confession of faith that was used at the beginning of morning and evening prayer in the temple (Deut. 6:4-5) and daily in the prayers of pious Jews. It stresses the oneness of God and the absolute priority of love for God. This love is to proceed from the whole person: heart (*kardia*, an expression for the whole person and understood to be the seat of will and intellect), soul (*psuche*, the soul or life principle, the seat of desire), mind (*dianoia*, seat of understanding and used in the LXX synonymously for *kardia*), and strength (*ischus*, understood as spiritual strength). What God requires of humans, Jesus suggests, is consonant with God's nature, which is love. And then Jesus gives the scribe a bonus, his view of the second most important commandment, which extends love from God to neighbor (see Lev. 19:18 where, however, "neighbor" seems to mean "fellow Jew"). Loving God naturally spills over to loving neighbor. Other similar formulations existed at the time; one is attributed to Rabbi Akiba (and see Paul in Gal. 5:14; Rom. 13:8; James 2:8).

The scribe recognizes Jesus' wisdom and affirms it with scriptural quotations (vv. 32-33; see Deut. 4:35, 39; Hos. 6:6). In fact, he extends the scope of what Jesus suggests. Jesus has compared laws with other laws; the scribe adds regulations about sacrificial offerings to law. The scribe introduces a theological theme in Mark's Gospel: that loving God and neighbor is more important than the cultic activity in the temple. (Remember that the setting of this exchange is still the temple, 11:27.) Jesus and this scribe seem to have come to a mutually respectful agreement, and this is important to remember: Jesus is not anti-Jewish, and his exchanges with Jewish officials are not universally negative. Jesus commends the scribe; "he answered wisely" (*nounechos*, intelligently or thoughtfully, used only here in the New Testament). The scribe is "not far from the kingdom of God," the reign of God that Jesus' coming signals and the subject of his teaching and preaching (1:15).

Although three more units of material follow in chapter 12, Mark seems to summarize the "temple interrogations" in v. 34b: "After that no one dared to ask him any question." Jesus has encountered the chief priests, the scribes and the elders (11:27ff.), Pharisees and Herodians (12:13ff.), and Sadducees (12:18ff.) and demonstrated his authority to each group by not only prevailing in debate, but by cutting to the heart of the principle involved in each case.[33] The controversy block of material certainly ends here and may, in fact, have concluded at v. 27.

In preaching this text, it is important not to introduce the old cliché that Judaism is about law and Christianity is about grace. This completely misunderstands the Jewish view of law or Torah, and thus Jesus' (and Paul's) view of it. To the Jew, Torah is a gift, God's greatest gift to human beings, because it reveals how humans may be related to God. What is at issue in Mark 12:28-34 is certainly *not* the validity of the law, which both the scribe and Jesus assume. The question is of the basic principle from which the law derived. What is the one, fundamental thing, the building block or cornerstone, on which all the rest of the law rests? (I am reminded here of Jesus' words to Martha in Luke 10:38-42: "there is need of only one thing.")

The text can be the beginning point for a sermon that stresses God's primacy. This is an important principle to stress in a culture where there are so many competing "gods" (the gods of wealth, youth, leisure, success, family, and so forth). Another homiletic possibility is to remind the congregation that this story summarizes a group of encounters, most of which are confrontational. What principles about how to behave and respond when challenged can be abstracted from Jesus' behavior in chapter 12 to this point?

For Further Reading
G. W. Hoyer, "Mk. 12:28-34," *Int* 33 (1979): 293–98.

12:35-44

Mark seems to have grouped these three pericopae together using a catchword principle. Although it is not confrontational, the conversation with the scribe in 12:28-34 introduces the word "scribe," which is repeated in vv. 32, 35, and 38. The word "widow" in v. 40 provides the link to the "widow's mite" account in vv. 41-44. While 12:35-37 could be treated in isolation, I think it is important to read 12:35-44 as a single unit of material. Otherwise we miss the stark implications about the temple system that 12:41-44 communicate.

With v. 35 Jesus raises publicly the question of the nature of his messiahship. He has been portrayed by Mark as characteristically taking the initiative by asking questions (8:27-29; 9:16, 33). As the questions in previous accounts were asked to uncover flaws in the disciples' thought, here the question is raised to critique ideas about the Messiah. What is at issue in vv. 35-37 is the interpretation of Ps. 110:1, which was understood to have been written by David and which became a key text for Christians (see Acts 2:34-35; Heb. 1:13). Jesus' probable intent is to point out that the Messiah is more than a descendant of David; he is David's lord. Verse 37 says even David himself affirmed this.

Morna Hooker's discussion of these verses is particularly illuminating.[34] She points out that the issue probably arose between Jews and Christians when Christians claimed that Jesus was the Messiah; it reflects an "inner church" debate. There is little reference to Jesus' Davidic descent in the New Testament (explicitly only Rom. 1:3 and 15:12), but Ps. 110:1 was widely used in Christian apologetic, especially to prove that the Messiah is greater than David. For Mark, then, this pericope is a statement about Jesus' messiahship. It may be included at this point to underline Jesus' authority to designate "the first commandment" in the previous pericope or to stress the importance of what follows, that is, Jesus' criticism of the scribes. Verse 37 certainly draws a sharp contrast between the religious leaders who opposed Jesus and the "large crowd" with whom he is still popular.

Criticism of the scribes' teaching in vv. 35-37 leads to the denunciation of their behavior in vv. 38-40. The pericope opens "as he taught," which is ambiguous at best and allows Mark to place the material here. The practice first condemned is wearing the "long robe," the *stolais*, generally the dress of dignitaries like kings and priests, but which here probably refers to the Jewish *tallith*, a floor-length, fringed garment representing scholarship and piety. It was intended for use during religious duties but was worn constantly by the scribes to attract attention to themselves. The attack is on those who want deference paid to them for their self-appointed religious superiority. This is also seen in a preference for "the best seats in the synagogues," the *protokathedrias*, the seat in front near the Torah scrolls, and "places of honor at banquets" (v. 39; and see also Luke 14:7-11). In a shame and honor culture, seating was an important matter, as it was a visible statement about status (cf. Matt. 23:1-26 and James 2:1-7, especially v. 3). Jesus condemns religious status consciousness and false piety. Mark's reader/hearer is meant to remember that it is in direct contrast to the requirements of discipleship (9:35; 10:23-27, 35-44).

Verse 40 originally may have been an independent saying. The show of false piety ("for the sake of appearance say long prayers") makes it appropriate here. The "devouring" (*katesthiontes*, to eat as an animal does) of widow's houses was, technically, governed by civil law, but represents an affront to divine law, which commends care for the widow, orphan, and stranger, those without power, the disenfranchised, and marginalized (Isa. 10:1-2; Zech. 7:8-14, especially v. 10). But there may be a real abuse in view here. The scribes were not paid a regular salary for their work, which left an opening for abuse of the sort we see in the following pericope. Verse 40 depicts those scribes who cover their greed with a pretense of piety. The comparative form of the adjective *greater* suggests they are more to be condemned because of their falseness, their hypocrisy. This image of judgment assumes a "final judgment" and thus begins to pave the way for the "last things" extensively treated in the discourse in chapter 13.

It should be noted that Jesus is consistently opposed to ostentation and unhealthy aspiration for position. It was exactly the root of the misguided request of James and John in 10:35-45. In 12:38-40 the focus is religious ostentation. The scribes are religious exhibitionists; they use ostentatious behavior and false piety to hide their unjust actions. Their lack of humanity is not hidden from Jesus by their showy piety. (As an aside, this pericope might well lead those of us in the clergy to question our day-to-day wearing of ecclesiastical garb, our collars, clergy shirts, or large pectoral crosses, and so forth. What is our *real* motivation for this? It might be benign. But it might not.)

It is the lack of humanity of the scribes, their devouring of widow's houses, that apparently determines Mark's placement of 12:41-44. In light of this placement, and with other recent commentators (see "For Further Reading" at the end of this section), I would suggest that what is at issue is not so much the widow's generosity (although she is certainly that) as a corrupt religious system (personified by the scribes) that would ask of her "all she had to live on" (v. 44). In short, the text is a classic example of one of the cardinal points in these homiletical notes: the placement of a text, its context in Mark's Gospel, is crucial to its interpretation.

It has been noted that 12:41-44 has parallels in both Hindu and Buddhist literature. In the Jewish tradition in *Leviticus Rabba* (III.5), there is the story of a priest who scorned a woman's offering of a handful of flour. He is rebuked in a vision, "despise her not; it is as though she offered her life." This has led D. E. Nineham to suggest that the story of the widow's mite was a story *by* Jesus that was transformed into a story *about* Jesus. "This beautiful story is perhaps best explained as originally a Jewish parable which Jesus took over in his teaching and which was later transformed into an incident in his life."[35] Perhaps, but there are other possibilities.

As the pericope opens, Jesus is sitting in one of the two outer courts of the temple, the Court of the Women, where thirteen trumpet-shaped (wider at the bottom and narrower at the top) collection boxes (*gazophulakeion*) were placed to receive offerings (cf. John 8:20 for the location). Jesus is watching people make their offerings. It is not the "many rich people" and their "large sums" (v. 41) that elicit his commentary, but the offering of "a poor widow" (v. 42). She contributes two *lepton*. A *lepta,* the smallest coin in circulation, was one-third of an *as;* ten *asses* equaled a denarius, which was a day's wage. Seeing this self-sacrificing act, Jesus calls his disciples (thus carrying on the Markan theme of special instruction to the disciples) and commends the widow (vv. 43-44). In light of what occurred in 10:17-31 and 32-45, Jesus especially wants them to notice an example of the sort of complete surrender to and trust in God that discipleship entails.

The standard interpretation of the text leans heavily on the comparison in v. 44 between "out of their abundance" and "out of her poverty." The idea carried by "abundance" (*perisseuontos,* literally, "that which abounds") is that the wealthy were not really endangering their resources to support the temple. Money values, the interpretation goes, are not the standard of gifts in the kingdom. As the older commentary by Gould puts it, only as a gift measures the moral value of the giver does it count with the God who looks on the heart.[36] This approach to the text moves from the widow's economic marginality and her generosity to her paradigmatic self-sacrifice. Carrying on the theme of 12:38-40, the interpretation suggests that it is not outward show but depth of surrender to God that matters. With John the Baptist and Jesus, the widow is one of three people in Mark's Gospel who give their whole life. Therefore she foreshadows Jesus' own sacrifice.[37] The widow exhibits the love of God and neighbor that Jesus commended in 12:30-33.

But is this Jesus' reason for calling attention to the widow? Both A. G. Wright and Elizabeth Struthers Malbon comment on the placement of the story.[38] In view of Jesus' strong condemnation of the scribes who devour widows' houses in 12:40, how could he approve of what he is seeing here in 12:41-44? And, of course, the text that immediately follows this one is Jesus' prediction of the destruction of the temple (13:1-2). Isn't it more than a little ironic that this widow gives "all she had to live on" to a doomed temple? Is Jesus calling the disciples to note the woman's generosity or the corruption of a religious system that would demand the resources of those least able to offer them? Furthermore, chapter 13, which predicts the destruction of the temple, is framed by two stories of exemplary women and evil men (12:38-44, the scribes and the widow; 14:1-11, the anointing woman and Judas). Unfortunately, we cannot recapture the tone of voice with which Jesus makes his remarks in 12:43-44, nor can we garner any hints from his "body language." If Jesus is in fact criticizing the temple system here, it is another example of his tacit elevation of women, his particular sensitivity to their circumstances (cf. 5:25-34; 10:2-12; 12:18-27; 14:3-9). Mark's placement of the story should be taken very seriously in its interpretation. Just because an interpretation is the "traditional" one does not mean that it is the correct one or the only one.

At least two approaches to the sermon suggest themselves. The more common is to view 12:41-44 as the summary of a series of stories that contrast outward ostentation and hypocritical piety with inward authenticity and faith. The barrenness of the scribes and temple practice is compared with the "true religion" of the widow. (Recall the scribe's own words in 12:32-33 and compare Matthew 23.) In taking this approach, the homilist must not be guilty of the thing that Jesus criticizes, that is, asking the most of the least. It is already the case in mainline churches that the financial burden of the church is carried by the retired people (those on fixed incomes) and women (those who still earn less for similar work than their male counterparts). Mark's placement of the widow's story certainly calls that into question. The church should provide for the needy and marginalized, not vice versa.

The second, and more daring approach to a sermon on this text, is to ask two very dangerous questions: what activities of Christians and church leaders exhibit an unhealthy, even hypocritical interest in self-aggrandizement and craving for status? And what practices in the contemporary church might be equivalent of asking of a widow "all she had to live on"? What acts of false piety do we use to hide injustice? In what ways are we outwardly generous but inwardly meager? Is our surrender to

God and God's kingdom complete? It is a frightening but enlightening exercise to subject personal religious and public ecclesial practice to the litmus tests of Mark 8:34-35; 10:43-44; and 12:28-44.

For Further Reading

Elizabeth Struthers Malbon, "The Poor Widow in Mark and His Poor Rich Readers," *CBQ* 53 (1991): 589–604.

A. G. Wright," The Widow's Mite: Praise or Lament?—A Matter of Context," *CBQ* 44 (1982): 256–65.

Introduction: 13

Chapters 4 and 13 are both blocks of teaching material, the only two in Mark's Gospel. In a sense, they form an inclusion around the active ministry of Jesus. The material in both chapters points to the ultimate success of the ministry of Jesus and of the reign of God, a success that is not without serious delays and hindrances. In both we see a Markan pattern: Jesus gives a general teaching that he later explains privately to his disciples. Mark's original audience must have found the chapters heartening.

Willem Voster has pointed out that the placement of chapter 13 is especially significant. Mark's narrative has been moving quickly forward. Conflict stories have been mounting, suggesting the inevitability of the passion. At this point, Mark inserts a speech into the narrative. Its effect is both to slow the pace of the narrative and to give special emphasis to the material in the discourse that is spoken "from an apocalyptic point of view in paraenetic style."[39] Chapter 13 has been called the "Markan apocalypse" or the "little apocalypse." This assumes familiarity with a type of literature well-known in Mark's day, but not necessarily in ours.

Excursus on Apocalyptic

As a theological perspective and a form of literature, apocalyptic arose in the history of Israel when Jews felt alienated from the dominant social and religious structures of the time. The Jewish literary form first appeared in postexilic times and flourished in the first centuries B.C. and A.D. (Examples include parts of Daniel and Ezekiel, the *Greek Apocalypse of Ezra*, and *1 Enoch*.) It was popular especially in times of catastrophe or persecution. (Sociologically, it continues to be a form popular among "fringe groups" or disenfranchised people.) "Apocalyptic usually arises when the values and structures of a society lose all meaning for some minority group within a particular society and are replaced by a new symbolic meaning system. It is therefore at once a crisis phenomenon and an all-embracing approach to life in which the future determines the present."[40]

The word *apocalyptic* means "uncovering" or "revelation." Its subject is eschatology, the end (*to eschaton,* the end; *logos,* word). It is, therefore, a teaching concerning last things. As a theological position, apocalyptic is characterized by dualism ("the world" is bad/ "the heavens" are good; the world is made up of "us and them"; we can expect everything from God and nothing from humans); by a sense of alienation from and despair about the dominant culture; by a conviction that the world is headed for destruction and the hope that God will intervene to save the faithful; and by the conviction that it is possible to see signs of the end in historical events. As a literary form, apocalyptic writings are often pseudonymous and rely heavily on metaphorical and symbolic language, speeches that detail events to be expected as the end-time draws near, descriptions of the "woes" that will precede it, and accounts of God's final intervention. The Society of Biblical Literature's working group on apocalyptic drew up the following definition: "'Apocalypse' is a genre of revelatory literature with a narrative framework, in which a revelation is mediated by an otherworldly being to a human recipient, disclosing a transcendent reality which is both temporal, insofar as it envisages eschatological salvation, and spatial, insofar as it involves another, supernatural world."[41]

Christian apocalyptic like Mark 13, Matthew 23-25, and the Revelation to John has two primary sources: scripture (either directly quoted or alluded to) and the author's own experience. Behind Christian apocalyptic is the belief that God's plan as foretold in scripture has been recently or soon will be fulfilled. The spiritual enemies of God's elect will "get theirs"! The ultimate purpose of Christian apocalyptic was to encourage the faithful to endure their suffering in the sure knowledge that God's purposes would prevail. So Mark's purpose in chapter 13 is both practical and pastoral.

Mark 13 has many characteristics in common with Jewish apocalyptic, and our knowledge of that material helps us to interpret this chapter, which brings into sharp focus the two levels on which we read a Gospel: the narrative level of the life of Jesus, and the life of the community of the evangelist (the Gospel's *sitz im leben*). Ralph Martin uses the image of trifocal lenses to get at this issue. He speaks of the "three ranges of vision" of Mark 13: the immediate situation of the apostolic church (which he thinks is in view in 13:5-13), the more distant scene of prediction about the Jewish War (13:14-23), and the most distant focus, the "end of the age" (13:24-47).[42] Mark 13 is one of the centers of scholarly activity on the Gospel, and I shall return to that discussion at the end of the notes on the chapter.[43]

For Further Reading

Dale C. Allison Jr., *The End of the Ages Has Come: An Early Interpretation of the Passion and Resurrection of Jesus* (Philadelphia: Fortress Press, 1985).

F. F. Bruce, "Unveiling the Apocalypse," *BR* 6 (1990): 14, 41.

Adela Yarbro Collins, "Mark 13: An Apocalyptic Discourse," in *The Beginning of the Gospel: Probings of Mark in Context* (Minneapolis: Fortress Press, 1992), 73–91.

_____. "The Apocalyptic Rhetoric of Mark 13 in Historical Context," *BR* 4 (1996): 5–36.

T. J. Geddert, "Apocalyptic Teaching," *DJG*, 20–27.

Charles L. Holman, *Till Jesus Comes: Origins of Christian Apocalyptic Expectation* (Peabody, Mass.: Hendrickson, 1996).

Joel Marcus and Marion L. Soards, *Apocalyptic and the New Testament*, JSNTSup 24 (Sheffield: JSOT Press, 1989).

13:1-2

These verses actually serve as the conclusion to the temple teaching sequence that began at 11:2 (see the introduction to this chapter above). The chapter is set between two stories contrasting faithful women with unfaithful men (12:38-44 and 14:1-11) that form a Markan inclusion or intercalation. Mark opens the chapter with the notation that Jesus "came out of the temple" (v. 1), a reference not only to the close of the teaching sequence but to Jesus' final separation from the temple cult. The temple to which the disciple of Jesus makes reference is the Second temple or Herod's temple (one of Herod's many massive building projects). Josephus' account corroborates the mammoth size of the stones, reporting they were white and thirty-seven feet long, twelve feet high, and eighteen feet wide. Some of these immense stones can be seen in Jerusalem today at the base of the Haram el Sharif.

The saying of Jesus in v. 2 appears in some form in all four Gospels and has good claim to being authentic. By means of it Jesus places himself in the line of the classical prophets who proclaimed the end of the temple because of the apostasy of Israel (see Jer. 26:6, 18; Mic. 3:12). It is this saying that is misquoted as evidence against Jesus in his trial before the council (14:57-59). Many interpreters take this word of Jesus to have been fulfilled in A.D. 70 when the Romans destroyed the city of Jerusalem and the temple and took its stones apart in order to recover the melted gold leaf that decorated them.

13:3-13

Verse 3 signals a shift of location and of audience. Jesus and at least four of the disciples are on the Mount of Olives opposite the temple. The material that follows is thus separate from Jesus' saying in v. 2, which Mark uses to introduce it. Jesus is sitting, the authoritative posture for a teacher, surrounded by the inner circle of disciples (Peter, James, John) and Andrew, who receive special teaching. Thus 13:1-2 and 3-37 parallel the model of public/private teaching that was apparent in the seed parable in chapter 4. (The same pattern occurred in chapter 10 as well.) They understand that the temple is the symbol of the nation and request this special instruction with the question in v. 4, which Mark has used as the link to vv. 1-2. The assumption that "signs" in the present signal an immanent divine intervention is characteristic of the apocalyptic worldview (see excursus above). Behind the words of Jesus that follow stands Zech. 14 (especially vv. 1-9), which says that in the last days the word of divine revelation is to come from the Mount of Olives. Verses 5-8 list things that disciples should not fear (Collins calls it a unit of paraenesis related to events called "birth pangs")[44] and vv. 9-13 things they should expect.

Jesus' answer to the disciples' question comes in the form of warnings. "Beware" (NRSV, *blepete*) is the characteristic word of the chapter (vv. 5, 9, 23, 33). The first two "signs" he enumerates are false messiahs (v. 6) and "wars and rumors of wars" (vv. 7-8). These events are not to alarm (*throeisthe,* used only here in Mark, and in the New Testament only in the passive voice, thus "be disturbed" or "be frightened"[45]) the disciples, because they are part of God's plan ("this must take place") and "the end is still to come" (v. 7; cf. 2 Thess. 2:1-12). The "birth pangs" to which v. 8 allude are the sufferings that precede the new order; the coming of the messianic age is compared to the travail of a mother before she gives birth to new life (Isa. 26:17; Jer. 22:23; Hos. 13:13; Mic. 4:9-10).

Verses 9-13 vividly depict what will be in store for Christians (and may, in fact, be Mark's retrospective view of his church's experiences). Jesus has already made clear to the disciples that discipleship involves suffering (8:34-35); here it is depicted in terms of conflict with religious and civil authorities (vv. 9-11) and of disruption within families (vv. 11-12). "Councils" (v. 9, literally *sunedria,* "sanhedrins") refers to the religious authority of the synagogue elders (who could sentence to flogging those who broke the law), "governors" to Roman magistrates. The vocabulary of the verse, especially "hand . . . over," echoes Jesus' predictions of his own sufferings (9:31; 10:33) and is characteristically Markan. Verse 10 introduces the typically Markan motifs of the suffering that results from preaching the Gospel and of the need to proclaim that Gospel to Gentiles. By A.D. 70 the Gospel was being proclaimed throughout the Empire. It must have been a great comfort to simple persons in Mark's original audience to know that the Holy Spirit would assist them when they were brought before powerful authorities (v. 11). Ralph Martin describes three ways the Holy Spirit helps believers in such times: the Spirit gives insight and perception to enable one to discern the true from the counterfeit, courage to stand for

Christ and his cause, and perseverance to maintain trust in him to the end.[46] The Holy Spirit is, in short, the believer's secret weapon.

Again, Jesus has already alluded to the fact that discipleship may "upset the filial apple cart" (3:31-35; 6:1-6; 10:28-31). In v. 12 he indicates that family members will actually betray one another to the authorities (cf. Mic. 7:2, 6; Isa. 3:5, 19:2; 1 Enoch 100:1-2.) The terms *brother* (*adelphos*), *father* (*pater*), and *child* (*tekna*) are all words that the New Testament uses to refer to Christians relationships with one another. Tacitus (Ann. 15.44) and Pliny (Ep. 10.96.6) both note that during the persecutions, members of the Christian community who were arrested betrayed other Christians. This has led Van Iersel to suggest that v. 12 is tied to a larger Markan intention, that of helping "failed followers" to come to terms with the suffering they have caused.[47] While family betrayal may be a common apocalyptic theme (Mic. 7:6; 2 Esd. 6:24), Mark's Jesus here generalizes it with the stark note, "You will be hated by all because of my name" (v. 13a; cf. Matt. 10:21-22; John 15:18-21).

If Mark 13 is understood primarily as the evangelist's encouragement to his persecuted community, then v. 13b is his central assertion. Perseverance assures salvation. The verb "endures" (*hupomeno*) means steadfastness under trial and opposition. The word is focal whenever New Testament writers urge endurance (see Heb. 3:14; 6:11-12; 10:36; 1 Pet. 4:14). It may, as well, provide the homiletical key to the passage. Throughout his Gospel, Mark warns his readers/hearers to count the cost of discipleship. To follow Jesus is to choose a difficult path, one that may lead to conflict and death. Mark's is not a Gospel of "health and wealth" or of be-happy attitudes. It is a Gospel that squarely confronts difficult realities. The preacher might well want to remind the congregation what it costs modern disciples to follow Jesus in today's Israel, Egypt, India, or East Asia (or wherever there is currently martyrdom for the faith), or what it cost men like Oscar Romero or the murdered women religious of Central America.

For Further Reading:

M. F. Van Iersel, "Failed Followers in Mark: Mark 13:12 as a Key for the Identification of the Intended Readers," *CBQ* 58 (1996): 244–63.

13:14-23

Verse 14 is one of the conundrums of Markan studies, as it raises both historical and literary issues. The "desolating sacrilege" is a term used by Daniel (9:27; 11:31; 12:11), probably for the heathen altar set up in the Temple by Antiochus Epiphanes in 168 B.C. But for Mark, it might also have referred to the statue of himself that Caligula set up in the temple in A.D. 40, or to the Roman standards that flew over the temple in A.D. 70.

"Let the reader understand" are obviously not the words of Jesus, but a reminder by Mark to his hearers/readers about how to interpret the passage. It is "just the kind of hint that a visionary writer of this period used to indicate that a phrase or image he had just used was a symbol or a cryptogram for some familiar person, place, or event. It shows that at some stage Jesus' teaching on the future has been assimilated to the conventions of a written apocalypse."[48] That we are not sure what we are to "understand" does not mean that Mark's original audience did not get it. Historically, it was the case that during the Maccabean revolt people hid in caves in the Judean hills (as they did during the Jewish revolt of A.D. 132–135).

Verse 14b-20 are a terrifying depiction of life "when the desolating sacrilege" is "set up." There will be no time for preparation or provision (vv. 15-16). The necessity for and speed of flight will be particularly hard for pregnant women (cf. 13:8) and the mothers of young children, who also serve as an image of any who are forced to flee in difficult circumstances (see 2 Esdras 5:8; 6:11). Winter increases the hardship because of inclement weather, rains, and swollen streams that impede the journey and magnify the unavailability of food and scarcity of shelter. Verse 19 is intended to indicate how terrible the trials will be that precede "the end." Mark quotes Dan. 12:1 both to give these historical events eschatological meaning and to remind his audience "at that time your people shall be delivered." That phrase, which follows the quotation from Daniel, serves to introduce the encouraging note of v. 20. God will shorten the suffering of "the elect, whom he chose." God is still in charge of human circumstances and sets limits to human tribulation.

Verses 21-23 reiterate the warnings of vv. 5-6. The focus of the warning is "false messiahs," which are not in short supply. The pronoun "it" that the NRSV supplies at the end of v. 21 does not appear in the Greek, which reads simply, "Do not believe," and indicates Mark's belief that no rival to Jesus Christ is possible. Even the false messiahs are able to produce "signs," actions done in proof of their claims. But the "elect," the followers of Jesus, are not only forewarned against them but forearmed in their knowledge that such things will occur. Disciples of Jesus are prepared for all sorts of tribulations and falsity by having been told of them before they occur. All this precedes the coming of the Son of Man (see *DJG* and Morna Hooker's *The Son of Man in Mark* [1967] for a discussion of this phrase).

Mark 13:14-23 is the lectionary text for the penultimate Sunday in Ordinary Time. Origen's comment on 13:22 provides an opening gambit for the sermon. "While Antichrist is generically one, there may be many species of him. It is as if one would say that falsehood is generically one, but according to the differences of false doctrines there are found many specific falsehoods."[49] In every age there will be persons and philosophies that compete with the Gospel of Jesus Christ. It is the duty of the responsible preacher to remind Christians of the uniqueness of Jesus and his "way" (cf. John 14:6-7; Acts 4:12.) This text invites the preacher to examine current "competing claims" or the present "species" of falsity in the light of the Markan Jesus.

13:24-27

"In those days" is an expression that the Hebrew Bible uses for the end of time or for turbulent times. "After that suffering" apparently refers to the tribulations of vv. 14-23 and indicates that more difficulties are to follow them. The quotation in vv. 24b-25 has affinities to Isa. 13:10; Ezek. 32:7-8; and Joel 2:10, 30-31. The sun, moon, and stars are symbols of the cosmic world and are another example of celestial portents, like the star at Jesus' birth (Matt. 2), which were familiar features of first-century thought. The "Son of Man coming in clouds" probably alludes to Dan. 7:13-14 and includes the notion of clouds as symbols of the power and glory of God (Exod. 19–20; Ps. 97:1-5). The ultimate outcome of this cosmic disruption is positive; the Son of Man sends his angels to gather the elect (v. 27). God gathers his scattered people (Isa. 11, especially v. 1; 43:1-7, especially vv. 5-7). Those familiar with Joel 2:30-32 (alluded to here) would have already understood this, for v. 32 asserts, "Then everyone who calls on the name of the LORD shall be saved; for in Mount Zion and in Jerusalem there shall be those who escape, as the LORD has said, and among the survivors shall be those whom the LORD calls." Again, the passage provides assurance to the faithful.

13:28-31

Mark 13:32 can be read after 13:24 with no sense of disjunction. This suggests that vv. 28-31, which are quite different in tone and subject matter, are not in their original context. Verses 28 and 29 are a mini-parable that picks up the theme of a sign (cf. 11:12-14, 20-24) and plays on the fact that in Jewish literature the fig tree is a symbol of the joys of the messianic age (recall 11:12-25). The signs of the coming of the Son of Man are as easy to recognize as the coming of spring. The great problem is the reference to "these things" (v. 29) in Greek. Does it refer to all the signs in vv. 5-23, just those in vv. 24-27, or to the "he" who is nigh?

Another difficulty is the temporal reference in vv. 30-31. What does Mark's Jesus mean by "this generation" (*he genea haute*)? Does he mean his present age? One generation? Or a race of people? Is "this generation" the persons living at the time of Jesus or those at the time of the evangelist? Elsewhere in Mark the term means people who are contemporaries of Jesus (9:1, 12, 19), and I am rather disposed to accept this commonsense meaning, even though it seems to place an unfulfilled prophecy on the lips of Jesus (cf. also 13:32). "All these things," then, are the events heretofore described in chapter 13.

The comparison of what is impermanent with what is permanent is the point to be stressed. The sufferings of "this generation" are temporary (a difficult idea to accept in the midst of suffering whenever it occurs). What is eternal is the word of God, Jesus' words ("my words") about the kingdom. Physical things, even "heaven," will pass away, but words/ideas are imperishable. Behind the verse stand the stirring words of Isa. 40:8 and Ps. 102:24-27, both of which are words of comfort, especially the Isaiah passage, which continues with a description of the coming of the God of comfort (cf. Isa. 40:1-11).

For Further Reading:

F. F. Bruce, "This Generation Will Not Pass Away," in *The Hard Sayings of Jesus* (Downers Grove: InterVarsity, 1983), 225–30.

13:32-37

Although v. 32 raises the theological problem of the Son's omniscience, Mark's concern is not systematic Christology, and his purpose in including the saying (about the authenticity of which there is great debate) is to introduce the main idea of the closing section of the discourse that, finally, Christians cannot know when the end with its attendant tribulations will come (cf. Acts 1:6-7, where the response of Jesus is consistent with this saying). The general idea is that one should not try to calculate when the end will occur. The disciples of Jesus can know that it will happen without knowing when, which is why it is so important to "beware" and "keep alert" (*agrupneite*, literally "be without sleep"). Some ancient manuscript traditions add "and pray" in v. 33, but it is omitted in most modern translations.

Verses 34-36 present a parable or a similitude that illustrates that the future is entirely in God's (the homeowner's) hands. A man leaves his home, puts his slaves in charge, and commands the porter to watch. Like those slaves, Christians are to keep awake, because they do not know whether the master will return during one of the four watches of the night (v. 35, phrases that will be echoed later in 14:17, 72; 15:1), and they must not be found sleeping when he comes (v. 36; cf. 12:1-11). In the larger context of Mark's Gospel, the implication is that the disciples have work to do, that is, spreading the Gospel. The charge to "keep awake" (which becomes the theme in the Garden of Gethsemane) is not just for the leaders but for "all" (cf. Matt. 24:36-51; Luke 12:35-48).

This passage (sometimes including the verses from 24 to the end of the chapter) is appointed for the first Sunday in Advent primarily because it issues the clear invitation to "watch" and to "be prepared." It signals the theme for the four weeks of Advent: Christians are to be alert and ready for the remarkable new thing that God is doing by means of the Incarnation. Thus vv. 25-27 can be preached in the light of Matthew's infancy material. Should the preacher use the text at other times of the year, it is perhaps best to stress the folly of trying to determine the precise moment of the "end" (as the Millerites in nineteenth-century America and other millenarian groups have discovered). In God's time, the Son of Man will come. In the meantime, his followers must be vigilant, and they have plenty of work to do!

Concluding Notes
Mark 13

As I noted earlier, chapter 13 is one of the centers of scholarly activity on Mark's Gospel. Its exegetical cruxes are the "desolating sacrilege," the phrase "let the reader understand" (v. 14), and the problem of Jesus' apparent lack of knowledge in v. 32. Many Markan theological themes also come together here. First, there is the christological issue raised by the fact that v. 30 seems not to have happened; it seems to foretell an imma-nent parousia that has yet to occur. Second, speculation about the date of the Gospel arises here. Are the events described here about to happen (a pre-70 date) or have they happened and thus fulfilled Jesus' prophecies (a post-70 date)? The "little apocalypse theory" suggests that Mark 13 was neither spoken by Jesus nor composed by Mark. It existed independently as a Christian apocalyptic, the argument goes, and was inserted here by Mark to serve his own narrative and theological purposes. Many scholars note that chapter 13 speaks directly to the life of Mark's community and its difficulties. They faced the threat of false messiahs (13:6, 21-22), per-secution from within families (13:12), and the dangers of falling victim to the "cares of the world" and the "delight in riches."

Several lines of interpretation of the chapter as a whole have been taken. Those who hold that it is predictive think it either: (1) predicts the destruction of the temple in Jerusalem (because it rejected Jesus?) or (2) predicts the end of all things and the coming of the Son in glory, the parousia. Others prefer to understand chapter 13 as primarily a pastoral document intended to encourage Mark's persecuted community (which, of course, implies a particular theory of when and where that community existed). Whatever theory the preacher adopts (or rejects), it is important to have thought through the literary and theological issues that Mark 13 raises, particularly because parishioners are so apt to have heard the text misinterpreted or preached irresponsibly on the radio or television (or from the pulpit!).

In chapter 13 Mark's Jesus has made clear that a final reckoning will come, but he has not said when. Such a clear prediction would not help faith. In fact, by terms of Heb. 11:1, it would not *be* faith. The comment of Victorinus of Petovium is instructive:

> We must not inordinately fix upon the chronology of what is said in Scripture, because frequently the Holy Spirit, having spoken of the last times, then returns again to address a previous time, and fills up what had before been left unsaid. Nor must we look for a specific chronology in apocalyptic visions, but rather follow the meaning of those things which are prophesied.[50]

The chapter as a whole makes clear that Jesus is the Lord of history and of all that will unfold in it. In the words of R. H. Lightfoot, it describes "the ultimate salvation of the elect after and indeed through unprecedented and unspeakable suffering, trouble, and disaster."[51] Seen with the eyes of faith, all of history is a series of highs and lows, of good times and bad for the Christian community. The key words of the chapter—*beware, watch, pray,* and *endure*—are the Christians' orders for the day, whenever and whatever day it is.

For Further Reading

George Beasley-Murray, "The Rise and Fall of the Little Apocalypse Theory," *ExpTim* 64 (1953): 346–49.

Adela Yarbro Collins, "Mark 13: An Apocalyptic Discourse," in *Beginning of the Gospel: Probings of Mark in Context* (Minneapolis: Fortress Press, 1992).

Conclusion

Because so much of the action of Mark 11–13 is set in the temple, I opened this chapter with a discussion of the figure of the temple in Mark. I want to close it with a discussion of the Jewish leaders in Mark's Gospel. They pose a particularly delicate problem for the evangelist, especially if the church in Rome has a large Jewish contingent (as Paul's letter to the church at Rome seems to suggest it did). The first thing to be said, then, is that the Jewish leaders are not universally presented as negative characters in Mark. Jairus is presented sympathetically (5:21-43), as are the scribes in 12:28-34, and Joseph of Arimathea in 14:42-47. The Jewish leaders are judged by Mark as everyone in the Gospel is, by their response to Jesus. "Being a foe of the Marcan Jesus is a matter of how one chooses to relate to him, not a matter of one's social or religious status and role."[52]

However, in Mark's Gospel, the movement toward the temple does not signify increasing holiness but increasing hostility. In 11:27—12:27, the conflict in the temple precincts (the locus of God's presence) is most confrontational. Jesus is questioned by and silences representatives of the major groups within Judaism. The chief priests, scribes, and elders are confronted on the question of authority (11:27-33) in an encounter that proves programmatic for the unit of material. The Pharisees and Herodians (who would normally be opposed to one another) are silenced with regard to taxes, a charged political issue (12:13-17). Finally, the Sadducees are corrected about resurrection from the dead in which, in any case, they do not believe (12:18-27). In each case the basic issue is authority. Mark has presented these various groups as a united front against Jesus, who has demonstrated his authority over them all. Mark wants the reader to understand that this is what leads to the final conflict in chapters 14 to 16.

We are, I think, to see the Jewish authorities in chapters 11 and 12 as polemical figures, composite characters who represent opposition to Jesus. As Neyrey has so eloquently proven, Jesus commands respect in the terms of ancient rhetoric.[53] The fact that he silences all opposition ("no one dared to ask him any question," 12:34) signals that he has won the rhetorical battles. His cleverness shames the Jewish leadership, who have been presented in terms of increasing hostility to Jesus. In the course of Mark's Gospel, they go from indirect to direct confrontation, from questioning him, to plotting against him, to openly accusing him, and, finally, condemning him to death. The focus on Jesus' confrontation with some Jewish authorities in chapters 11 and 12 leads inevitably to the final confrontation and Jesus' passion in chapters 14–16.

For Further Reading

Michael Cook, *Mark's Treatment of the Jewish Leaders* (Leiden: Brill, 1978).

Arland Hultgren, *Jesus and His Adversaries* (Minneapolis: Augsburg, 1979).

Jack Kingsbury, "The Religious Authorities in the Gospel of Mark," *NTS* 36 (1990): 42–65.

Elizabeth Struthers Malbon, "The Jewish Leaders in the Gospel of Mark," *CBQ* 60 (1989): 259–81.

8

The Passion and Resurrection

Mark 14–16

Introduction

Mark 14 opens the passion narrative proper. Scholars have generally assumed that the passion narrative was the first part of the Gospel tradition to be written down. The exact process is, of course, unrecoverable, but the passion narrative almost certainly "evolved" in several stages. Gerd Theissen argues intriguingly that the narrative originated in Jerusalem in the generation after Jesus, as early as A.D. 40 to 60.[1] Wherever and whenever it was written, the passion narrative seems related to a literary schema or genre called the "court conflict" or "vindication of the innocent sufferer." "Set against a legal or royal setting, the protagonists . . . are recognized for their outstanding qualities; their lives are endangered, usually through evil schemes; though innocent, they are persecuted; and finally, they are vindicated."[2]

A second literary feature, one of special importance to preachers, is the extensive use of the Hebrew Bible in the passion narrative. Two schools of thought about this use exist. One contends that the narrative is "created" around the fulfillment of Old Testament material. The other suggests that the Hebrew Bible is mined for its interpretive function vis-à-vis the passion of Jesus. I find the second view more persuasive, (1) because studies of the use of the Hebrew Bible at Qumran indicate "the direction of influence was primarily from event to Scripture rather than vice versa,"[3] and (2) because of the great scandal of the cross to early Christians, who had to explain the horrific death of their Messiah. They looked to their own scriptures to do so. As Howard C. Kee has noted, the Jewish biblical tradition is more important in chapters 11–16 of Mark than in 1–10, and more quotations from and allusions to it occur there.[4] The concern of the passion narrative was "to make clear what in the passion took place by God's will. This purpose was served by finding in the Old Testament the motivation which . . . penetrated the early narrative and was an essential element in Mark's Gospel."[5] Mark's use of these scriptural quotations and allusions often provides the focus for the homily or sermon, and the preacher should consult the Old Testament texts listed in the notes of study Bibles in preparing the sermon.

Mark's is the first complete canonical passion narrative and the basis of the other two synoptic accounts. As Pheme Perkins notes, Jesus' passion predictions in Mark 8:22—10:52 (8:31; 9:31; 10:33-34) have already given an outline of what will happen. Jesus will be handed over to the chief priests and scribes and condemned to death (14:43-65), then delivered to the Gentiles, mocked, spit upon, scourged (15:1-20), and killed (15:21-39), and after three days, he will rise from the dead (16:1-8).[6] The disciples' misunderstanding reaches its culmination here as almost every one of them abandons him. Sympathetic "outsiders," many of them unnamed, "highlight the failure of Jesus' disciples by doing what the disciples should have done."[7] Mark portrays the abandonment of Jesus in the starkest terms. But God acts to vindicate Jesus, as the rending of the temple curtain, the centurion's confession, and the resurrection itself attest. The identity of Jesus and the complete truth of his message are available to the characters in the narrative only after the cross and resurrection.

As I've noted before, the last week of Jesus is carefully set out by Mark. The passion is even more carefully organized, with time references as follows:

Wed.	Anointing in Bethany	14:1-11
	Betrayal by Judas	
Thu.	Preparation for Passover	14:12-72
	Last Supper	
	Gethsemane	
	Arrest & Sanhedrin Trial	
Fri.	Trial before Pilate	15:1-47
	Condemnation	
	Crucifixion	
	Burial	

Friday is arranged by three-hour Roman watches:

morning	15:1
third hour	15:25
sixth hour	15:33
ninth hour	15:34
evening	15:42

Sat.	Jesus in Tomb	15:42-47
Sun.	Resurrection	16:1-8

The Markan passion narrative is appointed to be read in Year B of the lectionary on Palm/Passion Sunday. When preaching any part of it during

Holy Week (or at other times of the year), the whole passion context should be kept in mind.

For Further Reading

The literature on the passion narrative is extensive and is readily found in general reference works like the *Anchor Bible Dictionary* or *Dictionary of Jesus and the Gospels*. The definitive work of our generation is Raymond Brown's two-volume work *The Death of the Messiah* (New York: Doubleday, 1994). Two small volumes by Fr. Brown provide helpful and accessible summaries: *A Crucified Christ in Holy Week* (Collegeville, Minn.: Liturgical, 1985), and *A Risen Christ in Eastertime* (Collegeville, Minn.: Liturgical, 1991) and are highly recommended to those who will preach and teach the Holy Week/Easter texts.

14:1-11

This passage opens with what is heretofore unusual in Mark, a continuous chronological narrative that ends only with the burial of Jesus. Verses 1-2 and 10-11, which deal with the plot to kill Jesus and his betrayal by Judas, form an inclusion around vv. 3-9, the anointing of Jesus at Bethany. The loving attention of an anonymous woman contrasts sharply with the behavior of the religious authorities (the chief priests and scribes) and his own disciple, Judas Iscariot.

The temporal reference in v. 1 introduces a series of complex problems regarding the dating of the passion.[8] In terms of Mark's narrative, the day must be Wednesday (see time schema above). The Jewish authorities are depicted as meeting ad hoc (not officially at this point) to seek a way to arrest Jesus "by stealth" (*en dolo,* "cunning" or "deceit"; the term appears in 7:20-23 in the list of things that defile). The phrase can mean either that they hoped to arrest Jesus secretly or that they were attempting to trick him into doing something or saying something that would provide the excuse for his arrest. (Recall the controversy dialogues in 11:27—12:27.) These religious leaders are aware of the problems connected with doing this during "the festival" (v. 2), Passover (Judaism's sacred commemoration of liberation from Egypt), when there were crowds of people in Jerusalem. The population of the city at the time of Jesus was around 50,000, but it swelled to as much as 180,000 at Passover.[9] Mark implies that these pilgrims are pro-Jesus, since his arrest would lead them to riot (cf. 11:1-10; 12:37).

At v. 3 the scene shifts to Bethany, where Jesus and his disciples are staying (11:11, 27; 13:3), probably because there was "no room in the inns" in the city. Mark contrasts the devious behavior of the religious authorities with the love of the anonymous anointing woman. (In John 12:3 she is Mary, the sister of Martha and Lazarus.) "Simon the leper" might well have been an associate of the Mary/Martha/Lazarus family or a friend of Jesus. That Jesus would dine with a leper is a striking indication of just how broadly he construed table fellowship, as is the presence of a woman (there is no indication in Mark's text that she came in off the street). The fact that they are reclining (*katakeimenou*) at table indicates that the meal is a feast. The alabaster container holding the nard, an expensive perfume essence from the plant of that name, which grew in India, would have been teardrop-shaped. When the slender neck was snapped off, the whole contents would have to be used. Thus the "ointment" and the jar serve as a symbol of the totality of the woman's giving. Joseph Grassi has pointed out several parallels between the generous widow in 12:41-44 and this woman. The "apocalyptic discourse" in chapter 13 is framed by stories of generous women. In each, the woman gives all she has, and her generosity is contrasted with others' stinginess.[10]

It is not insignificant that the woman anoints Jesus' head in Mark's Gospel (as opposed to his feet in John's). In the tradition of Israel, the heads of priests and kings were anointed as a sign of their reception of God's empowerment. This woman's anointing is her visible confession of Jesus as Messiah, literally "the anointed one." And since, culturally, dead bodies were also anointed for burial, her action points forward in the narrative to Jesus' immanent death. Mark may well be telling us that this woman (one of those who followed him from Galilee? cf. 15:41) has understood the intrinsic connection between Jesus' suffering and messiahship.

Not all those in attendance at the feast were so perceptive. Some, in fact, respond to generosity with anger (v. 4). Instead of seeing the anointing as an act of loving generosity, or understanding what it signified, they complained about the "waste" of three hundred denarii (about a year's wages if a denarius is the day's wage for a laborer). One wonders if their real concern is "the poor" or whether they are just uncomfortable with an extravagant and very intimate gesture of love for Jesus. In any case, "they scolded her" (v. 5). The word *enebrimonto* indicates that they expressed their displeasure with gestures as well as words.[11]

Jesus' response in vv. 6-9 is very different. He approves her action and silences her critics. His comment on her prophetic action is the longest and most positive on the words or deeds of any person preserved by Mark.[12] Perhaps Jesus perceives something specious in the outcry on waste and the needs of the poor. In any case, he indicates that there will always be opportunities to serve the poor (see Deut. 15:11), but he will not always be present. What is of crucial importance here, as it has been throughout Mark's Gospel, is the individual's response to Jesus, and the woman's has been extravagantly loving. Verses 7 and 8 together foreshadow what is about to happen and seem to indicate that Jesus is anticipating his own death. (And, in fact, only criminals were not anointed for burial, cf. 14:8 and 12:44.)

Every time v. 9 is read, its prediction comes true. In Mark's terms it picks up the theme of the universal proclamation of the Gospel by and to the Gentiles ("in the whole world," cf. 13:10). Jesus not only commends the woman, but says of her, as he says of no other disciple, that her fame will be proclaimed with the Gospel. The anointing woman is the first person in the Gospel to understand Jesus as the crucified Messiah. She looks forward to the anointing women at the tomb (16:1), and her action exemplifies the positive response of discipleship for which the whole Gospel calls.

In contrast to this picture of devotion, v. 10 picks up the theme of vv. 1-2, the plot against Jesus. Again, an unlikely person (a woman) is commended as an example of faith and contrasted with the male disciple, Judas, whom Mark emphasizes "was one of the Twelve," the inner circle of Jesus' associates, one who should have understood him and responded faithfully. Judas Iscariot (from Kerioth, about twelve miles south of Hebron) goes in order to "betray" Jesus. Mark's readers have known this since 3:19. Verse 11 communicates a sense of Judas's greed as well as the plotting of the religious leaders. Incidentally, the "thirty pieces of silver" that Matthew's Judas received to betray Jesus (26:15) was about four months' wages for a laborer and, ironically, much less than the value of the anointing woman's gift. Both vv. 10 and 11 use the word "betray" (*paradoi* from *paradidomi*, "hand over"), which by this point in Mark's Gospel has strong and negative associations (see 1:14; 9:31; 10:33; 14:41).

If this text is preached as a whole (and not vv. 3-9 alone), the sermon must obviously comment on the contrast between the religious officials and Judas and the woman. It might be fruitful to think about our response to the text. Are we more like Mary or Judas? How recently have we committed an extravagant act of love for anybody, much less Jesus? Are we slow to expend our resources at all? I find Jesus' response to what may be a commendable concern for the poor very interesting. He does not deny their need but suggests, albeit obliquely, that nobody lives by bread alone! We all need a little perfume in this life, and Jesus not only allows this, but commends it.

We may be comfortable with the anointing woman's act of extravagant love. We may even be able to imagine ourselves responding to Jesus in that way. But I wonder how many of us could be Jesus in the story, could accept such an act of love and generosity. Jesus sets an example for us in allowing people to love him. Although the sexual boundaries are clearer here than in John's telling of the story (John 12:1-11), both accounts confront the hearer/reader with a lavish and touching picture of loving and being loved. Both are standards against which we must measure our own responses. As 14:3-9 is the lectionary text for the Monday of Holy Week in Year B, it provides a useful basic question with which to approach all the texts of the week: in all honesty, with whom do I identify in this part of the passion story?

For Further Reading
Mary Ann Beavis, "Women as Models of Faith in Mark," *BTB* 18 (1988): 3–9.

14:12-25

Mark 14:12-25 depicts the preparation for and sharing of the Passover meal among Jesus and the disciples. Note that the references throughout are predominately to "disciples," not just to the "Twelve." Thus women are not excluded ipso facto (is it women Jesus sends in v. 13 to prepare the meal?), and if the meal were Passover, they would almost of necessity have been in attendance. In any case, the text consists of three units: vv. 12-16, preparation of the Passover; vv. 17-21, prediction of betrayal; vv. 22-25, institution of the "Lord's Supper."

14:12-21

Verses 12-16 may not have been part of the earliest version of the narrative. They are the means by which the Passover is introduced. In the text as a whole, Jesus appears to be cognizant of what is transpiring and to be making provision for a final meal with his disciples. That the Passover was usually celebrated in the family circle indicates both the closeness of the disciples to Jesus (recall 3:31-35) and suggests the presence of women at the meal.

The preparation for this Passover has something of a cloak-and-dagger quality. Since it was the job of women to carry water, a man carrying a water jar would be noticeable, v. 13. (Recall that water was a symbol of hospitality in the culture.) It was customary to rent out rooms to Passover pilgrims, and vv. 14-15 suggest Jesus had made prior arrangement for such a space. Church tradition has suggested that the room in question was in the house of the mother of John Mark (to whom this Gospel is traditionally ascribed); the place became a headquarters of the early Jerusalem church. (Was John Mark the "man with the water jug"?) That the designated room is "furnished and ready" (v. 15) suggests both that couches were supplied and that the place had been cleaned of leaven; that is, the ritual preparations for Passover had been completed. The disciples would have needed to provide the provisions for the meal—the unleavened bread, bitter herbs, wine, and lamb.

The "evening" of v. 17 would be Thursday of Passion week. (Recall that the Jewish day begins at sundown.) Jesus and the Twelve join the disciples who have made the preparations. In the course of the meal at which they are reclining (*anakeimenon*), Jesus predicts his betrayal by one who is sharing table fellowship (see Ps. 41:9). It is little wonder that the disciples are "distressed" (*lupeisthai*, to be sad or sorrowful), because betrayal by one who shares a meal is a terrible breach of the hospitality code. That "one after another" they inquire who would do this is a Markan detail, and the form of the question in v. 19 expects the answer "no" or "not I." Paul Achtemeier points out that the question is not so much self-reflective probing as an assertion that denial is impossible. This indicates just how great the gulf is between what the disciples' claim for themselves and what they understand and will need to do.[13]

The meat and bread of the meal were dipped in sauces (the word "dip" is the same root as "baptize"). Jesus' betrayer comes not from the general group of disciples, but from the inner group of the Twelve. Some early manuscripts of v. 20 indicate that Jesus says his betrayer is the one who dips "into the *same* bowl" as he, thus emphasizing the heinousness of the betrayal. Verse 21 indicates that what is happening is occurring in accordance with God's purposes. It is unclear whether Jesus has Isaiah 53 in mind or whether the reference is to Hebrew scripture generally. The word "goes" (*hupagei*) is used outside John's Gospel only here and points toward the death of Jesus.

As in 14:1-11, Mark's account brings together intimacy and betrayal. It is in this context of table fellowship, of a family religious celebration, Passover, and the shattering reality of a betrayer "in the midst," that what has come to be called "the institution of the Lord's Supper" occurs.

14:22-26

It is very difficult to comment on this text without being influenced by the theology and practice of one's own historic ecclesial tradition. The more the preacher knows about the Passover, the more faithfully he or she will be able to proclaim this text. The sermon is probably most helpful if it can keep the material firmly in the context of Mark's narrative, which in the immediately preceding passion prediction has cast the shadow of the cross over the event. The language here echoes the earlier account by Paul in 1 Cor. 11:23-26 and probably reflects eucharistic practice in Mark's own community.

During the meal Jesus acts as host and blesses the bread. The formula was: "Blessed art thou, O Lord our God, king of the world, who bringest forth bread from the earth." The word for bread in v. 22, *artos*, is the word for a common loaf, which is problematic if the setting is Passover. In the best manuscript traditions of v. 22, the imperative "eat" is absent (cf. 6:41; 8:6). Since the language Jesus spoke was Aramaic and there is no "to be" verb (is) in Aramaic, any literal interpretation of Jesus' saying is linguistically contraindicated. The word body, *soma*, means the whole person or the self.[14] Jesus is sharing all of himself with his disciples, establishing a covenant in his person.

At Passover, the third cup of wine was the cup of blessing. The formula of blessing is similar to that for blessing bread, but the last clause is "creator of the fruit of the vine." It is from "giving thanks" (*eucharistesas*) that the term *Eucharist* comes. Here in v. 23, "cup" may be intended to echo the exchange with James and John in 10:35-40 and to foreshadow the cup of suffering in 14:36. Note that "all of them drank from it." The common cup both emphasizes again the terrible betrayal that follows and predicts the suffering that will, indeed, come to the disciples. The words by which Jesus explained the meaning of this cup (v. 24) must have been extremely difficult for those Jews at Passover. In classical Greek, a "covenant" (*diatheke*) is a will or a testament. At many points in Hebrew scripture, covenant is tied to lifeblood (see Exod. 24:6-8; Zech. 9:11; Jer. 31:31-34, and the Christian interpretation in Heb. 8-10). As Moses sprinkled blood to assure participation in a covenant, so Jesus' blood, poured out in a violent death, assures participation in a "new" covenant, although the word "new" does not appear in all manuscript traditions (see Isa. 53:2, MT). But unlike Moses' covenant, this covenant is "for all"—another instance of Mark's concern for the Gentile mission (cf. 14:9). Again, the Aramaic original language reminds us that a literal equation of wine and blood probably ought not to be made. As "body" signified the whole self, "blood" signified life. Jesus says he pours out his life for many, which indeed he is about to do.

Verse 25, too, is laden with Semitic ideas and vocabulary. "Until" strikes a note of promise. It serves as another passion prediction but places the suffering that Jesus (and his disciples) undergo in the light of future feasting in the kingdom of God. It also brings Jesus and the disciples into a relationship that reaches beyond death. The Jewish Passover looked in two directions: back to the Hebrews' deliverance from Egypt and forward to a time when God would again liberate them. The Lord's Supper also has at least two temporal frames of reference. As Hugh Anderson notes in his commentary, we find here "the inauguration of a new covenental relationship between men and God secured by Jesus' sacrificial death and renewed always and again in the Lord's Supper, and the joyous expectation of the sure coming of the kingdom of God pledged to all who participate and enter into this new relationship."[15] The Lord's Supper is "for now" and "for then." Instead of engaging in polemics about what happens to the elements when the meal is reenacted, the sermon might better focus on the promissory character of the meal. It sustains in the face of present suffering and promises ever more joyous feasting in the future. And, in view of Mark's negative view of the temple (see the introduction of chapter 7 of this study), we see here a new sacrificial meal being instituted that replaces the sacrificial system of the temple.

Some commentators divide the pericopae between vv. 25 and 26, arguing that Mark often opens new accounts with geographic references.

While this is the case, I prefer to end what for Mark is a Passover account with the singing of the last hymn. Although Mark's account specifies no particular hymn, the Passover meal ended with singing a portion of the Hallel (Pss. 115–118). Jesus and the disciples withdraw from the city. That they "went out to the Mount of Olives" (v. 26) is significant. Jesus is outside the walls of Jerusalem, well on his way to Bethany and from there the road to Jericho and back to Galilee and safety. The Mount of Olives is a geographical point of decision. Here Jesus might have left "the cup" altogether.

The text usually appears in the lectionary for Holy Thursday and can also be used any time instruction in the meaning of the Lord's Supper is required. In either case, Mark's account of the supper points to a theology of Eucharist that issues a call to self-giving and to inclusivity. The first is focused on the person of Jesus, what he does here at table and what he will do in the next twelve hours. The second focuses on those present at table with him. Around that table were gathered, at the very least, those mentioned in 3:16-19 (and, in my view, more probably a larger group of disciples—including women; cf. 15:40-41). These persons might not have chosen each other for table fellowship, but each was chosen by Jesus to gather there for remembrance, sustenance, and mission. The text speaks powerfully of the diversity that should characterize our churches. Finally, the traditional approach to the text, which juxtaposes the intimacy of the event and the betrayer in the midst, is perennially appropriate.

For Further Reading

Robert H. Stein, "Last Supper" in *DJG*, 444–50.

Bonnie Thurston, "'Do This': A Study on the Institution of the Lord's Supper," *Restoration Quarterly* 30 (1988): 207–17.

14:27-31

As the positive event of the anointing of Jesus (14:3-9) in the context of a meal was flanked by images of betrayal, so the Lord's Supper text is bracketed by references to betrayal: Judas's (obliquely) in vv. 17-21 and Peter's in vv. 27-31. We are to understand the conversation as occurring on the way to Gethsemane. In v. 27 Jesus quotes Zech. 13:7, but v. 28 adds a surprising twist, suggesting that apparent human weakness (like betrayal) is, in fact, part of God's purposes. "Raised up" (*egerthenai*, v. 28) is Mark's usual word for resurrection. "Go before you" (*me proadzo humas*) can be taken either spatially as in "go ahead of" or "lead," or temporally as in "go before in time," "go first" (see notes on 16:6-7). In the midst of the two predictions of betrayal (v. 18 and v. 30) are two words of promise from Jesus (v. 25, which promises a reunion feast, and v. 28, which promises continued presence with the disciples). Verse 28 is quoted to the women by the angel at the empty tomb (16:6-7); the women, like Peter here, do not seem to "get it." Again, the text suggests there were women among those with Jesus on his last night, or they would have had no reason to remember later what was said there.

From what we have seen of him in Mark to this point, the Peter of vv. 29-31 is entirely in character. As previously, Peter speaks for all the disciples (cf. v. 31), who insist they will *not* do what Jesus has predicted in v. 27; they will not desert, fall away, or take offense (*skandalidzo*). "This day, this very night" (v. 30) indicates Jesus knows how very soon his passion will commence (and this adds to the "agony" in the garden that follows). The "cock crow" (*L. gallicinium*), a nickname for the bugle call for the change of the Roman guard and also for the Roman watch from midnight to 3:00 A.M., evinces Mark's interest in temporal specificity in the passion narrative. Jesus says they will not only desert; they will deny (literally disown, "with the sense of refusing to admit knowledge of, or relation to, Jesus"[16]) him (see 14:66-72, especially v. 71, where "deny" is used repeatedly). As he rebuked his master's teaching at 8:32b, so here Peter vehemently takes issue with what Jesus has stated as simple fact. It is a double irony that serves Mark's dramatic purposes well.

Peter and the disciples are no better and no worse than disciples today who pledge allegiance to Jesus until it costs something to follow him. We must not be too harsh on Peter. None of us knows how we will respond to mortal danger until we face it. But there is an interesting psychological truth here of the "methinks the lady doth protest too much" variety that might lead to an interesting sermon. Often what people most vehemently oppose publicly is what they most greatly fear privately or internally. How dangerous it is to insist on what we will or will not do until we know ourselves thoroughly, until we find that knowledge at the foot of the cross!

14:32-42

Although scholarship on this passage focuses on the source of the material and its redaction, those issues are not of focal importance for preachers.[17] The account of Jesus' prayer in Gethsemane does bring into sharp focus two important Markan themes: the blindness of the disciples and the close association of Jesus and God's purposes. Part of the Mount of Olives east of Jerusalem, "Gethsemane" means "oil press." It was geographically a place known to the disciples (Judas knows he will find Jesus there, v. 43) and symbolically a place where, as olives in a press, essence is extracted under pressure. The account has many eyewitness touches, and its historicity is bolstered by the entirely unflattering picture it presents of the disciples. The larger group of disciples is directed to "sit" while Jesus prays (v. 32), but his "inner circle"—Peter, James, and John (see 9:2ff; 13:3)—is invited to accompany him (v. 33). This is the very group who have boasted of their faithfulness and ability to "stick with" Jesus (recall 10:35-40; 14:29-31).

The words in vv. 33-34 that describe Jesus' emotional state indicate great distress and suffering. In v. 33, "distressed and agitated" (*ektham-beisthai kai ademonein*) "describe an extremely acute emotion, a compound of bewilderment, fear, uncertainty and anxiety, nowhere else portrayed in such vivid terms as here."[18] The word in v. 34 the NRSV translates "deeply grieved" (*perilupos*) is a picture word that literally means circled by grief. Jesus asks Peter, James, and John to watch and keep awake; it is the only personal request he makes in Mark's Gospel. "Keep awake" or "watch" (*gregoreite*) provides a connection to chapter 13 and means not just "look on" or "be on the look out" (as in a military watch), but "share vigil." These three disciples are being invited to participate in Jesus' suffering—exactly what Jesus said following would entail (cf. 8:34-35; see also Pss. 42:6; 43:5).

Jesus goes "a little farther" (v. 35), emphasizing his separation from the disciples and depicting what the leader does vis-à-vis followers. His posture is one of fervent supplication, and Mark's use of "the hour" and Jesus' of "the cup" both refer to a time of suffering and have apocalyptic precedents in Dan. 8:17, 19; 11:35, 40, 45 (and see also 13:11, 32). The content of Jesus' prayer is given in v. 36. Mark alone preserves the Aramaic address to God as *Abba*, Father, a term that, in his *The Prayers of Jesus*, Joachim Jeremias argues connotes "something of what the word 'Mother' signifies among us."[19] It is "a word of revelation. It represents the central statement of Jesus' mission."[20] (cf. Rom. 8:15; Gal. 4:6). The prayer begins with an acknowledgment of God's omnipotence, makes its request straightforwardly, and closes with acquiescence to God's will. (Note the strong similarity to the pattern of the Lord's Prayer.) The "cup" in question is clearly the cup of suffering (cf. 10:38; and see Ps. 11:6; Isa. 51:17, 22). And "cup" is also used in the Psalms as a metaphor for what is willed by God (Pss. 16:5; 116:13). Here we see the human Jesus struggling in his own will toward the will of God. Jesus' certainty of his special relationship with God does not take away his suffering. He knows God can do everything; the issue is what it is God's will to do. (I am reminded of the statement of Seneca, *"deo parari libertas est,"* God's will is freedom.)

Even in his distress, Jesus worries about his disciples. He returns to them (vv. 37-38), finds them sleeping, and addresses Peter as their representative. Watchfulness and prayer are now, more than ever before, important, especially for these three who have sworn special loyalty to Jesus (see Sir. 2:1). The word "trial" or "temptation," v. 38, literally means testing and carries cosmic connotations, as it does in the Lord's Prayer. The spirit/flesh dichotomy in v. 38 may refer to the two parts of the human person or may be a metaphor for a more cosmic conflict. I suggest this latter in light of the spiritual struggle that has been so much a part of Mark's understanding. (Recall, for example, 1:21-28, with which the Gospel opened, and see Job 34:14-15; Isa. 31:3.)

The repetitions of vv. 39-41a stress both the importance of what Jesus has asked of the three disciples and his own solitary struggle. Verse 40 provides a note of realism: the disciples are sleepy, and caught napping, their embarrassment leaves them speechless. In the synoptic tradition Jesus faces three temptations at the opening of his ministry. At the end of his ministry his disciples face three temptations and fail each time. The time for spiritual preparation has passed; the hour has come.

Verses 41b-42 are extremely vivid. The word that the NRSV translates "enough" (v. 41b) occurs only here in the New Testament and is something of a puzzle. Does it mean "it is enough" or "enough of that," referring to the disciples' shortcomings? Or does it refer to Jesus and mean something like "I am ready"? Or did Mark choose the word for its deliberate ambiguity? "The hour has come" leaves no doubt about what will happen next. The character of Jesus' death is made clear as he says, "the Son of Man is betrayed (literally "handed over") into the hands of [the] sinners." The Greek article, which the NRSV omits, indicates a class of people, not an individual (and so Mark implicates us in what transpires?). As Jesus has promised, he will go before the disciples (14:38); here he does so. The language is muscular. "Get up" uses the same verb at the root of "resurrection" or "be raised." "Let us be going" expresses Jesus' resolute acceptance of what is coming, his "going out to meet it." He apparently sees Judas coming, the one whom he knows is a betrayer (14:19-21).

This text is admittedly a difficult one to preach, not the least because it asks us to do something we would all rather avoid: to look fixedly at extreme human agony. In my view it is wrong to "deify" Jesus here, to suggest he really knows God will save him—that is to take away the very real suffering he underwent for our redemption, to make us less able to relate to him in our own darkest nights and deepest suffering. Jesus really is abandoned by his closest friends when he needs them most. Here he really suffers in an agony of decision. It is wrong to soften this, Jesus' nadir in Mark's Gospel. On Holy Thursday, or at any other time, it is appropriate to preach this text from the point of view of Heb. 2:10, 18; and 4:14-16.

Another way to approach the text is to mine it for what it teaches us about prayer. In it Jesus models for us the method ("apart," in humility, and persistently, vv. 35-36), content (intimate address, straightforward request, obedience to God's will, v. 36), reason (avoid temptation, weak flesh, v. 38), and results (clear vision, courage to face what comes, vv. 41-42) of Christian prayer.

For Further Reading

Werner Kelber, "Mark 14:32-42: Gethsemane Christology and Discipleship Failure," *ZNW* 63 (1972): 166–87.

Jerome Murphy-O'Connor, "What Really Happened at Gethsemane?" *BR* 14 (1998): 28–39, 52.

David Stanley, *Jesus in Gethsemane* (New York: Paulist, 1980).

14:43-52

Gethsemane was apparently known as a place of repose for Jesus and the disciples. The account of Jesus' arrest begins with Mark's favorite word, "immediately" (v. 43), which introduces the speed with which events will now transpire, and with the phrase "while he was still speaking," which indicates the abruptness and intrusiveness of the arrival of Judas and the Jewish police from the Sanhedrin. Mark cannot pass up another opportunity to remind the hearer/reader that Judas was "one of the Twelve," not an outsider (recall 3:19; 14:10-11, 18). Although Mark has drawn a picture of Jesus' popularity in Jerusalem (11:1-10; 12:12, 37; 14:2), that Jesus must be singled out with a kiss suggests that he was not well known in Jerusalem. "Although kisses were not unusual among family members, there was a reticence about public kisses in Greco-Roman society. Mostly they are described in scenes of reconciliation or of relatives meeting after separation."[21] The kiss is a particularly bitter means of betrayal since it was a token of respect, the way close friends greeted one another, and the way a disciple greeted his rabbi. In v. 45 the verb "kissed" (*katephilesen*) indicates profuseness, fervency, or tenderness (see Prov. 27:6). At the moment of the kiss, Jesus is arrested (v. 46).

Violence begets violence. The violence of Jesus' seizure sparks a violent response from his disciples. A follower of Jesus (John says it was Peter, John 18:10) draws his sword and cuts off the "little ear" (a Markan diminutive) of the high priest's slave (again, John supplies the name, "Malchus"). Although in both Luke's and John's Gospels Jesus rebukes such violence, in Mark he is silent, responding instead in vv. 48-49 to the general method of his arrest. Is he to be treated as a "bandit" (*lesten*)? The word can also be translated "robber" or "insurrectionist" and carries the idea of lawlessness. This, of course, is what Roman officials must decide about Jesus: *Is* he an insurrectionist? *Does* he claim to be a king? Jesus does not object to the arrest itself, but to its manner. Why is he being arrested by a mob and in secret, since he taught daily in that most public of places, the temple? (recall 4:22). The last word of Jesus before his trial is a word of resignation, "let the scriptures be fulfilled." At least the final petition of his prayer in 14:36 has been answered (see Isa. 53; Zech. 13:7).

Mark closes the scene of Jesus' arrest with a vivid picture of abandonment. In spite of their protestations (14:19, 29, 31), all the disciples flee, fulfilling Jesus' prediction in 14:27 (and see also Amos 2:16). One particular escapee is singled out by Mark, the young man in vv. 51-52 who flees naked. Ironically Peter has said that the disciples left all they had to follow Jesus (10:28); here someone leaves all he has to get away from him. That the garment left behind is linen suggests its owner was a person of means (cf. Prov. 31:24).

The naked young man has garnered all sorts of speculation. Some scholars think his inclusion is a historical reminiscence, signaling an eye-witness account, perhaps even the source of the Gethsemane narrative.[22] Others suggest that the young man is Mark himself, who is "painting himself in" as did Renaissance painters in their canvases. The young man has been seen as anticipating the angel at the tomb in 16:5. And one of the most ingenious explanations notes that in the early church, persons were baptized in the nude and then given white robes. Furthermore, in the New Testament, receiving baptism and new life in Christ is described as stripping off old clothes (see Colossians and Ephesians). Thus in the naked young man, the dying and rising of a believer in baptism is woven into the narrative of the dying and rising of Christ.[23]

I tend to agree with Morna Hooker that the detail is "a total enigma."[24] And for preaching purposes, I think Harry Fledderman's approach is most helpful. He explains that "the flight of a naked young man is a commentary on 14:50; it is a dramatization of the universal flight of the disciples." Fledderman continues, "he is a concretization of the fleeing disciples, and his flight is an action that is opposed to Jesus' act of acceptance."[25] I agree with Fledderman that if he is a symbol, it is of those who oppose God's will in the passion. The naked young man is a Markan signature that summarizes Mark's theology especially as it focuses on the disciples' lack of understanding of Jesus' passion (see 8:31-33).

For Further Reading
Harry Fledderman, "The Flight of a Naked Young Man," *CBQ* 41 (1979): 412–18.

Excursus on the Trial of Jesus
In Mark's Gospel, the trial of Jesus is a block of material that encompasses 14:52 through 15:20. It opens as "they took Jesus to the high priest" (14:53) and closes when "they led him out to crucify him" (15:20). The two parts of Jesus' trial, before the Sanhedrin (14:53-65) and before Pilate (15:1-15), form an inclusion around the narrative of Peter's denial (14:66-72). Each trial scene is constructed of a cross-examination of Jesus

(14:60-62; 15:2-5), a sentencing (14:63-64; 15:15), and Jesus' mistreatment (14:65; 15:16-20).

The trial before the Sanhedrin had three parts: a preliminary hearing before Annas, the former priest (reported only by John in John 18:12-14, 19-23); the trial before the high priest Caiaphas (14:53-65); and the end of the Sanhedrin's all-night session (15:1). The Sanhedrin was the council of chief priests and scribes and included both Pharisees and Sadducees. Its full size was seventy or seventy-one; twenty-three constituted a quorum. (What would be the likelihood that a quorum could be gathered on Passover eve?) It had its own police force and authority to arrest and inflict all but capital sentences, a power it lost some forty years before the destruction of the temple (see *Baraita TJ Sanhedrin* 1:1; 7:2). A trial normally began with the reasons why the accused was *not* guilty. Technically the Sanhedrin could not meet at night, during the Sabbath, or on a Holy Day. Any capital sentencing (when it was allowed) took two days, the second of which could not be Sabbath or a Holy Day. The purpose of this "unofficial" meeting was to find a charge the Romans would execute. The witnesses against Jesus do not agree with each other, and even to declare one's self Messiah (which Jesus did not unequivocally do) was not blasphemy, although to speak against the temple was.

The trial before the Romans also had three parts: a trial before Pilate (15:2-5); a trial before Herod Antipas (only in Luke 23:6-12); and the conclusion of the trial before Pilate (15:6-15). Pilate was the Roman procurator of Judea from A.D. 25 to 36. He normally resided at Caesarea Maritima but came to Jerusalem at Passover because of the danger of political unrest with so many pilgrims in the city and so inflammatory a commemoration: that of liberation. Pilate sees no great threat in Jesus, but he is sensitive to popular opinion. He therefore bows to the will of the crowd, which had few of Jesus' supporters in it because he was taken by stealth and at night. Or perhaps the crowd was pro-Jesus, and Pilate's ignorance of Aramaic worked against him. The crowd cries for "Barabbas," in Aramaic, *bar* (son) *abbas* (of the father). People like Pilate normally transacted business between early morning and noon. There is no independent confirmation of the practice of releasing a prisoner, but the way Jesus is treated by the soldiers is entirely consonant with the behavior of occupation forces in any age.

The differences among the Gospel accounts of the trial of Jesus suggest that the early church did not know with great exactness what transpired. The general attitude, however, is that the death of Jesus came about because of the Jews, the Romans, and Pilate: Jesus' trial was a perversion of justice by both the Jewish and the Roman system, and in spite of it all, Jesus' death was in accord with the will of God as revealed in the Hebrew scriptures. What Mark in particular wants the hearer/reader to understand is that Jesus' trial is conducted in two "kangaroo courts." There is no serious attempt to give him a fair trial. Mark's narrative lays the blame for Jesus' death on the Jewish officials. In view of the fact that the Gospel may have been written in Rome, I think it is fair to ask whether this emphasis might have been to protect his own community. If official Rome reads the Gospel (or hears it recounted), the "really bad guys" are not the Romans or even official Rome. Jesus dies because of the cunning of the Jewish officials and the indecisiveness of a particular Roman official.

For Further Reading

For an extensive treatment of the trial of Jesus, see the first volume of Raymond Brown's *The Death of the Messiah* (New York: Doubleday, 1994), which provides an extensive bibliography, and John R. Donahue, *Are You the Christ? The Trial Narrative in the Gospel of Mark*, SBLDS 10 (Missoula: Scholars, 1973).

14:53-65

Mark begins his account of the trial of Jesus by reminding his hearers/readers of the three groups that made up the Sanhedrin: chief priests, elders, and scribes (v. 53). Verse 54 serves not only to introduce the Peter narrative that follows in 14:66-72 (and perhaps to suggest a certain courage on Peter's part; he did, at least, follow into the "lion's den," as it were), but reveals that the meeting is at the high priest's house and at a season of the year when nights were cool enough to require a fire for warmth. That they met at Caiaphas's house provided some security for the conspirators, but it made the proceedings irregular from the beginning, since official meetings of the council were not to take place at a private residence.

Verses 55-59 make it clear that what is happening is an attempt to find a charge against Jesus; this is an arraignment, not a trial. That they were "looking for testimony against Jesus" (v. 55) suggests a last-minute search for witnesses (see Pss. 27:12; 35:11-15). Since according to the Mishnah a trial begins with reasons for acquittal, here the council members are acting like prosecutors rather than judges. In a Jewish trial, witnesses functioned as prosecution, and a person could not be convicted unless two or more men gave consistent testimony (Deut. 17:6; 19:15). This is obviously not the case here (v. 56), where Jesus is also misquoted (cf. v. 58 and 13:2). To criticize the temple was a grave offense (cf. Acts 6:13-14), but Jesus' criticism of it cannot be corroborated.

What apparently amazes Caiaphas is Jesus' silence in the face of his accusers (vv. 60-61). Jesus' silence not only fulfills scriptural expectation (Ps. 38:12-14; Isa. 53:7), but is a clear sign of his surrender to the will of

God in whatever way it plays itself out. However, when asked directly if he is the Messiah, "the Son of the Blessed One" (v. 61, a way to refer to God without speaking the divine name), Jesus answers simply, directly, and truthfully. His "I am" seems surprising to scholars who hold the "messianic secret" (see introduction to this volume) to be of paramount theological importance to Mark. But the hearer/reader of Mark already knows Jesus was proclaimed God's Son at his baptism (1:11) and transfiguration (9:7). Jesus' answer combines Ps. 110:1 and Dan. 7:13-14 (a characteristically Markan conflation of two verses of scripture). Note that it points to the future ("you *will* see"). The allusion to Ps. 110:1 does suggest divine appointment but, as F. F. Bruce notes, "the historical sequel may be allowed to rule on the question whether it was blasphemy or an expression of faith in God which was justified in the event."[26]

Jesus' response is enough for the high priest. Tearing the clothes, which was originally a sign of grief (cf. Job 1:20), became a juridical act of the high priest at the end of a trial when the accused was guilty of blasphemy. And in Mark, it prefigures the rending of the temple curtain in 15:38, which signifies something very different indeed. But blasphemy implies cursing God, which Jesus has not done. Not even the false witnesses accused him of this (see vv. 56-59). Caiaphas sets aside the need for witnesses and asks the chief priests, elders, and scribes for their verdict. Mark records that "all of them condemned him as deserving death" (v. 64b); no one escapes guilt for Jesus' death, which follows the sentence that they pass but cannot execute (Lev. 24:16). The gruesome details of spitting and striking are gestures of condemnation and rejection (Num. 12:14; Deut. 25:9). An interpretation of Isa. 11:2-4 said that the Messiah would be able to judge by smell without seeing, so perhaps the blindfolding here serves the same ironic function as the "crowning ceremony" in 15:17-18 (see also Isa. 50:6). What began as a parody of a trial has degenerated into an unruly mob attack on an innocent man. As Raymond Brown notes in *A Crucified Christ in Holy Week,* "at the very moment when Jesus is being mocked by the Sanhedrin challenge to prophesy, his prophecies are coming true"[27] in what is transpiring in the courtyard (14:66-72).

It is important that the sermon on this dark passage not be an exercise in anti-Semitism. Mark's Jewish leaders are not today's Jewish people. As noted above, the *Sitz im Leben* of Mark may have influenced his narration of the trial narrative. What I think the passage exemplifies is how very dangerous a motive for action fear is. It is clearly fear for their own prestige, position, and authority that motivates the Jewish officials' covert and unjust action here. That "preaches" in any age. The metaphor of night might be a helpful sermon-starter as well. Why does this action need to be carried out under the cover of night? Is it a good, general moral principle that what must be done in secret is better left undone? (Recall Jesus' words on this very subject at 4:22.) Matt. 10:26-31 (Luke 12:2-7) is most interesting read in conjunction with Mark 14:53-65. As early as the fourth century, Hilary of Poitiers suggested we could learn from Christ's accusers: "If you will not learn who Christ is from those who received him, at least learn from those who rejected him."[28] Finally, a powerful sermon could be preached focusing on the example Jesus sets for those who are falsely accused and roughly treated by a "system of justice": he is silent. It is the silence of St. Thomas More, of Gandhi, of Dorothy Day. How mightily the silence of the innocent rings when history passes judgment on the powerful!

For Further Reading

Darrell L. Bock, *Blasphemy and Exaltation in Judaism: The Charge against Jesus in Mark 14:53-65* (Grand Rapids: Baker, 2000).

14:66-72

Peter's threefold denial follows his threefold inability to watch with Jesus in 14:32-42. This "trial" of Peter is intercalated with Jesus' trial as a way of linking the stories of Jesus and Peter. The note in The Orthodox Study Bible softens somewhat the picture of Peter, who "denies the Lord, but at least he is there to do so. His intentions are commendable (v. 29), but his strength fails."[29] While the innocent Jesus remains silent, Peter incriminates himself by repeated denials. (Note how often this narrative is in sharp contrast with the parallel Jesus story.) The historicity of the account has seldom been called into question. Who would fabricate such an unflattering account of one of the "heroes" of the early church (and perhaps Mark's eyewitness source)?

John's account of Peter's denial explains that one of Jesus' disciples was known to the high priest. That disciple secured Peter's admittance to the courtyard where the slaves and police had made a fire to warm themselves (John 18:15-18). Mark relates none of this. He simply notes that a servant girl of the high priest saw Peter warming himself and recognized him as one who had been with Jesus. Peter seeks creature comfort (v. 67) while Jesus is being abused (v. 65). Peter denies association with Jesus with the ironic statement, "I do not know or understand what you are talking about" (v. 68). Indeed, throughout the Gospel Peter has been depicted as lacking understanding of Jesus and his message (8:32-33; 9:5-6). The encounter alarms him enough that he withdraws from the warmth and light of the fire to the "forecourt," the *proaulion*, the passageway that leads from courtyard to gate. Is he embarrassed? Or is he positioning himself for a quick getaway should it prove necessary? Symbolically, Peter moves from light into greater darkness as the cock crows for the first time.

The servant girl "won't let it go." With the persistence of the Syrophoenician woman of 7:24-30, she insists that Peter was one of Jesus' followers. For the second time, Peter denies the association (v. 70). "That it is a . . . maid whose comment prompts Peter's . . . denial . . . contrasts his babbling weakness with the quiet strength of Jesus, who resisted pressure from a personage no less imposing than the high priest."[30] But attention has been called to Peter, and, perhaps by his dress or accent, "bystanders" identify Peter as a Galilean. Jesus, of course, is known as Jesus of *Nazareth*, a town in Galilee, so the identification is particularly telling. For the third time, Peter denies Jesus. His denial is particularly vehement and final; "with an oath," Peter insists that "I do not know this man" (v. 71). Peter, who has confessed Jesus as the Christ (8:29), seen his transfigured glory (9:2-8), and sworn loyalty to him (14:29); Peter, whose last vehement word has been that he will die with Jesus (14:31), denies even knowing "this man" (v. 71). As Gundry notes, Peter's first denial was private and evasive; the second, while evasive, is public; the third is direct, public, and strong.[31]

With great sensitivity to the drama of the moment, Mark records "the cock crowed for the second time" (v. 72). Jesus' prediction (14:30) has come true. Unlike the religious authorities in the previous pericope who show no human feeling, Peter, remembering what Jesus has said (cf. 14:21), "broke down and wept" (v. 72). Although there is little agreement on the translation of *epibalon*, the consensus is that the word expresses deep emotion. This is the last view we have of Peter in Mark's Gospel. Having denied his Lord, he is a broken man.

This was not, however, the end of Peter's story. Peter was included in the promise of 14:28. In Mark's Gospel, Peter is singled out by the young man at the tomb and thus "rehabilitated" (16:7). The historic connection between Mark's community and Peter allows for a sermon lifting up the good news that even those who have denied Jesus (or, like Paul, persecuted his followers) are embraced by his love and forgiveness. And perhaps it is not amiss to note that those who have been forgiven much not only "love much," but ought to be more compassionate toward others who have "fallen" (cf. Luke 7:40-43). As Augustine noted, "the blessed Peter earnestly repented, having denied the Lord, and shed such bitter tears, yet remained an apostle."[32]

Focusing on Peter's later leadership in spite of his denial would not be the most appropriate way to preach the passage during Holy Week. In that context, the traditional approach that asks us to compare ourselves to Peter seems more helpful. Even Peter, who was so close to Jesus, denied him when the circumstances became difficult. How many of the members of Mark's persecuted church understood all too well Peter's experience? If Peter could apostatize, who of us can exempt ourselves from the same possibility?

Most sermons on this text quite rightly focus on Peter. But what insights might be garnered from looking at the text from the point of view of the servant girl, who had apparently seen Peter with Jesus and perhaps, therefore, herself heard something of Jesus' teaching? And what of the bystanders about whom John's Gospel tells us a bit more than Mark does? What do they know of Jesus and Peter? Since the narrative itself is so dramatic, a little "dramatic license" might be exerted by the preacher.

15:1-20

Jesus' trial before Pilate contains the same elements as the trial before the high priest: Jesus is asked about himself (15:2-5; 14:60-62); the opinions of "the crowd" are sought (15:6-15; 14:55-59); Jesus is sentenced (15:15; 14:63-65) and subsequently abused (15:16-20; 14:65). The structure of this, the second part of Jesus' trial, is as follows: Pilate questions Jesus (vv. 1-5), Pilate questions the crowd (vv. 6-14), and Pilate delivers Jesus to be crucified (vv. 15-20).

Mark's narrative continues without interruption from the previous scene. "Morning" (NRSV translation of *proi*, v. 1) is literally "at an early hour." Mark made it clear that the whole Sanhedrin conferred and concurred in Jesus' sentence (14:64). They "handed him over to Pilate." "Handed over" forms a leitmotif in the pericope (vv. 1, 10, 15; cf. also 10:33 and 14:10, where "betray" is the same root as "hand over") and ties the fate of Jesus to that of John the Baptist, who was also "handed over." Pilate, as Roman governor of Judea from A.D. 26–36, was probably in Jerusalem because of the high tension surrounding Passover and customarily did transact all his official business early in the morning.

Verse 2 is central to what happens to Jesus. "King of the Jews" is a title first found here and, in Pilate's ears, would be political, and thus seditious if true (cf. 14:61, the religious equivalent of Pilate's political question). The central issue in Jesus' trial before Pilate is whether he is a king and poses a threat of some sort to Caesar. In Greek, the "you" of Pilate's question is emphatic. Jesus' response is practically silence. He makes no direct claim for himself and throws the question back on the questioner (as has been typical of his teaching and confrontational style, 2:8-9, 25; 3:4; 11:29-30). At this point, the chief priests chime in with their own accusations (v. 3). In the face of these charges, vv. 4-5 emphasize the silence of Jesus that continues from the Jewish trial (14:61). In response to a real question, Jesus responds (14:61-62); in the face of false accusation, he is silent. Even Pilate realizes that he is dealing with an unusual person; Mark says he was "amazed" (*thaumazo*, he "marveled" or "wondered"). Ralph Martin's comment on Jesus' silence is important enough to quote at length. He notes that Jesus speaks only three times after his arrest in the garden (14:62; 15:2, 34). When provoked, mocked, taunted, he remains silent.

> Mark's readers would find immense comfort and strength at this point. They were experiencing suffering and persecution . . . they would recall the example of Jesus himself who did not answer back when he was incriminated but endured to the end. . . . 1 Peter—a document which tradition associates with Mark in time and circumstance—encourages Christians in persecution with precisely this appeal to the picture of the suffering Jesus (1 Pet 2:20-23; 3:15-17).[33]

Verses 6-8 introduce a practice for which there is no independent confirmation in any ancient source. The imprisoned Barabbas (a common family name composed of *bar,* son of, and *abba,* father;[34] see excursus on the trial of Jesus above) is called a rebel and is associated with those who led an "insurrection." Perhaps in Pilate's mind he would have been connected with a title like "King of the Jews." Mark presents him as a popular figure, one for whom the crowd seeks release. Instead, Pilate offers them "the King of the Jews" (v. 9), understanding that the issue is the religious officials' jealousy of Jesus (cf. 14:1-2). Pilate may be weak and indecisive, but he is no fool. Again, Mark's narrative focuses on the Jewish officials as responsible for Jesus' death. They incite the crowd to call for Barabbas (v. 11). The crowd, which Mark has depicted as pro-Jesus since his entry into Jerusalem (chapter 11), now, like his disciples, deserts him.

Popular opinion is notoriously fickle and never firm ground for moral decision making. But like many politicians, Pilate is unduly influenced by it. Pilate's second questioning of the crowd (vv. 12-14) makes it clear that they, too, are implicated in Jesus' death. Three times Pilate asks the crowd what should become of Jesus (vv. 9, 12, 14), and we are to assume that, just as Peter denied Jesus three times, they call for his execution three times. There is nothing in Roman law and certainly nothing in what Mark presents of Pilate's response to Jesus to indicate that Jesus had to be crucified. Pilate's last words, "Why, what evil has he done?" (v. 14), make clear that the governor finds Jesus guilty of no capital offense. The sentence is really that of the crowd, not Pilate, who could have ignored it and prevented the execution but did not because he wished "to satisfy the crowd" (v. 15). "Jesus goes to his execution without even the formality of a verdict, false though a verdict of guilty would have been."[35] In one of the most heinous acts of weakness in human history,[36] Pilate releases Barabbas, who was clearly implicated in rebellion and murder, and "hands over" the innocent Jesus to flogging and crucifixion. Mark's account passes quickly over the exceedingly bloody business of flogging, which was carried out with leather thongs into which bits of bone and metal had been woven. The effect was to shred the flesh of the back; many people died from such floggings or the subsequent loss of blood.

It is possible that the account of the mocking of Jesus in vv. 16-20 is a later insertion into Mark's passion narrative. It is, however, typical of

Markan irony: the true (and now hideously beaten) king is mocked and humiliated. The praetorium (v. 16) was the governor's official headquarters when he came from Caesarea Maritima to Jerusalem and the barracks of part of the Roman legion. The whole cohort (v. 16) would have been between two hundred and six hundred soldiers. The behavior here of the occupying army toward a representative of its subject people is all too realistic (cf. Isa. 50:6; Mic. 5:1). Jesus is given the mock trappings of kingship and wrapped in the soldier's scarlet cloak. Verse 18 is a parody of the *Ave Caesar, victor, imperator* ("Hail Caesar, conqueror, emperor"; compare the mocking homage of v. 19 to Phil. 2:10). When the soldiers tire of their brutal game, they lead Jesus out to crucifixion. Exactly what he predicted in 10:33-34 has come to pass.

Sermons on this passage usually focus on either Pilate, whose refusal to act for the right is a great evil, or on the fickleness of the crowd, which a week earlier cried, "Hosanna!" and now cries, "Crucify!" Because Mark's narrative focuses on Pilate as he bounces back and forth between the religious leaders and the crowd, it is easy to overlook Jesus, who stands silently in the midst of this whirlwind of activity. Jesus' silence here is dramatic evidence of the depth of his prayer at 14:36: "Not what I want, but what you want." It is this quiet resignation to the will of God that stands as the model for all Christians as we face the apparent catastrophes of life.

For Further Reading

T. E. Schmidt, "Mark 15:16-32: The Crucifixion Narrative and the Roman Triumphal Procession, " *NTS* 41 (1955): 1–18.

15:21-41

Any preaching of this material must try to recapture for modern audiences the horror of the cross for first-century people. The empty crosses of Protestant churches and attractive "cross jewelry" blunt the reality of the cross for us. What modern person would wear a gold electric chair around her or his neck? Crucifixion was the Roman penalty for slaves, and it was intended as a deterrent. Those convicted of the most horrible crimes were crucified naked and publicly, often at a crossroads. Death was by slow strangulation or exhaustion and could take several days. The corpses were left to rot on the cross or be eaten by birds to remind passersby what happened to those who defied the Roman order. (Perhaps the most helpful explanation of the meaning of the cross in the first century occurs in Morna Hooker's *Not Ashamed of the Gospel,* Eerdmans, 1994.)

As Raymond Brown notes, Mark's is the shortest account of the crucifixion, and every detail is important. Mark continues to order the passion narrative in threes (Jesus' threefold prayer in Gethsemane, Peter's threefold denial; Pilate's threefold questioning of the crowd), here the third, sixth, and ninth hours. Between the third and sixth, three groups mock Jesus: those crucified with him, passersby, and the religious leaders.[37]

The officials of Israel and Rome have retired and left the Roman soldiers to do the dirty work; "they led him out to crucify him" (v. 20). (Watch the repetition of "they crucified" in what follows: vv. 24, 25, 27.) Verse 21 introduces men who may have been known to Mark's original audience. Rom. 16:13 mentions a Rufus, though whether this is one is impossible to say. Simon was from Cyrene, a city in North Africa (now in Libya) that had a large Jewish population (see Acts 6:9; 11:20; 13:1). Even though Roman law said that a criminal must carry his own cross, Jesus was so exhausted by the rigors of the night, and especially his flogging (v. 15), that he was apparently unable to carry the crossbeam (the vertical bar of the cross was stationary and was left in place from execution to execution), so Simon, who is coming in from the country and presumably his work, is conscripted to do so. The prisoners are taken to Golgotha, slightly north of first-century Jerusalem, called the Place of the Skull, either because its topography resembled a skull (so the British General Gordon thought early in this century) or because it was the place of execution (v. 22). Jesus is offered a sedative (v. 23, cf. *Talmud Baba Sanhedrin* 43a), which he refuses, either because he has vowed not to taste wine again until he enters the kingdom (14:25) or because he does not want to die drugged (see Ps. 69:31; Prov. 31:6).

Criminals were executed naked, and their clothes were spoils for their executioners, but v. 24 also serves to echo Ps. 22:18. Allusions to this Psalm are abundant in Mark's narrative, and some commentators suggest it shaped the passion traditions. The crucifixion commences at 9:00 a.m., the third hour of the Roman day. It was the practice to affix to the criminal's cross his name and crime. Verse 26 reflects that practice and assigns to Jesus a title that is profoundly, if in this context ironically, true. Again, it was common to execute criminals in groups, and this is the case at Jesus' crucifixion, where two "bandits" (NRSV translation of *lestas,* the word Jesus uses in 14:48, Mark associates with Barabbas in 15:7, and Josephus associates with insurrectionists) are given the places on his right and left, places requested by James and John (10:37), who are nowhere to be found. Verse 28 is omitted by the oldest manuscript traditions and, in any case, Mark seldom quotes Hebrew scripture directly.

The mocking of Jesus begun in vv. 16-20 is continued in vv. 29-32. To Jesus' physical agony is added the suffering of total misunderstanding, indeed misrepresentation, of what he has taught (cf. vv. 29-30 with 13:2). Although the scribes might well attend an execution, what are the high priests doing at a location where contact with corpses might defile them (and so near Passover!)? The mocking described in v. 29 employs scriptural terms (Pss. 22:7; 109:25). Careful readers already know from 8:11-13 that the demand for a sign is evidence of unbelief. Even the political criminals executed with Jesus mock him. (Note how many of the details in these verses echo texts from Hebrew scripture: Pss. 22:7-8, 109:5; Wis. 2:17-18.)

Mark's narrative moves swiftly from 9:00 A.M. (v. 25) to noon (v. 33) when darkness covers the land until 3:00 P.M. Although I have been in Jerusalem when a Hamseen wind blew in dust from the desert that did, indeed, cause darkness in the afternoon, a naturalistic explanation like this (or an eclipse) is not the point. The darkness signals a terrible event, like the portents chronicled at the deaths of other great men in the ancient world. Mark would have us understand that, as human nature abases Jesus, the creation itself sympathizes with him (see Isa. 60:2; Amos 8:9).

Verse 34 has occasioned as much commentary as any verse in the Gospel. Jesus seems to be quoting Ps. 22:1. As is typical at dramatic moments in the narrative, Mark retains the original Aramaic (5:41). But what does the quotation signify? Some have suggested that because the psalm moves from despair to confidence in God, this ought not to be called a "cry of dereliction." They argue that the psalm means Jesus knows he is vindicated by God. In my view, this undercuts the radical humanity of Jesus, a humanity with which Mark's tradition has been profoundly in touch. As I view Jesus' agony in the garden as real agony (14:32-42), I view Jesus' scream here as one of real suffering. He experiences not only horrific physical (crucifixion) and emotional (abandonment and mocking) suffering, but the most terrible thing any deeply religious person can face: the sense that God has abandoned him, that he is completely alone in a hostile universe. In this moment, Jesus enters into the darkest experience that humanity can face.

If scholars and theologians have disputed the meaning of the cry, the original bystanders also were confused by it. Some thought he called for Elijah, who in Jewish tradition rescues the righteous (v. 35). In a fascinating article, Harald Sahlin suggests the bystanders heard Jesus say *Elia' ta'* or "Elijah, come" in Aramaic. Sahlin posits that Jesus cried out in Hebrew *Eli 'atta* or "My God, it's you." This Hebrew phrase occurs in Pss. 22:11; 31:15; and Isa. 44:17.[38] In fact, we cannot recover exactly what Jesus said or what the bystanders heard. The preacher must decide how to interpret v. 34 in the context of Mark's understanding of Jesus' passion. This would include the Markan theme of hearing and seeing but not understanding (4:12; 8:14-21). In any case, the last human words Jesus hears are those of continued mockery (vv. 35-36).

Mark's narrative preserves the tradition of John's Jesus who cries, "I thirst" (v. 36; Ps. 69:21; John 19:28). It is a severe mercy, but Jesus lingered on the cross only six hours (twelve was average, and some poor wretches lived several days) before dying (the Greek word *exepneusen* means literally "expired" or "breathed his last," suggesting to some scholars a voluntary death) with a loud cry (v. 37). What that cry meant only God knows. At the beginning of the Gospel, the heavens are torn open and God's Spirit descends on Jesus (1:10-11). At the end of the Gospel, Jesus returns that Spirit with a great cry and "the curtain of the temple was torn in two from top to bottom" (v. 38, as a priest tears his clothes in making a capital charge, cf. 14:63). The "curtain of the temple" was the curtain separating the Holy of Holies from the inner court of the temple (Exod 26:31-37). It was the holiest space in the holiest place, the place where God was understood to dwell. The temple itself provided progressive exclusion from it (the Court of the Gentiles, the Court of the Women, the Court of Israel, the Inner temple, and, finally the Holy of Holies, where only the High Priest, and only on the Day of Atonement, entered to atone for Israel's sins). Its rending symbolizes that the barrier between God and humans is removed (cf. Eph. 2:14-16, especially v. 14). Further, it presages for Mark the destruction of the temple and the end of Israel's cult, which is no longer needed, since Jesus, who has "given himself for many," has effected a once-and-for-all atonement (cf. Heb. 6:19-20 and 10:19-20). Symbolically and ironically at v. 38, what Jesus is accused of in 14:58 comes to pass.

Similarly, the centurion's confession in v. 39 is a theological high point of Mark's Gospel. The textual traditions disagree about exactly what was said. Did the centurion say, "This man was God's Son" (does the Greek have an anarthrous noun, one without an article?), or "This man was *a* son of God"? Mark's narrative here is quiet but dramatic. The centurion stood "facing" Jesus, watching his response to the abuses, watching him die. Perhaps he has been in attendance since the praetorium events (vv. 16-20). In any case, seeing led to his confession. The point for Mark is that it is only *after* Jesus' death on the cross that his connection with God can be grasped and fully confessed, *first* by a centurion, a Gentile, who represents the first of many Gentile believers and a group in whom Mark has a special interest. (Recall earlier accounts in the Gospel in which the "wrong" or unlikely person understands Jesus—2:13-14; 5:1-20; 7:24-30.) Again, what Jesus was mocked for admitting at 14:61-65 becomes a confession here.[39] And again in Mark's Gospel, the wrong person responds rightly.

Verses 40-41 seem almost an afterthought, but they are of crucial importance to the picture of discipleship in Mark and need to be read back on the whole of Jesus' ministry in the Gospel. The male disciples have fled, but the women—the two Marys and Salome (the "female inner circle" who parallel Peter, James, and John?)—have followed to the place of execution and stood watch with the dying Jesus. And they and "many other women" have been with him since the beginning in Galilee and "come up with him to Jerusalem" (v. 41). These women "followed," (*ekolouthoun*), the technical term for discipleship in Mark and the same word used of Andrew, Simon, and Levi (1:18; 2:14). It is inaccurate to think of Jesus traveling about with twelve men. In fact, there were many disciples, some of them women, who traveled with him. And the women "provided for him" (NRSV; cf. Luke 8:1-3), *diekonoun*, literally "served," the word from which the word *deacon* comes. Of the disciples of Jesus, only the women stood by him. It will be these women who link the historical Jesus with the risen Christ.[40] The women followers witnessed the death, burial (15:47), and resurrection (16:1-8) of Jesus and are a source of evidence for all three; and thus they are at the basis, indeed the eyewitnesses, of the church's most sacred tradition.

These texts are usually preached in the context of Holy Week: either on Passion (Palm) Sunday or Good Friday (in the Arabic-speaking Christian community, termed more appropriately "Sad Friday"). The liturgical context, however, should focus the sermon; the preacher might note that the narrative is framed by two strangers (Simon of Cyrene, 15:21; the centurion, 15:39), neither of whom have previous knowledge of Jesus, but whom Mark intends us to see in a positive light. They represent other unlikely characters in Mark's Gospel who respond appropriately when those who should have understood Jesus and his message do not (here, for example, the chief priests and scribes who mocked). Have modern Christians become so "close to" and "comfortable with" the cross that they are unable to see what it means and what it asks?

I, personally, have a particular distaste for sermons that try to "cheer up" this scene, either by interpreting v. 34 as a cry of triumph or by rushing too quickly to the garden of resurrection, which is still three days away in the narrative. Life is full of dark events and terrible suffering. Why should we pretend that our Gospel is not? I, at least, find in the suffering Jesus a profound point of identification and comfort. As Fr. Franklin Brookhart, rector of a church in which I worship regularly, told us, "Calvary is a window into the heart of God." Surely there is a brokenheartedness about our God, who is "not unable to sympathize with our weaknesses" (Heb. 4:15). In spite of some historic abuses, I am grateful that some branches of the Christian family have not abandoned prayer practices that facilitate serious reflection upon our Lord's passion (for example, the stations of the cross or the "sorrowful mysteries" of the rosary). Preparation for the sermon might best begin with one of them.

For Further Reading

J. D. Kingsbury, "The Significance of the Cross within Mark's Story," *Int* 47 (1993): 370–79.

Jerome Murphy-O'Connor," The Geography of Faith: Tracing the Via Dolorosa," *BR* 12 (1996): 32–41, 52–53.

Harald Sahlin, "Mk 15, 34," *Biblica* 33 (1952): 62–66.

Winsome Munro, "Women Disciples in Mark?" *CBQ* 44 (1982): 225–41.

15:42-47

The New Testament record and the historical confessions of the church insist that Jesus was "crucified, dead *and* buried" (italics mine). The burial of Jesus confirms that he was really dead. No sleight of hand occurred; no drugged person was resuscitated. Jesus was really dead and buried, and Isa. 53:9 was fulfilled.

Again, the Markan passion narrative evinces great exactitude with regard to time. "Evening" (v. 42) must have been before sunset or the Sabbath would have begun; thus Mark's narrative supports John's dating here. Joseph of Arimathea is an important part of the tradition. He is himself a Jew and a member of the Sanhedrin, which indicates that not all of Jewish officialdom opposed Jesus (contra 14:64, thus making false by definition blanket anti-Jewish statements in connection with the proclamation of Jesus' passion). Mark's description of him is interesting. He is from Arimathea, a city in Judea northwest of Jerusalem. Only Mark describes him as "respected" (*euschemon,* "prominent," "of repute," "noble," perhaps "wealthy,"[41] as having linen cloth on hand and access to a tomb suggest; cf. Matt. 27:57). He was "waiting expectantly for the kingdom of God" (v. 43), a suggestion that ties him to the preaching of John the Baptist and the early message of Jesus. This member of the council, who has much to lose in being associated with a troublemaker and "insurrectionist" whom his colleagues have condemned, "went boldly to Pilate" (v. 43), to whom he must have been known or he would not have gained access.

Noting that v. 46 could follow seamlessly from v. 43, some scholars think vv. 44-45 are a later addition. They serve the apologetic purpose of proving that Jesus was really dead, a fact stressed by the use of the word "corpse," *to ptoma,* in v. 45. But Pilate's response is perfectly reasonable, since some criminals lingered on the cross for days before dying. He summons "the centurion" (the same one who confessed in v. 39?) to corroborate Jesus' death before giving his corpse to Joseph. He by no means is required to do so. Bodies of those who died by capital punishment were not denied to their families, but bodies of those guilty of treason might be. Suetonius and Tacitus tell of many who were refused burial. The burial practices described in v. 46 are those of the time. Corpses were wrapped in linen, anointed with oil (or, less commonly, with spices) and placed in rolling stone tombs, tombs cut into rock faces and closed by flat, circular stones that moved in grooves cut into the ground at their openings. Later, when the flesh had decayed, the bones were placed in ossuaries.

The traditional approach to Joseph of Arimathea (which I have outlined) paints him as a noble figure. But Raymond Brown suggests another possibility. He notes that Joseph was a member of the Sanhedrin, and Mark says all of them had agreed on Jesus' guilt. If he were "looking" or "waiting" for the kingdom, he had not found it in Jesus. Brown suggests he buried Jesus because the law demanded it, not because he was a follower of Jesus (see Deut. 21:22-23). The problem of the ritual impurity he would have incurred would have been overridden by the command to bury the dead. None of the burial customs mentioned elsewhere in the New Testament are done for Jesus here, and in Mark the tomb is "a tomb," not Joseph's. According to Brown, Jesus is conveniently and quickly buried by a member of the Sanhedrin, who simply wanted the corpse off the cross before the Sabbath. The women disciples in v. 47 are not allowed to participate because Joseph did not know them. He was not a disciple of Jesus at the time, but is remembered because *later* he became a follower of Jesus.[42] However one decides to assign motives to Joseph, the women remain an important (and universal) part of the burial tradition. The two Marys who saw Jesus die (v. 40) now see where the corpse is laid (v. 47). They are the continuous witnesses of the passion narrative and are thus credible witnesses to proclaim Jesus' resurrection.

Traditional preaching of the passage is straightforward. At great risk to himself, Joseph seeks to do a final service for Jesus and is remembered for his devotion. But even if Joseph is understood in terms of Raymond Brown's interpretation, he serves as an interesting object lesson. Joseph, who has no real loyalty to or concern for Jesus, carries out a religious duty, burying the indigent. And in the course of doing his duty something else happens to him. He comes into contact with Jesus. And that contact is transforming. He is like Paul. Once an opponent of Jesus (a member of the council who condemned him), he comes to be remembered in the most sacred and important part of the tradition about him. Or the sermon might focus on the two Marys. What courage they must have had and how strong emotionally they were to have stood by Jesus at his execution, followed Joseph to Pilate to see what would happen to the body, and looked on as Jesus is hastily buried (without ceremony)! And they do not go home and collapse. They go away to make preparations to return and carry out a more complete burial. I find it a comfort at the end of this terrible story to think that Jesus had friends like that.

For Further Reading

Raymond Brown, "The Burial of Jesus (Mark 15:42-47)," *CBQ* 50 (1988): 233–45.

Excursus on the Ending of Mark's Gospel

Most good translations of the New Testament in English now offer three endings to the Gospel: 16:8 (which scholars prefer); 16:8 with a sentence added that describes the women's proclamation (the "shorter ending"); and 16:9-20, which include postresurrection appearances of Jesus and an account of his ascension (the "longer ending"). While scholarly consensus holds that 16:8 is, in fact, the ending of Mark and that the other material represents later additions, a discussion of the issue provides an opportunity to visit again some overarching themes in Mark's Gospel. (As an aside, let me say that I have thought a good deal about this issue and read widely in the literature on it. Some of the ideas I have read may well have embedded themselves so deeply in my thinking that I can no longer cite their source. If, as a result, I have neglected to note a source, I beg pardon in advance.)

Admittedly 16:8 is a perplexing ending for "good news": "and they said nothing to anyone, for they were afraid." Some scholars postulate that for some reason Mark was prevented from finishing the Gospel or that the real conclusion was somehow torn from the autograph (the original manuscript). Others think the original ending was deliberately suppressed early on. But there is strong evidence that 16:8 is the intended ending. Of the 163 words in the longer ending, nineteen words and two phrases appear nowhere else in Mark. The summarizing of appearances found in these verses is not characteristic of Mark's otherwise vivid, detailed style. The handling of snakes and drinking of poison are the sort of thaumaturgy to which Mark's Jesus objected; he and his disciples faced the ordinary consequences of their actions in the earlier parts of the Gospel. And, finally, the appearances described in vv. 9-20 do not agree with the first eight verses of the chapter.

On the other hand, some students of the Gospel prefer to see 16:20 as the authentic ending of the Gospel. They argue that elsewhere (15:3-8) the reality of Jesus' resurrection depends upon appearances in his risen form. Since resurrection is predicted in the passion predictions, hearers/readers expect them at the end. If the Gospel ends at 16:8, the hearers/readers are left with the problem of Peter's denial and the psychologically unsatisfying ending with "fear." Furthermore, v. 8 ends with the particle *gar* (for), which usually requires an object. To expect that hearers or readers would understand Jesus' resurrection on the basis of vv. 1-8 is too much to expect, suggest advocates of the longer ending, and, in any case, 14:28 and 16:7 point forward to Galilee and appearances there.

Such objections have received compelling responses. Theologically, in Mark, the empty tomb is but a pointer to what really matters: the encounter of the living Jesus with his disciples. Throughout Mark, Jesus has restrained the tendency to disclose himself in manifestations of power for all to see. An ending at 16:8 is consistent with this practice. Recent investigations have found that "for" could end a sentence, and the LXX has many "for" endings to which no one objects (cf. Gen. 18:15, LXX). In any case, Mark is fond of short sentences with "for" (1:16; 5:42; 9:6; 11:18).[43] Finally, proponents of v. 8 as the ending note that 16:1-8 are not that hard to understand. An angelic messenger announces that Jesus is no longer among the dead. "Fear" is an appropriate and frequent biblical response to angelic figures. The reverence and silence at the end of Mark suggest the realization that the old world is "finished" and a new day of God has begun.

Attestation, style, content, and theology all suggest (to me at least) that what comes after 16:8 is non-Markan. There are two practical responses to this vis-à-vis how to treat vv. 9-20. First, the longer ending is canonical, even if it is not Markan, and is thus fully scriptural and should be treated accordingly. Or the material represents an early tradition of the church even if it is not Markan; thus it should not be rejected, but theology ought not to be based upon texts that appear only here.

This may close the scholarly issue, but it does not address the pastoral issues that arise when people figure out "where Mark ended." What if our parishioners are upset by the fear and silence with which Mark closes? The ending of Mark, I would suggest, points once again to the cross and its meaning as central to Mark's thinking. (This, of course, is the whole premise of Robert Gundry's magisterial commentary, *Mark: A Commentary on His Apology for the Cross*, to which I have referred so often.) Jesus' resurrection is presupposed and certainly known even by Mark's original audience, but it must be understood in terms of the cross. As Lightfoot noted, the crucified Messiah as the fulfillment of God's promise is the chief theme of Mark's Gospel.[44] In Mark's Gospel, the resurrection serves the cross, not vice versa.

Mark's ending is consistent with what has gone before in the Gospel. The passion story presents a beautiful account of the devotion of the women and a dark picture of the Twelve, who are nowhere to be seen. This is consistent with the whole of Mark, in which the disciples misunderstood Jesus and the "unlikely" persons responded positively. And v. 7 makes clear that the Twelve are not rejected by Jesus, but are called to meet him in Galilee; Peter is singled out and thus reconciled. With regard to the women's fearful silence, perhaps it is another instance of Mark's realism. The women have come to deal with the body of one whom the Jewish leaders have condemned and the Romans killed. Will they meet soldiers? Under the circumstances, they have reason to fear both Roman and Jewish authorities. The women are afraid because they are standing by an empty tomb and they expect a corpse. "Fear" is the usual response to the unexpected in Mark (and to heavenly beings in the Bible) and is a powerful symbol of human inadequacy in the presence of divine action.

A. T. Lincoln argues that the juxtaposition of 16:7 and 16:8 are important in that they provide a paradigm of Christian existence according to Mark. They present a word of promise and of human failure, but the word of promise predominates for the future. The Gospel closes with encouragement to persevere despite failure and disobedience. If disciples and witnesses fail, the Gospel is not lost.[45] This would have been a powerful message for Mark's original audience, among whom, no doubt, there were those who had not lived up to complete fidelity to Jesus in the face of difficulty.[46]

To raise the issue another way, what concerns of Mark would have led him to omit appearances of the risen Jesus? The answer has to do with another pastoral issue for Mark: the growth and spread of faith as he has understood it and depicted it throughout the Gospel. Mark has wanted to make clear that faith is generated by the word of Jesus, not by miracles. Jesus is the teacher in Mark; his message is more important than his miracles (even if we get more miracle stories than teaching units). Indeed, to seek signs denotes unbelief (recall 8:11-13). Mark places no special value on "being there," on seeing the risen Jesus, precisely because faith in him comes through the proclamation of the Word.

Mark 16:1-8, then, is a beginning as much as an ending. It pushes the narrative into the "present tense" of the hearer/reader. It reminds us that dread and fear as well as love and faith are essential notes in Christianity. This has been vividly depicted in the realism of the passion narrative, in which Jesus struggles in the garden and screams from the cross. Mark's purpose is to get the hearer/reader to understand that to confess Jesus as Messiah and Son of God is to confess him as the one God appointed to die on the cross. This is why the confession of Jesus as Son of God comes only at his death, at the foot of the cross, and on the lips of a Gentile centurion. Whether we like it or not, crucifixion is God's way in the world. A "happily ever after" ending is not appropriate for Mark's community or for Mark's theology. But the renewed promises of Jesus to the disciples in 16:7 are a word of grace in spite of denial and of suffering. It is, in the words of Morna Hooker, a call to the failed disciples to begin again.[47] Mark 16:8 works theologically as the end of Mark and reminds us of what he is doing in the rest of the Gospel. And ironically, it leaves the hearer/reader in the position of the women: will we or will we not take up the heavenly charge to "go, tell"?

For Further Reading

Michael W. Holmes, "To Be Continued: The Many Endings of the Gospel of Mark," *BRev* 17 (2001): 12–23, 48–50.

R. H. Lightfoot, "St. Mark's Gospel—Complete or Incomplete," in *The Gospel Message of St. Mark* (Oxford: Oxford Univ. Press, 1962), chap. 7.

A. T. Lincoln, "The Promise and the Failure: Mark 16:7, 8," *JBL* 108 (1989): 283–300.

Norman Petersen, "When Is the End Not the End? Reflections on the Ending of Mark's Narrative," *Int* 34 (1980): 15–66.

16:1-8

Chapter 16 opens with a double time reference: "when the Sabbath was over" (v. 1) and "very early on the first day of the week, when the sun had risen" (v. 2). Throughout the passion narrative Mark has had a special interest in time sequences (see the opening of chapter 7 and of this chapter). Here the time references are important to communicate that the Sabbath is over, so the women are not breaking Sabbath observance; also because in that culture it was customary for relatives and friends to visit the grave of the deceased for three days after burial (see also John 11). The resurrection account opens on "Sunday" or the first day of the Jewish week, not on the Sabbath.

The women who accompanied the ministry and attended the death of Jesus (15:40-41) now come to attend to his burial. Their careful identification is noteworthy. Mary of Magdala appears in all four resurrection accounts. "Mary the mother of James" may be the mother of James, son of Alphaeus" (3:18, one of the Twelve). Her ties to Jesus would thus go back to his Galilean ministry (cf. 15:40), as would those of Salome, traditionally the mother of James and John, the sons of Zebedee (cf. 1:19; Matt. 27:56). That the women come with "spices" (v. 1, literally *aromata,* "spices" or "aromatic salves") is noteworthy on two counts. First, it indicates that they did not expect resurrection; they expected to find a corpse. Second, "oils" were normal for burial anointing (see notes on 14:2-9 above); "spices" are associated with the burial of a king (see 2 Chron. 16:14). Mark indicates that the crucified criminal is being treated exactly "as charged," as "King of the Jews" (15:2, 9, 12, 18, 26). The women know the tomb has been closed with a stone (15:46), and they speculate about who will remove it for them (v. 3). Mark stresses the stone in v. 3, and the "stone, which was very large" in v. 4 to make clear that the body cannot have been stolen. If the women are to complete their task, they know they will need help. And it has already come, but in a manner beyond their wildest dreams!

Seeing that the large stone "has already been rolled back" (v. 4), the women do not hesitate or cower. They "entered the tomb" (v. 5). Only after they enter the tomb are they "alarmed" (NRSV, *exethambethesan* might better be translated "they were astonished"; the compound verb, which occurs only here in the New Testament, indicates intense emotion).[48] Their fear is not of grave robbers, nor is it natural reticence at entering a tomb. It is a response to seeing a heavenly being (Mark's description of their response in v. 6a is the typical biblical reaction to an angelic being), for so Mark characterizes the "young man" of v. 5. The "white robe" suggests the great whiteness associated with the glory of the Transfiguration (9:3). Some commentators have associated this figure with the young man of 14:51-52, but in my view he is more like the angelic beings in 2 Macc. 3:26, 33. That he is "sitting on the right side" is not just a Markan detail; the "right side" is the place of authority.

It is from this place of authority that he issues the word of comfort and commission in vv. 6-7. Biblical angelophanies always include a word of reassurance. In fact, as noted earlier, the characteristic heavenly word to earthly beings is "fear not." While reassuring the women, v. 6 contains in miniature the substance of the early Christian kerygma. The "young man" knows they "are looking for Jesus of Nazareth who was crucified." He indicates divine prescience about their intentions (which legitimates his right to command them in the next verse) and also that this was, indeed, the correct tomb. No mistake has been made. But Jesus of Nazareth (so designated by the "unclean" spirit world at the outset of the Gospel, 1:23) "has been raised" (*egerthe*). This may be Mark's most important use of what I have called the "Divine passive." The point is that God has raised Jesus from the dead. God has vindicated the message and person of Jesus by raising him from the dead. Mark's aorist passive here is consistent with its parallel uses in other places in the New Testament where the kerygma is rehearsed (cf. Acts 2:24; 1 Cor. 15:4). But the women are not to take even an authoritative angel's word for it. They are invited to see "the place where they laid him" (v. 6). They are to carry back a report on the basis of firsthand evidence.

The charge to "go, tell" comes in v. 7. The women are to report what they have heard and seen to "his disciples and Peter." Peter is singled out because he has both insisted he will remain faithful (14:26-31) and failed miserably in doing so (14:32-42, 66-72). A word is given especially to Peter, who must have felt his betrayals placed him forever outside the circle of discipleship. He is called back into the circle. The Jesus who has been raised "is going ahead (*proagein*) of you to Galilee." This can be taken both spatially (Jesus is again leading them; they are to follow) and temporally (Jesus has preceded them, in death, and to Galilee). "Galilee" is a symbol for Gentiles (Isa. 9:1) and thus reflects Mark's interest in the Gentile mission, but it was also the place where Jesus' message was well received (versus Jerusalem, which has been the place of opposition). Additionally, Galilee is the normal, ordinary "home place" of the original disciples. Jesus is not to be found "in the tomb," but in the normal round of daily activity, precisely because he has "gone before." "*There* you will see him" (italics mine), not in the place of opposition (which he has over-come) or the tomb (from which he has been raised). All of this is "just as [Jesus] told you." The brief verses of the resurrection account fulfill many of the "predictions" of Jesus in the Markan passion narrative (14:21, 28).

Verse 7 is crucial to Mark's picture of discipleship. Throughout the Gospel the disciples have been ambiguous figures, sometimes completely misunderstanding Jesus, sometimes having partial insight. Heretofore the women disciples have been presented as more faithful than the men. But in the following verse their discipleship, too, will be called into question. But Jesus is not ashamed of failed disciples. The narrative suggests that a divine messenger has been dispatched to call them back. As Brown notes, "the Marcan readers are not left in total suspense about the fate of Jesus' disci-ples: he has no intention of losing them permanently."[49]

The Gospel closes with a great Markan irony. The women who were strong enough to attend Jesus' passion, brave enough to follow Joseph of Arimathea, courageous enough to go to the place of burial and enter a tomb not knowing what they would find—now, even they fail. Mark's last word is "they were afraid" (v. 8), and this in a Gospel in which fear signals lack of faith (4:40-41; 6:50-52). "This uncomplimentary portrait is in har-mony with Mark's somber insistence that none can escape suffering in the following of Jesus."[50] The Gospel ends on the chord it has struck through-out: one note is the call to discipleship and following, the other is the fear of what it will mean to do so. As Thomas Boomershine puts it, "flight into silence was the supreme danger as well as the ultimate irony."[51]

But attentive hearers/readers of the Gospel of Mark have known since chapter 4 that God's word is more powerful than human witness. The women may say nothing because they are afraid, but the power of the word of the kingdom is greater than human fear. Here, certainly, is the personal, psychological "good news," which parallels the public, historic "good news" of the resurrection itself. In the final analysis, Mark's Gospel is about the power of God, not the failure of human beings. "In this light the juxtapo-sition of 16:7 and 16:8 provides a paradigm for Christian existence accord-ing to Mark—the word of promise and the failure of the disciples, and yet the word of promise prevailing despite human failure."[52]

The resurrection of Jesus itself is the heart of the "good news" of this pas-sage and should be the focus of the sermon. But there are other possibilities here in the liturgical context of Easter preaching or at other times of the year. What a comfort it can be to our parishioners to remind them that, when they fail (and we all do from time to time), Jesus is faithful in seeing that his mis-sion is accomplished anyhow, in calling them back "into the circle," and in continuing to love those who have failed. Jesus just keeps reaching out to people who do not quite measure up: to Peter, to the spice-bearing women, to us. Indeed, nothing "will be able to separate us from the love of God in Christ Jesus our Lord" (Rom 8:39), not even our imperfect selves.

The text also provides an opportunity to lift up the importance of women in the ministry and mission of Jesus. Because we are so familiar with the story, we are prone to forget what a startling thing it is that the apostolic commission is entrusted to women. History's most important message is given to those who could not give legal testimony in court in their own culture. Here is a Markan irony with an important message for those who still question the legitimacy of women's ministry in the church. In the Orthodox tradition, Mary Magdalene is called "apostle to the apostles," an apt designation.

Finally, I am intrigued by the phrase "he is going ahead of you to Galilee" (v. 7). In a few words, Mark's notion of discipleship is encapsulated: Jesus "goes before," disciples follow. The phrase suggests many levels of meaning. Disciples are never "lost" so long as their master "goes ahead" of them. If the phrase is understood temporally as well as spatially, then it suggests that there is nothing that a disciple will face that the Master has not already experienced. Jesus has already faced all that we will face; he knows it and understands it. And the locus of this profound identification between the one who "goes before" and the "followers" is "Galilee," the place of the daily routine and home. Now is the time and here is the place where we "follow Jesus," and he "goes before." (This was Jesus' word to the former demoniac in 5:19.)

For Further Reading

Thomas E. Boomershine, "Mark 16:8 and the Apostolic Commission," *JBL* 100 (1981): 225–39.

Andrew T. Lincoln, "The Promise and the Failure: Mark 16:7, 8," *JBL* 108 (1989): 283–300.

16:9-20

As noted in the excursus above, vv. 9-20 are almost certainly a second-century appendix to Mark's Gospel[53] and do not appear in the earliest manuscripts of the Gospel. There are four distinct units of material, each of which seems to allude to a resurrection appearance of Jesus in another Gospel, often Luke's. These units are as follows: vv. 9-11, an appearance to Mary Magdalene; vv. 12-13, an appearance to travelers; vv. 14-18, an appearance and commissioning; vv. 10-20, the ascension.

The appearance to Mary Magdalene in vv. 9-11 does not seem to assume the account just related in vv. 1-8. It does echo information provided by Luke (8:2; 24:11) and by John (20:1-18). (Cf. 16:6 and 11. Jesus' associates reject an eyewitness report. Is that because it came on the lips of a woman?) Similarly vv. 12-13 provide in outline the Emmaus Road encounter that is told in full in Luke 24:13-35. The commissioning event described in vv. 14-18 echoes similar material in Matt. 28:19 and Acts 1:8. The "upbraiding" (*oneidisen*, reproached, rebuked) in v. 14 seems slightly out of character for Mark's Jesus but does depict two of the characteristic attitudes of disciples in this Gospel: lack of faith and stubbornness. Interestingly, Jesus scolds them for the behavior described in v. 11, not believing the witnesses "who saw him after he had risen" (v. 14). In the entire Gospel tradition, these witnesses were, of course, the women. As he has throughout Mark (and in other Gospels), Jesus defends the legitimacy of female disciples, and Jesus' rebuke in v. 14 recalls the general Markan theme of belief/faith from unlikely sources.

It has been noted that the commission in vv. 15-16 seems abrupt after the rebuke of v. 14. Nevertheless, it is the case that all of the Gospels end with some form of commissioning of Jesus' disciples. (And this is also true of the authentic ending of Mark, with the charge to the women in v. 7.) Verse 16 underlines the importance of belief/faith as a Markan theme, although the verse itself sounds more like John 3:18. With regard to vv. 17-18, Nineham remarks that "the argument to the truth of Christianity from the ability of the Christians to work miracles is typical of second-century apologetic."[54] But the same idea appears in the New Testament in Heb 2:3-4. In Mark's Gospel, the disciples have already healed and performed exorcisms (3:15; 6:13), and all the other "signs" except drinking poison appear in the New Testament, again usually in Lukan settings (cf. Acts 2:4; 28:3-6). (Also cf. 1 Cor. 17; James 5:14-15. Eusebius does preserve a tradition in which Barsabbas Justus [Acts 1:23] drinks poison and survives.)

Similarly, the ascension account in vv. 19-20 seems to echo in substance Luke 24:50-53 and Acts 1:6-11 (and Acts 1:11 in language). Verse 19 makes use of Ps. 110:1, a key christological text for the early Christians that depicts the heavenly existence and cosmic authority ("at the right hand of God," cf. 16:5) of the ascended Lord Jesus. (Cf. 14:62; Rom. 8:34; 1 Pet. 3:22.) In contrast to the authentic ending of Mark at 16:8, v. 20 closes with the disciples' obedience to the commission given in v. 15. They "proclaimed the good news everywhere," which was Jesus' understanding of his own mission (1:38), "while the Lord worked with them and confirmed the message by the signs that accompanied it (v.20)." Work accomplished in mission is work carried out in company with Jesus and by means of his empowering. The passage closes with another reference to the "signs," which were prominent in the previous section (vv. 17-18) and give the "longer ending" of Mark a Johannine theological cast.

Hugh Anderson's commentary on the alternative endings of Mark is helpful. Anderson notes:

These Endings can hardly be regarded as canonical. Yet they do have their own intrinsic significance. They show us how the church continued to think of Easter as central and decisive, as the hinge of its history and belief and above all of its missionary proclamation and service. The Longer Ending represents one of the earliest attempts we know to construct a harmony of Easter events out of the varied data of the Gospels and Acts.[55]

In my view this "harmony" relies heavily on the events in Luke's Gospel and the theology of John's. Texts from the longer ending of Mark do not appear in the Sunday lectionaries but do occasionally appear in the Roman Catholic daily Mass lectionary and in the Easter Week daily lectionary, and they can, with care, be preached at other times as well. The crucial point in such preaching, of course, is the centrality of the Easter events. The theme that runs throughout vv. 9-20 is that of seeing/proclaiming/believing (vv. 10-11, 13, 14, 15-16, 20). This is a more theologically solid approach to the passage than a focus on the "signs" in vv. 17-18. As were miracles in the body of Mark's Gospel, the signs here are secondary proofs of the truth of the message (and the authority of those who proclaim it), which is of primary importance. The reality of the risen Jesus and his continued involvement with his disciples provides both continuity with the resurrection account in vv. 1-8 and a word of hope for today's disciples. The Gospel continues to spread and the Lord continues to work with us (v. 20), and that is very good news indeed.

For Further Reading

Raymond Brown, "Mark 16:9-20 (The "Long Ending"): Three Appearances of Jesus," in *A Risen Christ at Eastertime* (Collegeville, Minn.: Liturgical, 1991), 17–22.

Robert Bratcher and Eugene Nida, "Additional Note: The Ending of the Gospel of Mark," in *A Translator's Handbook on the Gospel of Mark* (New York: United Bible Societies, 1961), 517–22.

Appendix 1
Lectionaries

Mark is the focal gospel for Year B of the three-year lectionary cycle. Gospel texts given here are for the principal service on the Sunday or for major feasts/holidays/commemorations of Year B.

Roman Catholic: Year B

Advent I	Mark 13:33-37
Advent II	Mark 1:1-8
Advent III	John 1:6-8, 19-28
Advent IV	Luke 1:26-38
Christmas Day	John 1:1-18
Holy Family	Luke 2:22-40
Epiphany	Matthew 2:1-12
Baptism of the Lord	Mark 1:7-11
[Markan texts for daily Mass begin here.]	
Ordinary Time 2	John 1:35-42
Ordinary Time 3	Mark 1:14-20
Ordinary Time 4	Mark 1:21-28
Ordinary Time 5	Mark 1:29-39
Ordinary Time 6	Mark 1:40-45
Ordinary Time 7	Mark 2:1-12
Ordinary Time 8	Mark 2:18-22
Ordinary Time 9	Mark 2:23—3:6
Lent I	Mark 1:12-15
Lent II	Mark 9:2-10
Lent III	John 2:13-25
Lent IV	John 3:14-21
Lent V	John 12:20-33
Passion/Palm	Mark 14:1—15:47
Easter	John 20:1-9
Easter 2	John 20:19-31
Easter 3	Luke 24:35-48
Easter 4	John 10:11-18
Easter 5	John 15:1-8
Easter 6	John 15:9-17
Ascension	Mark 16:15-20
Easter 7	John 17:11b-19
Pentecost	John 20:19-23
Holy Trinity	Matthew 28:16-20
Body & Blood of Christ	Mark 14:12-16, 22-26
Ordinary Time 13	Mark 5:21-43

Ordinary Time 14	Mark 6:1-6
Ordinary Time 15	Mark 6:7-13
Ordinary Time 16	Mark 6:30-34
Ordinary Time 17	John 6:1-15
Transfiguration	Mark 9:2-10
Ordinary Time 19	John 6:41-51
Ordinary Time 20	John 6:51-58
Ordinary Time 21	John 6:60-69
Ordinary Time 22	Mark 7:1-8
Ordinary Time 23	Mark 7:31-37
Ordinary Time 24	Mark 8:27-35
Ordinary Time 25	Mark 9:30-37
Ordinary Time 26	Mark 9:38-43, 45, 47-48
Ordinary Time 27	Mark 10:2-16
Ordinary Time 28	Mark 10:17-30
Ordinary Time 29	Mark 10:35-45
Ordinary Time 30	Mark 10:46-52
Ordinary Time 31	Mark 12:28b-34
Ordinary Time 32	Mark 12:38-44
Ordinary Time 33	Mark 13:24-32
Christ the King	John 18:33b-37

The Episcopal Church: Year B

Advent I	Mark 13:(24-32) 33-37
Advent II	Mark 1:1-8
Advent III	John 1:6-8, 23-30 (John 3:3-30)
Advent IV	Luke 1:26-38
Christmas Day I	Luke 2:1-14 (15-20)
Christmas I	John 1:1-18
Holy Name	Luke 2:15-21
Christmas 2	Matthew 2:13-15, 19-23
Epiphany	Matthew 2:1-12
Epiphany 1	Mark 1:7-11
Epiphany 2	John 1:43-51
Epiphany 3	Mark 1:14-20
Epiphany 4	Mark 1:21-28
Epiphany 5	Mark 1:29-39
Epiphany 6	Mark 1:40-45
Epiphany 7	Mark 2:1-12
Epiphany 8	Mark 2:18-22
Last Epiphany	Mark 9:2-9
Lent I	Mark 1:9-13
Lent II	Mark 8:31-38
Lent III	John 2:13-22
Lent IV	John 6:4-15

Lent V	John 12:20-33
Liturgy of Palms	Mark 11:1-11a
Palm Sunday	Mark (14:32-72) 15:1-39 (40-47)
Easter (Principal Service)	Mark 16:1-8
Easter 2	John 20:19-31
Easter 3	Luke 24:36b-48
Easter 4	John 10:11-16
Easter 5	John 14:15-21
Easter 6	John 15:9-17
Ascension	Mark 16:9-15, 19-20 (second text)
Easter 7	John 17:11b-19
Pentecost	John 20:19-23
Trinity Sunday	John 3:1-16
Proper 1 (5/11)	Mark 1:40-45
Proper 2 (5/18)	Mark 2:1-12
Proper 3 (5/23)	Mark 2:18-22
Proper 4 (6/1)	Mark 2:23-28
Proper 5 (6/8)	Mark 3:20-35
Proper 6 (6/15)	Mark 4:26-34
Proper 7 (6/22)	Mark 4:35-41 (5:1-20)
Proper 8 (6/29)	Mark 5:22-24, 35b-43
Proper 9 (7/6)	Mark 6:1-6
Proper 10 (7/13)	Mark 6:7-13
Proper 11 (7/20)	Mark 6:30-44
Proper 12 (7/27)	Mark 6:45-52
Proper 13 (8/3)	John 6:24-35
Proper 14 (8/10)	John 6:37-51
Proper 15 (8/17)	John 6:53-59
Proper 16 (8/24)	John 6:60-69
Proper 17 (8/31)	Mark 7:1-8, 14-15, 21-23
Proper 18 (9/7)	Mark 7:31-37
Proper 19 (9/14)	Mark 8:27-38 or 9:14-29
Proper 20 (9/21)	Mark 9:30-37
Proper 21 (9/28)	Mark 9:38-43, 45, 47-48
Proper 22 (10/5)	Mark 10:2-9
Proper 23 (10/12)	Mark 10:17-27 (28-31)
Proper 24 (10/19)	Mark 10:35-45
Proper 25 (10/26)	Mark 10:46-52
Proper 26 (11/2)	Mark 12:28-34
Proper 27 (11/9)	Mark 12:38-44
Proper 28 (11/16)	Mark 13:14-23
Proper 29 (11/23)	John 18:33-37 or Mark 11:1-11

The Common Lectionary

Advent I	Mark 13:24-37

Advent II	Mark 1:1-8
Advent III	John 1:6-8, 19-28
Advent IV	Luke 1:26-38
Christmas Day	John 1:1-14
Christmas 1	Luke 2:22-40
Christmas 2	John 1:(1-9) 10-18
Epiphany	Matthew 2:1-12
Baptism of the Lord	Mark 1:4-11
Ordinary Time 2	John 1:43-51
Ordinary Time 3	Mark 1:14-20
Ordinary Time 4	Mark 1:21-28
Ordinary Time 5	Mark 1:29-39
Ordinary Time 6	Mark 1:40-45
Ordinary Time 7	Mark 2:1-12
Ordinary Time 8	Mark 2:13-22
Transfiguration	Mark 9:2-9
Lent I	Mark 1:9-15
Lent II	Mark 8:31-38
Lent III	John 2:13-22
Lent IV	John 3:14-21
Lent V	John 12:20-33
Liturgy of the Palms	Mark 11:1-11
Passion/Palm Sunday	Mark 14:1—15:47 or Mark 15:1-39 (40-47)
Easter	Mark 16:1-8
Easter I	John 20:19-31
Easter II	Luke 24:36b-48
Easter III	John 10:11-18
Easter IV	John 15:1-8
Easter V	John 15:9-17
Ascension	Luke 24:44-53
Easter VII	John 17:6-19
Pentecost	John 15:26-27; 16:4b-15
Trinity	John 3:1-17
Ordinary Time 9	Mark 2:23—3:6
Ordinary Time 10	Mark 3:20-35
Ordinary Time 11	Mark 4:26-34
Ordinary Time 12	Mark 4:35-41
Ordinary Time 13	Mark 5:21-43
Ordinary Time 14	Mark 6:1-13
Ordinary Time 15	Mark 6:14-29
Ordinary Time 16	Mark 6:30-34, 53-56
Ordinary Time 17	John 6:1-21
Ordinary Time 18	John 6:24-35
Ordinary Time 19	John 6:35, 41-51
Ordinary Time 20	John 6:51-58
Ordinary Time 21	John 6:56-69

Appendix 2
Helps for Preaching Mark

The following is not intended to be an exhaustive list of current scholarship on Mark's Gospel. Such a list would be very extensive. Rather, I think of these as "suggestions for the pastor's library." They are works that I have found of particular help specifically in preaching and teaching Mark and in using Mark as a starting point for prayer and meditation. These are the criteria for inclusion, and no negative judgment is to be inferred on the many excellent works on Mark that do not appear in this list.

General Reference Works

I assume that most pastors own a good study Bible and a synopsis of the Gospels (those in Greek and English prepared by the United Bible Societies are recommended). *The Anchor Bible Dictionary* and *The Dictionary of Jesus and the Gospels* provide excellent introductory essays on Mark and many articles on issues of specific interest. Nor is the older *Interpreter's Dictionary of the Bible* without value. For students of Mark who know Greek, Bruce M. Metzger's *A Textual Commentary on the Greek New Testament,* 2d ed. (New York: United Bible Societies, 1994); Fritz Reinecker and Cleon Rogers, *Linguistic Key to the Greek New Testament* (Grand Rapids: Zondervan, 1983); and Robert Bratcher and Eugene Nida, *A Translator's Handbook on St. Mark* (New York: United Bible Societies, 1961), are invaluable.

Commentaries

An exhaustive recent commentary on Mark's Gospel is Robert H. Gundry's *Mark: A Commentary on His Apology for the Cross* (Grand Rapids: Eerdmans, 1993), which, in addition to the excellent commentary itself, provides an extensive bibliography. For preaching purposes, I have found two commentaries by British scholars to be of particular interest: Morna D. Hooker's *The Gospel according to St. Mark* (Peabody, Mass.: Hendrickson, 1991) and D. E. Nineham's *The Gospel of St. Mark* (Harmondsworth: Penguin, 1963). Both provide a wealth of information on the historical and cultural context of Mark and on his literary skill, and both deal solidly and responsibly with the text. Hooker's commentary has the added advantage of addressing theological issues as they arise (often in an excursus), and if the preacher/teacher can afford only one commentary, this is the one I recommend. Although it has been out of print for some time, Ralph Martin's commentary in the Knox Preaching Guide series, *Mark* (Atlanta: John Knox, 1981), is a concise and helpful thought-starter for sermons.

A work I have found of particular help, edited by Thomas Oden and Christopher Hall, is *Ancient Christian Commentary on Scripture: Mark* (Downers Grove: InterVarsity, 1998). The editors have excerpted material on the texts of Mark from the church fathers (mothers, alas, are largely omitted). This is a convenient way for the student/preacher to place a Markan text in the wider context of what the historic church has thought about it. I have found the volume a useful place to find sermon-starters. And when the preacher includes material from the volume in the sermon, parishioners get a bit of painless church history.

Book-Length Studies of Mark

Happily, Mark's Gospel has been the focus of much scholarly attention in recent years, with the result that there are many studies on the Gospel available. Two are of particular help in introducing the general issues connected with the study of the Gospel as they relate to the church and to Christian life: Adela Yarbro Collins, *The Beginning of the Gospel: Probings of Mark in Context* (Minneapolis: Fortress Press, 1992), and Frank Matera, *What Are They Saying about Mark?* (New York: Paulist, 1987). The latter is a summary of the scholarly questions raised in connection with Mark in the latter half of the twentieth century and provides a broad and concise overview of the issues. Although it is an older work, I have found R. H. Lightfoot's solid presentation of issues in *The Gospel Message of St. Mark* (Oxford: Oxford Univ. Press, 1962) to be of ongoing relevance and help.

Two collections of essays on Mark will deepen the interpreter's understanding of Mark the writer and theologian: Ernest Best's *Disciples and Discipleship: Studies in the Gospel according to Mark* (Edinburgh: T. & T. Clark, 1986), which is especially helpful for understanding the practical issues confronting Mark's original audience; and William Telford's edited volume, *The Interpretation of Mark* (Edinburgh: T. & T. Clark, 1995), which is a wide-ranging collection of important scholarly articles on Mark written over the past fifty years.

The student of Mark will find many other helpful works. Preachers are especially encouraged to consult the publishing houses of their own denominations for materials on Mark. I have recommended these few books because I think they are ecumenically appropriate for any Christian and exhibit solid scholarship, general accessibility, practical applicability, and theological moderation.

Notes

Preface

1. Notable exceptions include Ralph Martin, *Mark* (Atlanta: John Knox, 1981), now unfortunately out of print; Robert S. Reid, *Preaching Mark* (St. Louis: Chalice, 1996); Lamar Williamson Jr., *Mark* (Atlanta: John Knox, 1983); *The Interpreter's Bible*, ed. G. A. Buttrick et al., 2 vols. (New York: Abingdon, 1951–1957); and Leander E. Keck et al., eds., *NIB* (Nashville: Abingdon, 1995).

2. Pheme Perkins, "The Gospel of Mark," in Leander E. Keck et al., eds., *NIB*, vol. 8 (Nashville: Abingdon, 1995), 513.

Introduction

1. See, for example, Paul J. Achtemeier, "Mark, Gospel of," in *ABD* 4:541–57; Frederick Grant, "Mark: Introduction," in *The Interpreter's Bible*, vol. 8, ed. George A. Buttrick et al. (New York: Abingdon, 1951), 629–47; R. A. Guelich, "Mark, Gospel of," in *DJG*, 512–25; Raymond A. Brown, *An Introduction to the New Testament* (New York: Anchor, 1997), chap. 7. Paul J. Achtemeier's book in the Proclamation Commentary series, *Mark* (Philadelphia: Fortress Press, 1986), also provides a good brief introduction.

2. The following books are good places to begin a survey of Markan scholarship over the last fifty years: Joanna Dewey, "Recent Studies on Mark," *RelSRev* 17 (1991): 12, 14–16; H. C. Key, "Mark's Gospel in Recent Research," *Int* 32 (1978): 353–68; Frank J. Matera, *What Are They Saying about Mark?* (New York: Paulist, 1987); Vernon Robbins, "Text and Context in Recent Studies of Mark's Gospel," *RelSRev* 17 (1991): 16–22; William Telford, "Introduction: The Interpretation of Mark—A History of Developments and Issues," in *The Interpretation of Mark,* ed. William Telford (Edinburgh: T. & T. Clark, 1995), 1–61.

3. Note, however, that reputable scholars like C. S. Mann and William Farmer hold what is called, after its early proponent, the Griesbach Hypothesis, which agrees that Matthew was the first Gospel to be written.

4. For exemplary discussions of such narrative units in Mark, see Paul J. Achtemeier's articles "Toward Isolation of a Pre-Marcan Miracle Catenae," *JBL* 89 (1970): 265–91, and "The Origin and Function of the Pre-Markan Miracle Catenae," *JBL* 91 (1972): 198–221.

5. This hypothesis was first suggested by Emil Wendling in *Die Entstehung des Marcus-Evangeliums* (1908). For more recent discussions, see John Brown, "An Early Revision of the Gospel of Mark," *JBL* 78 (1959): 215–27, and Helmut Koester, *Ancient Christian Gospels* (Philadelphia: Trinity, 1990), 284–86, 293–303.

6. Thomas C. Oden and Christopher A. Hall, eds., *Ancient Christian Commentary on Scripture: Mark* (Downers Grove: InterVarsity, 1998), xxix.

7. See Harry Fledderman, "The Flight of a Naked Young Man," *CBQ* 41 (1979): 412–18.

8. For discussions of the Gospel genre, see David Aune, *The New Testament in Its Literary Environment* (Philadelphia: Westminster, 1987), chap. 1 and 2; Adela Yarbro Collins, *The Beginning of the Gospel* (Minneapolis: Fortress Press, 1992), chap. 1; Helmut Koester, *Ancient Christian Gospels* (Philadelphia: Trinity, 1990), sect. 1; Robert C. Tannehill, "The Gospels and Narrative Literature," in Leander E. Keck et al., eds., *NIB*, vol. 8. (Nashville: Abingdon, 1995), 56–70; Clyde Votaw, *The Gospels and Contemporary Biographies in the Greco-Roman World* (Philadelphia: Fortress Press, 1970).

9. For a creative understanding of what this means for Mark, see Mary Ann Tolbert, "How the Gospel of Mark Builds Character," *Int* 47 (1993): 347–57.

10. Werner Kümmel, *Introduction to the New Testament*, 17th ed. (Nashville: Abingdon, 1975), 37.

11. For literary and narrative analyses of Mark, see John Drury, "Mark," in *The Literary Guide to the Bible*, ed. Robert Alter and Frank Kermode (Cambridge, Mass.: Belknap, 1987), 402–17; Mark Powell, "Toward a Narrative-Critical Interpretation of Mark," *Int* 47 (1993): 341–46; David Rhoads and Donald Michie, *Mark as Story* (Philadelphia: Fortress Press, 1982). Elizabeth Struthers Malbon consistently uses literary analysis perceptively and effectively in her work on Mark.

12. Paul J. Achtemeier, "Mark as Interpreter of the Jesus Traditions," *Int* 32 (1978): 340, 346.

13. Achtemeier, "Mark as Interpreter," 339, 343.

14. James Hoover, *Mark: Follow Me* (Downers Grove: InterVarsity, 1985), 8.

15. Jack Kingsbury, "The 'Divine Man' as the Key to Mark's Christology—The End of an Era?" *Int* 35 (1981): 256.

16. Koester, *Ancient Christian Gospels*, 291.

17. The best description I have encountered of what the cross meant in Jesus' day is found in Morna D. Hooker's book *Not Ashamed of the Gospel* (Grand Rapids: Eerdmans, 1994).

18. Robert H. Gundry, *Mark: A Commentary on His Apology for the Cross* (Grand Rapids: Eerdmans, 1993).

19. R. H. Lightfoot, *The Gospel Message of St. Mark* (Oxford: Oxford Univ. Press, 1962), 31.

Chapter 1

1. Morna D. Hooker, *The Gospel according to St. Mark* (Peabody, Mass.: Hendrickson, 1997), 31.

2. Lewis Hay, "The Son-of-God Christology in Mark," *JBR* 32 (1964): 109. For a classic scholarly discussion, see Martin Hengel, *The Son of Man* (Philadelphia: Fortress Press, 1976). Also helpful are Bruce Chilton, "The Son of Man: Who Was He?" *BRev* 12 (1996): 34–39, 45–46, and James Hoffmeier, "Son of God: From Pharaoh to Israel's Kings to Jesus," *BRev* 13 (1997): 44–49, 54.

3. For good, general discussions of John the Baptist, see Paul W. Hollenbach, "John the Baptist," *ABD* 3:887–988; G. E. Ladd, "John the Baptist," in *Theology of the New Testament* (Grand Rapids: Eerdmans, 1993); Ben Witherington III, "John the Baptist," *DJG*, 383–91. Two helpful book-length studies are Robert L. Webb, *John the Baptizer and Prophet: A Socio-Historical Study*, JSNTSup 62 (Sheffield: JSOT Press,

1991); and Walter Wink, *John the Baptist in Gospel Tradition* (Cambridge: Cambridge Univ. Press, 1968).

4. Howard C. Kee, "The Function of Scriptural Quotations and Allusions in Mark 11-16," in *Jesus und Paulus,* ed. E. E. Ellis and E. Grässer (Göttingen: Vandenhoeck & Ruprecht, 1975), 176–77, 181.

5. Paul J. Achtemeier, "Mark as Interpreter of the Jesus Traditions," *Int* 32 (1978): 342.

6. Dale C. Allison Jr., "Elijah Must Come First," *JBL* 103 (1984): 256–58.

7. For a discussion of this matter, see Otto Betz, "Was John the Baptist an Essene?" *BRev* 6 (1990). For another view of the Baptist and his significance, see Flavius Josephus (ca. A.D. 37–100) *Antiquities* XVIII. 5, which describes the arrest and death of John.

8. For a succinct and helpful discussion of "Kingdom of God," see Morna D. Hooker, *The Gospel according to St. Mark* (Peabody, Mass.: Hendrickson, 1997), 55–58. Other resources include C. C. Caragounis, "Kingdom of God/Kingdom of Heaven," in *DJG* and "Kingdom of God/Kingdom of Heaven," in *ABD* 4:49–69, which also provides a full bibliography on 67–69.

9. Location also figures in Elizabeth Struthers Malbon's "Disciples, Crowds, Whoever: Markan Characters and Readers," *NovT* 28 (1986a): 104–30, especially 111–13.

Chapter 2

1. R. H. Lightfoot, *The Gospel Message of St. Mark* (Oxford: Oxford Univ. Press, 1962), 29.

2. J. D. Kingsbury, "The Religious Authorities in the Gospel of Mark," *NTS* 36 (1990): 47.

3. Joanna Dewey, "The Literary Structure of the Controversy Stories in Mark 2:1—3:6," *JBL* 92 (1973): 394–401 (reprinted in Telford).

4. For quite different general treatments of miracle see B. L. Blackburn, "Miracles and Miracle Stories," in *DJG,* 549–60; Jarl Fossum, "Understanding Jesus' Miracles," *BRev* 10 (1994): 16–23, 50; and C. S. Lewis, *Miracles* (New York: Macmillan, 1947).

5. Adela Yarbro Collins, *The Beginning of the Gospel: Probings of Mark in Context* (Minneapolis: Fortress Press, 1992), 57.

6. As does Morna D. Hooker in her commentary on Mark. See Hooker, *The Gospel according to St. Mark* (Peabody, Mass.: Hendrickson, 1977), 79–80, and, for the other view, Bruce M. Metzger, *A Textual Commentary on the Greek New Testament* (New York: United Bible Societies, 1975), 76–77. Metzger thinks the confusion may have arisen from similar Aramaic words.

7. Elizabeth Struthers Malbon, "*Th Oikia Aytoy:* Mark 2:15 in Context," *NTS* 31 (1985): 282–92.

8. Jerome H. Neyrey, "Questions, *Chreiai,* and Challenges to Honor: The Interface of Rhetoric and Culture in Mark's Gospel," *CBQ* 60 (1998): 657–81. Perhaps the most extensive treatment of controversy material is Arland Hultgren's *Jesus and His Adversaries: The Form and Function of Conflict Stories in the Synoptic Tradition* (Minneapolis: Augsburg, 1979).

9. For concise treatments of "Son of Man," see Hooker, *The Gospel according to St. Mark,* 88–93, and I. H. Marshall, "Son of Man," in *DJG,* 775–81. For more extended

treatments, consult Morna D. Hooker, *The Son of Man in Mark* (London: S.P.C.K., 1967); Barnabas Linders, *Jesus Son of Man* (Grand Rapids: Eerdmans, 1983). See also note 2 in chapter 1.

10. F. F. Bruce, *Jesus: Lord and Savior* (Downers Grove: InterVarsity, 1986), 66.

11. John Donahue, "Tax Collectors and Sinners," *CBQ* 33 (1971): 39–61.

12. Bruce, *Jesus*, 71.

13. Neyrey, *Questions*, 677–78.

14. Hugh Anderson, *The Gospel of Mark*, NCBC (Grand Rapids: Eerdmans, 1984), 115.

15. Elizabeth Schüssler Fiorenza, "The Twelve," in Leonard and Arlene Swidler, eds., *Women Priests* (New York: Paulist, 1977), 117.

16. For an interesting Roman Catholic exchange on this matter see Richard Bauckham, "The Brothers and Sisters of Jesus: An Epiphanian Response to John P. Meier," *CBQ* 56 (1994): 686–700; and John P. Meier, "The Brothers and Sisters of Jesus in Ecumenical Perspective," *CBQ* 54 (1992): 1–28.

17. For an immensely helpful study of this issue, see Carolyn Osiek and David L. Balch, *Families in the New Testament World* (Louisville: Westminster John Knox, 1997).

18. For more detailed commentary, see Robert H. Gundry, *Mark: A Commentary on His Apology for the Cross* (Grand Rapids: Eerdmans, 1993), 182–86; D. E. Nineham, *Saint Mark* (Harmondsworth: Penguin, 1963), 120–22, 124–25.

19. Nineham, *Saint Mark*, 119.

Chapter 3

1. Paul J. Achtemeier, "He Taught Them Many Things: Reflection on Marcan Christology," *CBQ* 42 (1980): 473, 475.

2. Greg Fay, "Introduction to Incomprehension: The Literary Structure of Mk 4:1-34," *CBQ* 51 (1989): 65–81.

3. Ibid., 79.

4. Much of this material comes from the very fine discussion of parables in D. E. Nineham, *Saint Mark* (Harmondsworth: Penguin, 1963), 125–33.

5. Quoted in *Ancient Christian Commentary on Scripture: Mark,* ed. Thomas C. Oden and Christopher A. Hall (Downers Grove: InterVarsity, 1998), 55.

6. Pheme Perkins, "The Gospel of Mark," in Leander E. Keck et al., eds., *NIB,* vol. 8 (Nashville: Abingdon, 1995), 568–69.

7. Nineham, *Saint Mark*, 133.

8. Perkins, "Gospel of Mark," 568.

9. Ibid., 569.

10. Morna D. Hooker, *The Gospel according to St. Mark* (Peabody, Mass.: Hendrickson, 1997), 126.

11. C. S. Mann, *Mark: A New Translation with Introduction and Commentary,* Anchor Bible, v. 27 (Garden City, N.Y.: Doubleday, 1986), 263–65; cf. E. P. Gould, *The Gospel according to St. Mark,* ICC (New York: Scribners, 1913), 71–74, and J. Schmid, *The Gospel according to Mark* (Regensburg: Alba, 1968), 97–99.

12. Howard C. Kee, "The Function of Scriptural Quotations and Allusions in Mark 11-16," in *Jesus und Paulus,* ed. E. E. Ellis and E. Grässer (Göttingen: Vandenhoeck & Ruprecht, 1975), 179–80.

13. Paul J. Achtemeier, "Mark as Interpreter of the Jesus Traditions," *Int* 32 (1978): 344–45.

14. Mary Ann Tolbert, "How the Gospel of Mark Builds Character," *Int* 47 (1993): 347–57.

15. Nineham, *Saint Mark,* 144.

16. Achtemeier, "He Taught Them," 475.

17. Schuyler Brown, "The Secret of the Kingdom of God (Mark 4:11)," *JBL* 92 (1973): 66.

18. John D. Crossan, "The Seed Parables of Jesus," *JBL* 92 (1973): 265.

Chapter 4

1. Paul J. Achtemeier, "Toward the Isolation of a Pre-Markan Miracle Catenae," *JBL* 89 (1970): 265–91. Cf. Norman Petersen, "The Composition of Mark 4:1— 8:25," *HTR* 93 (1980): 194–97.

2. Paul J. Achtemeier, "The Origin and Function of the Pre-Markan Miracle Catenae," *JBL* 91 (1972): 198–221.

3. I am not at all troubled by the miracles of Jesus. For me, the issue is not miracles per se, but the nature of God and Christology. If God is God (that is, creator and omnipotent), then God can do what God wants to do with God's "stuff," with creation. And by extension, if Jesus is God, then Jesus can do what God does, in this case miracles of various sorts.

4. Hugh Anderson, *The Gospel of Mark,* NCBC (Grand Rapids: Eerdmans, 1984), 142.

5. Ibid., 143.

6. A helpful source for such material is James B. Pritchard, ed., *Ancient Near Eastern Texts,* 3rd ed. (Princeton: Princeton Univ. Press, 1969). Although the material is collected for its relevance to study of the Old Testament, it is a rich source for New Testament preaching as well.

7. For a concise but detailed discussion of the matter, see Robert H. Gundry, *Mark: A Commentary on His Apology for the Cross* (Grand Rapids: Eerdmans, 1993), 255–57.

8. For an account of this, see Josephus, *Antiquities* VIII. 48.

9. Achtemeier, "Toward the Isolation of a Pre-Markan Miracle Catenae," 278.

10. Pheme Perkins, "The Gospel of Mark," in Leander E. Keck et al., eds., *NIB,* vol. 8 (Nashville: Abingdon, 1995), 588. In her discussion, she relies upon H. C. Kee, *Medicine, Miracle, and Magic* (New Haven: Yale Univ. Press, 1983).

11. Elizabeth S. Malbon, "Fallible Followers: Women and Men in the Gospel of Mark," *Semeia* 28 (1983): 36.

12. Morna D. Hooker, *The Gospel according to St. Mark* (Peabody, Mass.: Hendrickson, 1991), 150.

13. Perkins, "Gospel of Mark," 589–90.

Chapter 5

1. J. D. Kingsbury, "The Religious Authorities in the Gospel of Mark," *NTS* 36 (1990): 42–65.

2. Paul J. Achtemeier, "The Origin and Function of the Pre-Markan Miracle Catenae," *JBL* 91 (1972): 198–221; and "Toward the Isolation of Pre-Markan Miracle Catenae," *JBL* 89 (1970): 265–91.

3. Hugh M. Humphrey, *He Is Risen! A New Reading of Mark's Gospel* (New York: Paulist, 1992).

4. Ibid., 56.

5. Ibid., 69.

6. For a fascinating study of the theological reasons for Jesus' movements, see Jerome Murphy-O'Connor, "Why Jesus Went Back to Galilee," *BR* 12 (1996): 20–29, 42–43.

7. For a very helpful gloss on "carpenter" see C. S. Mann, *Mark: A New Translation with Introduction and Commentary,* Anchor Bible, v. 27 (Garden City, N.Y.: Doubleday, 1986), 289. He points out that the Aramaic word behind *tekton, naggara,* can mean anything from a maker of furniture to a builder.

8. Richard Bauckham, "The Brothers and Sisters of Jesus," *CBQ* 56 (1994): 698.

9. Morna D. Hooker, *The Gospel according to St. Mark* (Peabody, Mass.: Hendrickson, 1991), 157.

10. For an interesting discussion of how Mark inserts his own material by the repetition of phrases, see F. C. Synge, "Intruded Middles," *ExpTim* 92 (1981): 329–33.

11. Paul J. Achtemeier, "He Taught Them Many Things: Reflection on Marcan Christology," *CBQ* 42 (1980): 479.

12. Robert G. Bratcher and Eugene A. Nida, *A Translator's Handbook on the Gospel of Mark* (New York: United Bible Societies, 1961), 216.

13. Ibid.

14. Ibid.

15. Ibid., 218.

16. For a clear description of the issue see Graham Stanton, "A Gospel among the Scrolls?" *BR* 11 (1995): 36–42, in which Carsten Thiede's argument is that the fragment is Markan and Graham Stanton marshals the evidence against his view.

17. Schuyler Brown, "The Secret of the Kingdom of God (Mark 4:11)," *JBL* 92 (1973): 68.

18. Elizabeth Struthers Malbon, "The Jewish Leaders in the Gospel of Mark: A Literary Study of Marcan Characterization," *JBL* 108 (1989): 271.

19. See, for example, Robert H. Gundry, *Mark: A Commentary on His Apology for the Cross* (Grand Rapids: Eerdmans, 1993), 347–49, 357–62; D. E. Nineham, *St. Mark* (Harmondsworth: Penguin, 1963), 188–94.

20. Martin Hengel, *Studies in Early Christology* (Edinburgh: T. & T. Clark, 1995), 388.

21. Jerome H. Neyrey, "Questions, Chreiai, and Challenges to Honor: The Interface of Rhetoric and Culture in Mark's Gospel," *CBQ* 60 (1998): 657–81.

22. Gundry, *Mark,* 354.

23. F. C. Synge, "Intruded Middles," 331, has an interesting alternative reading for the word "defile," *koinosai.* He notes that it comes from the root *koinoo,* "common," which in ordinary Greek means "having in common." The point, he thinks, is that the process of elimination "commonizes" all people.

24. Gundry, *Mark,* 347.

25. Kingsbury, "Religious Authorities," 45–47.

26. Quoted in John Moses, *The Desert: An Anthology for Lent* (Harrisburg, Pa.: Morehouse, 1997), 74.

27. Hugh Anderson, *The Gospel of Mark*, NCBC (Grand Rapids: Eerdmans, 1984), 183.

28. F. F. Bruce, *The Hard Sayings of Jesus* (Downers Grove: InterVarsity, 1983), 111.

29. Sharon H. Ringe, "A Gentile Woman's Story," in Letty M. Russell, ed., *Feminist Interpretation of the Bible* (Philadelphia: Westminster, 1985), 69.

30. Ibid., 65, 72.

31. Quoted in *Ancient Christian Commentary on Scripture: Mark*, Thomas Oden and Christopher Hall, eds. (Downers Grove: InterVarsity, 1998), 104.

32. Austin Farrar, *A Study in Mark* (New York: Oxford Univ. Press, 1952), chap. 8.

33. Hooker, *St. Mark*, 189.

34. Ibid., 191.

35. David Hawkin, "The Incomprehension of the Disciples in the Marcan Redaction," *JBL* 91 (1972): 495.

Chapter 6

1. A particularly accessible discussion of the structure of this material is found in Norman Perrin, *What Is Redaction Criticism?* (Philadelphia: Fortress Press, 1969), 40–63. My own thinking about this material has been highly influenced by Perrin's schema.

2. Ernest Best, *Disciples and Discipleship: Studies in the Gospel according to Mark* (Edinburgh: T. & T. Clark, 1986), 3.

3. Ibid., 13.

4. Pheme Perkins, "The Gospel of Mark," in Leander E. Keck et al., eds., *NIB*, vol. 8 (Nashville: Abingdon, 1995), 619.

5. David Hawkin, "The Incomprehension of the Disciples in the Markan Redaction," *JBL* 91 (1972): 498.

6. F. F. Bruce, *The Hard Sayings of Jesus* (Downers Grove: InterVarsity, 1983), 146.

7. See the discussion in C. S. Mann, *Mark: A New Translation with Introduction and Commentary*, Anchor Bible, v. 27 (Garden City, N.Y.: Doubleday, 1986).

8. For more on this, see F. R. McCurley Jr., "'And After Six Days' (Mk 9:2): A Semitic Literary Device," *JBL* 93 (1974): 67–81.

9. Robert Bratcher and Eugene Nida, *A Translator's Handbook on the Gospel of Mark* (New York: United Bible Societies, 1961), 272.

10. See M. E. Thrall, "Elijah and Moses in Mark's Account of the Transfiguration," *NTS* 16 (1970): 305–17.

11. Robert H. Gundry, *Mark: A Commentary on His Apology for the Cross* (Grand Rapids: Eerdmans, 1993), 478.

12. Hubert Basser, "The Jewish Roots of the Transfiguration," *BR* 14 (1998): 35.

13. Gundry, *Mark*, 457.

14. So also Murphy-O'Connor, "What Really Happened at the Transfiguration?" *BR* 3 (1987): 19. "Mark became aware of the primitive version of the Transfiguration in a somewhat garbled form."

15. Ralph Martin, *Mark,* Knox Preaching Guides (Atlanta: John Knox, 1981), 56.

16. Morna D. Hooker, *The Gospel according to St. Mark* (Peabody, Mass.: Hendrickson, 1997), 228.

17. Bruce, *Hard Sayings,* 37.

18. Ibid., 38.

19. Hugh Anderson, *The Gospel of Mark,* NCBC (Grand Rapids: Eerdmans, 1984), 239.

20. Anderson's commentary speaks of the "extreme stringency of Jesus' stance on marriage and divorce." Ibid., 242.

21. Bruce, *Hard Sayings,* 172.

22. Robert H. Gundry, "Mark 10:29: Order in the List," *CBQ* 59 (1997): 467, 473.

23. John P. Keenan, *The Gospel of Mark: A Mahayana Reading* (Maryknoll: Orbis, 1995), 248.

24. Ibid., 242.

25. See M. Selvidge, "And Those Who Followed Feared . . . ," *CBQ* 45 (1983): 396–400.

26. Bratcher and Nida, *Translator's Handbook,* 105.

27. Hooker, *St. Mark,* 249. Professor Hooker's discussion of atonement on 247–51 is particularly helpful.

28. Vernon K. Robbins, "The Healing of Blind Bartimaeus (10: 46-52) in Marcan Theology," *JBL* 92 (1973): 242.

29. Joel F. Williams, *Other Followers of Jesus: Minor Characters as Major Figures in Mark's Gospel,* JSNTSup 102 (Sheffield: JSOT Press, 1994), chap. 4, "The Characterization of Blind Bartimaeus in Mark 10:46-52," 151–71.

30. Earl S. Johnson Jr., "Mark 10:46-52: Blind Bartimaeus," *CBQ* 40 (1978): 199, 201.

31. Robert C. Tannehill, "The Disciples in Mark: The Function of a Narrative Role," in *The Interpretation of Mark,* ed. William R. Telford (Edinburgh: T. & T. Clark, 1995), 185.

Chapter 7

1. For an excursus on the chronology of Mark 11, see Robert H. Gundry, *Mark: A Commentary on His Apology for the Cross* (Grand Rapids: Eerdmans, 1993), 671–82.

2. John Paul Heil, "The Narrative Strategy and Pragmatics of the Temple Theme in Mark," *CBQ* 59 (1997): 76–100.

3. Sharyn Echols Dowd, *Prayer, Power and the Problem of Suffering: Mark 11:22-25 in the Context of Markan Theology,* SBLDS 105 (Atlanta: Scholars, 1988).

4. Howard C. Kee, "The Function of Scriptural Quotations and Allusions in Mark 11–16," in *Jesus und Paulus,* ed. E. E. Ellis and E. Grässer (Göttingen: Vandenhoeck & Ruprecht, 1975), 165–88. In 167–71 Kee provides an extensive listing of the quotations and allusions in Mark 11–16.

5. Ibid., 176.

6. I am indebted to the lecture by Paul B. Duff entitled "Fools Rush In: Entry in Jerusalem in Mark" (given at the Society of Biblical Literature meeting in Anaheim, Calif., Nov. 19, 1989), for my knowledge of some of the Greco-Roman

backgrounds of the text.

7. Robert G. Bratcher and Eugene A. Nida, *A Translator's Handbook on the Gospel of Mark* (New York: United Bible Societies, 1961), 346.

8. Morna D. Hooker, *The Gospel according to St. Mark* (Peabody, Mass.: Hendrickson, 1991), 253.

9. F. F. Bruce, *The Hard Sayings of Jesus* (Downers Grove: InterVarsity, 1983), 208–9.

10. For a survey of the exegesis on the phrase see William R. Telford, *The Barren Temple and the Withered Fig Tree*, JSNTSup 1 (Sheffield: JSOT Press, 1980), 1–48. Helpful articles include J. D. M. Derrett, "Fig Trees in the New Testament," *Heythrop Journal* 87 (1968): 249–65, and articles by Heirs and Cotter (see notes 11 and 12 below).

11. Richard H. Hiers, "Not the Season for Figs," *JBL* 87 (1968): 394–400.

12. Wendy Cotter, "For It Was Not the Season for Figs," *CBQ* 48 (1986): 62–66.

13. R. H. Lightfoot, *The Gospel Message of St. Mark* (Oxford: Oxford Univ. Press, 1962), 64.

14. Dowd, *Prayer, Power, and the Problem of Suffering.*

15. Bruce, *Hard Sayings,* 211.

16. This schema is taken from Ralph Martin, *Mark,* Knox Preaching Guides (Atlanta: John Knox, 1981), 69.

17. Lightfoot, *Gospel Message of St. Mark,* 60.

18. Hugh Anderson, *The Gospel of Mark,* NCBC (Grand Rapids: Eerdmans, 1984), 265.

19. Bruce, *Hard Sayings,* 213.

20. A similar parable appears in the noncanonical Gospel of Thomas.

21. See Bonnie Thurston, "Faith and Fear in Mark's Gospel," *The Bible Today* 23 (1985): 305–10.

22. Bruce, *Hard Sayings,* 213.

23. For more on the Pharisees, see D. E. Cook, "A Gospel Portrait of the Pharisees," *RevExp* 84 (1987): 221–33; Stephen Westerholm, "Pharisees," *DJG,* 609–14.

24. For more on the Herodians, see Harold Hoenher, "Herodian Dynasty," *DJG,* 317–26, especially 325.

25. For more information on groups within Judaism, see Anthony J. Saldarini, *Pharisees, Scribes and Sadducees in Palestinian Society: A Sociological Approach* (Wilmington: Michael Glazier, 1988); and Marcel Simon, *Jewish Sects at the Time of Jesus* (Philadelphia: Fortress Press, 1967).

26. Robert H. Gundry, *Mark: A Commentary on His Apology for the Cross* (Grand Rapids: Eerdmans, 1993), 692–93.

27. For an interesting discussion of the word see Bratcher and Nida, *Translator's Handbook,* 224–25.

28. Gundry, *Mark,* 695.

29. For more on the Sadducees, see Josephus, *Wars* II.8.14; *Antiquities* XIII.10.6, XVIII.1.4; Gary Porton, "Sadducees," *ABD* 5:892–94. See also note 24 above.

30. Hooker, *Gospel according to Mark,* 284.

31. Bratcher and Nida, *Translator's Handbook,* 379.

32. Gundry, *Mark,* 704.

33. Jerome H. Neyrey's article, "Questions, *Chreiai,* and Challenges to Honor: The Interface of Rhetoric and Culture in Mark's Gospel," *CBQ* 60 (1998): 657–81, provides crucial insight into these exchanges.

34. Hooker, *Gospel according to Mark,* 290–94.

35. D. E. Nineham, *St. Mark* (Harmondsworth: Penguin, 1963), 334.

36. Ezra Gould, *A Critical and Exegetical Commentary on the Gospel according to St. Mark,* ICC (New York: Scribners, 1913), 239.

37. Mary Ann Beavis, "Women as Models of Faith in Mark," *BTB* 18 (1988): 6.

38. A. G. Wright, "The Widow's Mite: Praise or Lament?—A Matter of Context," *CBQ* 44 (1982): 256–65; Elizabeth Struthers Malbon, "The Poor Widow in Mark and Her Poor Rich Readers," *CBQ* 53 (1991): 589–604.

39. Willem S. Vorster, "Literary Reflections on Mark 13:5-37: A Narrated Speech of Jesus," first appeared in *Neotestamentica* 21 (1987): 203–24, reprinted in William Telford, *The Interpretation of Mark* (Edinburgh: T. & T. Clark, 1995), 269–88. Quotation from this edition, 281.

40. Ibid., 283.

41. John Collins, *Semeia* 14 (1979): 9.

42. Martin, *Mark,* 76.

43. This is witnessed to by the fact that in August, 1998, John R. Donahue, S.J. shared a ten-paged, single-spaced bibliography of works on Mark 13 with the members of the Mark Study Group of the Catholic Biblical Association.

44. Adela Yarbro Collins, *The Beginning of the Gospel: Probings of Mark in Context* (Minneapolis: Fortress Press, 1992), 81.

45. Bratcher and Nida, *Translator's Handbook,* 399.

46. Martin, *Mark,* 78.

47. Bas M. F. Van Iersel, "Failed Followers in Mark: Mark 13:12 as a Key for the Identification of the Intended Readers," *CBQ* 58 (1996): 244–63.

48. A. E. Harvey, *The New English Bible Companion to the New Testament* (New York: Oxford Univ. Press/Cambridge Univ. Press, 1970), 188.

49. Thomas C. Oden and Christopher A. Hall, *Ancient Christian Commentary on Scripture: Mark* (Downers Grove: InterVarsity, 1998), 185.

50. Ibid., 187.

51. Lightfoot, *Gospel Message of St. Mark,* 48.

52. Elizabeth Struthers Malbon, "The Jewish Leaders in the Gospel of Mark: A Literary Study of Marcan Characterization," *JBL* 108 (1989): 276.

53. Neyrey, "Questions, *Chreiai,* and Challenges to Honor," 657–81.

Chapter 8

1. Gerd Theissen, "A Major Narrative Unit (The Passion Story) and the Jerusalem Community in the Years 40–50 C.E.," in *The Gospels in Context: Social and Political History in the Synoptic Tradition* (Minneapolis: Fortress Press, 1991), 166–99.

2. Joel B. Green, "Passion Narrative," in *DJG,* 601.

3. Ibid., 602.

4. Howard C. Kee, "The Function of Scriptural Quotations and Allusions in Mark 11-16," in *Jesus und Paulus,* ed. E. E. Ellis and E. Grässer (Göttingen:

Vandenhoeck & Ruprecht, 1975), 166.

5. Martin Dibelius, *From Tradition to Gospel* (New York: Scribners, 1934), 186.

6. Pheme Perkins, "The Gospel of Mark," in Leander E. Keck et al., eds., *NIB*, vol. 8 (Nashville: Abingdon, 1995), 695.

7. Ibid., 695.

8. For discussions see Robert H. Gundry, *Mark: A Commentary on His Apology for the Cross* (Grand Rapids: Eerdmans, 1993), 801–2, 805–8, and Morna D. Hooker, *The Gospel according to St. Mark* (Peabody, Mass.: Hendrickson, 1991), 325–26.

9. See Joachim Jeremias, *Jerusalem in the Time of Jesus* (Philadelphia: Fortress Press, 1975); and John Wilkinson, "Ancient Jerusalem—Its Water Supply and Population," *Palestine Exploration Quarterly* 106 (1974): 49.

10. Joseph Grassi, "The Secret Heroine of Mark's Drama," *BTB* 18 (1988): 11.

11. Robert Bratcher and Eugene Nida, *A Translator's Handbook on the Gospel of Mark* (New York: United Bible Societies, 1961), 429.

12. Mary Ann Beavis, "Women as Models of Faith in Mark," *BTB* 18 (1988): 7.

13. Paul J. Achtemeier, "Mark as Interpreter of the Jesus Traditions," *Int* 32 (1978): 349.

14. For another view, see Gundry, *Mark*, 831.

15. Hugh Anderson, *The Gospel of Mark*, NCBC (Grand Rapids: Eerdmans, 1984), 312.

16. Bratcher and Nida, *Translator's Handbook*, 444.

17. Those interested in the source question can consult Robert H. Gundry's commentary or Martin Dibelius, "Gethsemane," *Crozier Quarterly* 12 (1935): 254–65; the dissertation by J. W. Holleran, *The Synoptic Gethsemane* (Rome: Università gregoriana, 1973); Barbara Saunderson, "Gethsemani: The Missing Witness," *Biblica* 70 (1989): 224–33.

18. Bratcher and Nida, *Translator's Handbook*, 446.

19. Joachim Jeremias, *The Prayers of Jesus* (Philadelphia: Fortress, 1984), 11.

20. Ibid., 53.

21. Raymond Brown, *An Introduction to the New Testament* (New York: Doubleday, 1997), 418.

22. The last is the view of Barbara Saunderson in "Gethsemane."

23. This is the position of Robin Scroggs and Kent Groff in "Baptism in Mark: Dying and Rising with Christ," *JBL* 92 (1973): 531–48.

24. Hooker, *Gospel according to St. Mark*, 352.

25. Harry Fledderman, "The Flight of a Naked Young Man," *CBQ* 41 (1979): 415, 417.

26. F. F. Bruce, *The Hard Sayings of Jesus* (Downers Grove: InterVarsity, 1983), 247.

27. Raymond Brown, *A Crucified Christ in Holy Week* (Collegeville, Minn.: Liturgical, 1986), 27.

28. Quoted in Thomas Oden and Christopher Hall, *Ancient Christian Commentary on Scripture: Mark* (Downers Grove: InterVarsity, 1998), 218.

29. *The Orthodox Study Bible* (Nashville: Thomas Nelson, 1993), 124.

30. Gundry, *Mark*, 888.

31. Ibid., 890.

32. Oden and Hall, *Ancient Christian Commentary: Mark*, 221–22.

33. Ralph C. Martin, *Mark*, Knox Preaching Guide (Atlanta: John Knox, 1981), 88–89.

34. A variant reading of Matt. 27:16 calls him "Jesus Barabbas," increasing the possibility of confusion.

35. Gundry, *Mark*, 928.

36. In a major address to the Catholic Biblical Association of America in August 2001, "Matthew's Pilate (Matt. 27:11-26): Roman Justice Is All Washed Up," Professor Warren Carter gave a very different reading of the trial before Pilate. By highlighting neglected "imperial dynamics" like the alliance between Jerusalem's leaders and the Roman elite, the Roman legal bias toward the elite, and the immense power of Roman governors, Carter argues that Pilate is *not* a weak person who knows Jesus is innocent but is easily swayed by the crowd. On the contrary, Pilate quickly establishes Jesus' guilt (because he is "King of the Jews" and therefore seditious), polls the crowd to establish the extent of Jesus' threat, and then manipulates the audience to call for Jesus' death. In Carter's reading, Pilate is a powerful, skillful, and unscrupulous politician who manipulates the people to accomplish his will. Understood in this way, the narrative is intended to expose the nature of Roman "justice." If Carter is correct, and if, as I have suggested, Mark's original audience was Roman, certainly this view of the workings of the Roman legal system would have resonated with Mark's audience.

37. Brown, *Crucified Christ*, 29–30.

38. Harald Sahlin, "Mk 15, 34," *Biblica* 33 (1952): 62–66. I am grateful to Michael Patella, OSB, whose paper on the death of Jesus given to the Mark study group of the Catholic Biblical Association in August 2000 alerted me to this article.

39. Brown, *Crucified Christ*, 32.

40. Winsome Munro, "Women Disciples in Mark?" *CBQ* 44 (1982): 236.

41. Bratcher and Nida, *Translator's Handbook*, 497.

42. Raymond Brown, "The Burial of Jesus (Mark 15:42-47)," *CBQ* 50 (1988): 233–45.

43. For a discussion of some of the narrative techniques in the ending of Mark see C. H. Bird, "Some *gar* Clauses in St. Mark's Gospel," *JTS* 4 (1953): 171–87; Thomas E. Boomershine and G. L. Bartholomew, "Narrative Technique of Mark 16:8," *JBL* 100 (1981): 213–23; and P. W. Van der Horst, "Can a Book End with *gar*? A Note on Mark 16:8," *JTS* 23 (1972): 121–24.

44. R. H. Lightfoot, *The Gospel Message of St. Mark* (Oxford: Oxford Univ. Press, 1962), 31.

45. A. T. Lincoln, "The Promise and the Failure: Mark 16:7, 8," *JBL* 108 (1989): 283–300.

46. Bas Van Iersel spells out other implications of the fact that during persecutions, members of the Roman church who were arrested betrayed other Christians in his article "Failed Followers in Mark: Mark 13:12 as a Key for the Identification of the Intended Readers," *CBQ* 58 (1996): 244–63.

47. For Hooker's discussion of the ending of Mark see *Gospel according to St. Mark*, 382–94, especially 391–94.

48. Bratcher and Nida, *Translator's Handbook,* 503.

49. Raymond Brown, *A Risen Christ in Eastertime* (Collegeville, Minn.: Liturgical, 1991), 15.

50. Ibid., 16.

51. Thomas E. Boomershine, "Mark 16:8 and the Apostolic Commission," *JBL* 100 (1981): 238.

52. Andrew T. Lincoln, "The Promise and the Failure: Mark 16:7, 8" in *The Interpretation of Mark,* ed. William Telford (Edinburgh: T. & T. Clark, 1995), 237.

53. D. E. Nineham, *Saint Mark* (Harmondsworth: Penguin, 1963), 449.

54. Ibid., 452.

55. Anderson, *Gospel of Mark,* 361.

Index